SPECTRAL ANALYSIS OF ORGANIC COMPOUNDS

An Introductory Programmed Text

by

CLIFFORD J. CRESWELL
OLAF RUNQUIST

Hamline University
St. Paul, Minnesota

Burgess Publishing Company

426 South Sixth Street • Minneapolis, Minn. 55415

COMMUNICATION OF KNOWLEDGE

Copyright © 1970 by Burgess Publishing Company
Printed in the United States of America
Library of Congress Catalog Card Number 72-93674
ISBN 8087-0330-7

PREFACE

Spectroscopy has provided the chemist with powerful tools for the determination of structures and conformations of organic compounds. Competence in interpreting and using spectral data is essential to any serious student of chemistry. The primary purpose of this book is to assist in developing the ability to interpret spectra and use the information in determining the structure of organic compounds.

This is a programmed book. It is organized into a logical set of questions which, wnen answered correctly, will lead the student to the desired learning goals. Each question is accompanied by a correct response so that proposed answers may be immediately checked. This book differs from many programmed texts in that topics are covered in more depth, and the questions require a greater degree of independent thought. Some questions may be answered quickly. Other questions are more involved and will require plotting of graphs, solving equations, or deriving mathematical relationships.

This programmed text is divided into six chapters, each of which has a short introduction indicating what should be accomplished. Following the introduction are statements (marked S), questions (marked Q), answers (marked A), and review statements (marked R). The statements give some basic information and are followed by a series of graded questions and answers. *This manual will be a useful learning aid only if each question is answered by the student before the correct response is consulted.* Reading the question and then reading the answer *is not* satisfactory. The following steps are recommended for using this book:

1. Cover each page of the book with a piece of scratch paper in such a way that you can see only a statement. Read the statement carefully.
2. Uncover the first question. *Write out* the answer to the question on the piece of scratch paper.
3. Move the scratch paper down the page so that a correct response to the first question can be seen. Read the entire answer given and compare it with your answer.
4. If your answer is correct, proceed to the next question. If your answer is incorrect, restudy the previous statement and questions. DO NOT PROCEED UNTIL YOU UNDERSTAND AND CAN CORRECTLY ANSWER EACH QUESTION. To become expert in the interpretation of spectra and the art of structural determination requires considerable practice. There is no substitute for experience.

We are indebted to the helpful suggestions made by colleagues and the many students at Hamline University who have used this book. We wish particularly to thank Deborah Johnson for her effort in proofreading the manuscript.

C.J.C.
O.A.R.

CONTENTS

Chapter 1 | THE INTERACTION OF LIGHT WITH ATOMS AND MOLECULES

After completing this chapter, you should be able to:

a) determine the period, frequency, energy, and wave number for light of any wavelength
b) explain why atoms and molecules will absorb light of only certain wavelengths
c) understand the origin of vibrational, rotational, and electronic spectra
d) determine the difference between rotational, vibrational, and electronic energy levels of a molecule from a knowledge of the wavelengths of light absorbed by the molecule
e) diagram the bonding and anti-bonding orbitals for simple molecules and determine if the orbitals are sigma, pi, or nonbonding.

S-1   Spectroscopy is the study of interactions of light with atoms and molecules. Light or electromagnetic radiation can be regarded as being wavelike or corpuscular. Some physical properties of light are best explained by its wave characteristics while other properties are best explained by its particle nature. Thus, light is said to be dualistic in nature. The wave nature of light will be considered first.

A diagram of a wave, with its essential features labeled, is shown below:

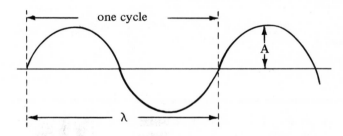

λ = wavelength: distance that the wave moves during one cycle.
unit: unit of length/cycle.
A = wave amplitude: the maximum disturbance from the horizontal axis.
unit: unit of length.
τ = period: the time for one complete cycle.
unit: sec/cycle.
ν = frequency of oscillation: the number of cycles that occur in every second.
unit: cycle/sec or Hertz.

When referring to λ, τ, and ν, the word cycle is understood and is not usually used. The relationship between wavelength (λ) and frequency (ν) for a light wave is

$\nu \lambda = c,$

where c is the velocity of light (3.0×10^{10} cm/sec).

	Calculate the period and frequency of light with a wavelength of 2.0×10^5 cm.
A-1 $\nu = c/\lambda$ $\nu = \dfrac{3.0 \times 10^{10}\ \text{cm/sec}}{2.0 \times 10^5\ \text{cm}} = 1.5 \times 10^5\ \text{sec}^{-1}$ $\tau = 1/\nu$ $\tau = \text{sec}/1.5 \times 10^5 = 6.7 \times 10^{-6}\ \text{sec}$	**Q-2** If the period of a light wave is 2.0×10^{-17} sec, what is the length of this wave in Angstrom units? $(1\ \text{Å} = 10^{-8}\ \text{cm})$
A-2 $\nu = 1/\tau = 1/2.0 \times 10^{-17}\ \text{sec}$ $\quad = 5.0 \times 10^{16}\ \text{sec}^{-1}$ $\lambda = c/\nu = \dfrac{3.0 \times 10^{10}\ \text{cm/sec}}{5.0 \times 10^{16}\ \text{sec}^{-1}}$ $\quad = 6.0 \times 10^{-7}\ \text{cm} = 60\ \text{Å}$	**Q-3** Calculate the period of electromagnetic radiation with $\lambda = 4.0 \times 10^3$ cm.
A-3 $\nu = c/\lambda = \dfrac{3.0 \times 10^{10}\ \text{cm/sec}}{4.0 \times 10^3\ \text{cm}}$ $\quad = 7.5 \times 10^6\ \text{sec}^{-1}$ $\tau = 1/\nu = 1/7.5 \times 10^6\ \text{sec}^{-1}$ $\quad = 1.3 \times 10^{-7}\ \text{sec}$	**Q-4** What is the frequency of green light with a wavelength of 5000 Å?
A-4 $\nu = c/\lambda = \dfrac{3.0 \times 10^{10}\ \text{cm/sec}}{5000\ \text{Å}} \left\|\dfrac{1\ \text{Å}}{10^{-8}\ \text{cm}}\right.$ $\quad = 6.0 \times 10^{14}\ \text{sec}^{-1}$	**R** $\nu = 1/\tau$, where ν is the frequency of the wave and τ is its period. $\lambda \nu = c$, where ν is the frequency, λ is the wavelength and c is the velocity of light.

S-2   Light which can be described as an oscillating wave may also be considered as a stream of energy packets or particles traveling with a high velocity (3.0×10^{10} cm/sec). These energy packets are called photons. The frequency (ν) of the wave theory can be related to the energy of the photons (E) of the particle theory through Planck's equation.

$$E = h\nu$$

where h is Planck's constant, a proportionality factor whose value is 6.63×10^{-27} erg-sec (erg = g-cm^2/sec^2).

Wave number, $\bar{\nu}$, is a wave characteristic that is proportional to energy and is defined as the number of waves per centimeter.

$$\bar{\nu} = 1/\lambda$$

	Q-5
	Q-5 Find the energy of the photons which correspond to light of frequency 3.0×10^{15} sec^{-1}.
A-5 $E = h\nu = (6.63 \times 10^{-27}\ \text{erg-sec})(3.0 \times 10^{15}\ \text{sec}^{-1})$ $\quad\quad = 2.0 \times 10^{-11}\ \text{erg}$	**Q-6** Find the frequency of light which corresponds to photons of energy 5.0×10^{-5} erg.

A-6 $\nu = \dfrac{E}{h} = \dfrac{5.0 \times 10^{-5} \ \text{erg}}{6.63 \times 10^{-27} \ \text{erg-sec}}$

  $= 7.5 \times 10^{21} \ \text{sec}^{-1}$

Q-7 From the equation $E = h\nu$ and $\lambda \nu = c$, derive an equation which relates energy to wavelength.

A-7 $E = h\nu \quad \nu = c/\lambda$

  $E = hc/\lambda$

Q-8 What is the energy of photons with a wavelength equal to 0.50Å?

A-8 $E = h\nu = hc/\lambda$

  $E = \dfrac{6.63 \times 10^{-27} \text{erg-sec}}{0.50 \times 10^{-8} \ \text{cm}} \left| \dfrac{3.0 \times 10^{10} \ \text{cm}}{\text{sec}} \right.$

  $E = 4.0 \times 10^{-11} \ \text{erg}$

Q-9 Show that $\bar{\nu}$ is proportional to energy

A-9 $E = h\nu$ and $\nu = c/\lambda$

  Therefore, $E = hc/\lambda$

  $1/\lambda = \bar{\nu}$

  Therefore, $E = hc\bar{\nu}$

  $hc = \text{constant}$

Q-10 What is the wave number for light with a wavelength of 4000Å?

A-10 $\bar{\nu} = \dfrac{1}{\lambda} = \dfrac{1}{4000\text{Å}} \left| \dfrac{1\text{Å}}{10^{-8} \ \text{cm}} \right.$

  $= 2.5 \times 10^{4} \ \text{cm}^{-1}$

Q-11 What is the energy of photons which have a wave number of $2.5 \times 10^{-5} \ \text{cm}^{-1}$?

A-11 $E = hc\bar{\nu}$

  $= \dfrac{6.63 \times 10^{-27} \text{erg-sec}}{} \left| \dfrac{3 \times 10^{10} \ \text{cm}}{\text{sec}} \right| \dfrac{2.5 \times 10^{-5}}{\text{cm}}$

  $= 5.0 \times 10^{-21} \ \text{erg}$

R $E = h\nu$ where E is the energy of the photon, ν is the frequency of light, and h is a proportionality constant with a value of 6.63×10^{-27} erg-sec. $\bar{\nu} = \dfrac{1}{\lambda}$ where $\bar{\nu}$ is the wave number.

S-3 Electromagnetic radiation is divided into several regions called radio wave, microwave, infrared, visible, ultraviolet, and x-ray. The wavelengths, wave numbers, frequencies, and energies associated with each of these regions are given on the diagram below.

$\bar{\nu}$, cm^{-1}

	0.1	1.0	10	10^2	10^4	10^5	10^6
	radio wave	micro-wave		infra-red	visible	ultra-violet	x-ray
λ, cm	10	1.0	0.1	10^{-2}	10^{-4}	10^{-5}	10^{-6}
λ, Å	10^9	10^8	10^7	10^6	10^4	10^3	10^2
E, erg	2×10^{-17}	2×10^{-16}	2×10^{-15}	2×10^{-14}	2×10^{-12}	2×10^{-11}	2×10^{-10}
ν, sec^{-1}	3×10^9	3×10^{10}	3×10^{11}	3×10^{12}	3×10^{14}	3×10^{15}	3×10^{16}

		Q-12	In what region of the electromagnetic radiation will the following wavelengths be located? 1 cm 0.8μ (micron) (1 micron = 10^{-4} cm) 10μ 100 mμ m = milli (1/1000) 100Å
A-12	1 cm microwave 0.8μ visible 10μ infrared 100 mμ ultraviolet 100Å x-ray	Q-13	In what region of the electromagnetic radiation will the following wave numbers be located? 983 cm^{-1} 3.0 x 10^4 cm^{-1} 5.0 cm^{-1} 8.7 x 10^4 cm^{-1}
A-13	983 cm^{-1} infrared 3.0 x 10^4 cm^{-1} visible 5.0 cm^{-1} microwave 8.7 x 10^4 cm^{-1} ultraviolet	Q-14	Arrange the following regions of light in order of increasing energy. microwave x-ray visible ultraviolet infrared
A-14	microwave < infrared < visible < ultraviolet < x-ray	R	Electromagnetic radiation is grouped into regions called radio wave, microwave, infrared, visible, ultraviolet, and x-ray.

S-4   When continuous light (i.e., light which consists of all possible wavelengths within a given range) is passed through a prism, the light is dispersed into its component wavelengths. When these dispersed wavelengths are passed through cells containing samples of atoms or molecules, the emergent light is no longer continuous. Some of the light waves have interacted with and have been absorbed by the atoms or molecules in the cells. The missing wavelengths can be detected by permitting the light emerging from the sample cell to fall on a photographic plate or some other detecting device. This procedure is called *absorption spectroscopy* and the recorded image is called a spectrum. A spectral "line" is the wavelength at which light has been absorbed. Absorption spectroscopy is illustrated by the following diagram:

Continuous
visible
light
source

prism

sample
cell

photographic
plate

photographic plates (spectra)

no sample
in cell

sample in cell
(some wavelengths missing)

	Q-15 What happens to the light waves missing from the spectrum given by an atom or molecule?
A-15 These light waves interact with the atoms or molecules in the cell and are absorbed.	Q-16 Each different type of atom and molecule interacts with light in its own characteristic way. What effect will this have on the absorption spectrum of different types of atoms and molecules?
A-16 Each different type of atom and molecule interacts differently with light to absorb its own characteristic wavelengths of light. Therefore, the spectrum for different types of atoms or molecules will be different.	Q-17 An atom interacts with light by absorbing an amount of energy equivalent to a given wavelength of light. If an atom has a spectral "line" at 4000Å, what energy has this atom absorbed?
A-17 $E = h\nu$ $\nu = c/\lambda$ $E = hc/\lambda$ $E = \dfrac{6.63 \times 10^{-27}\ \text{erg-sec}}{4000\ \text{Å}} \left\lvert \dfrac{3.0 \times 10^{10}\ \text{cm}}{\text{sec}} \right\rvert \dfrac{1\ \text{Å}}{10^{-8}\ \text{cm}}$ $= 5.0 \times 10^{-12}\ \text{erg}$	Q-18 An atom is known to absorb energy of 3.0×10^{-12} erg. At what wavelength (in Å) would there be a spectral "line" in the spectrum of this atom?

A-18 $E = \dfrac{hc}{\lambda}$ $\lambda = \dfrac{hc}{E}$

$\lambda = \dfrac{6.63 \times 10^{-27}\,\text{erg-sec}}{3.0 \times 10^{-12}\,\text{erg}}\left|\dfrac{3.0 \times 10^{10}\,\text{cm}}{\text{sec}}\right|\dfrac{1\text{Å}}{10^{-8}\,\text{cm}}$

$= 6600\text{Å}$

Q-19   An atom is known to absorb energy equal to 5.0×10^{-12} erg. At what wave number would there be an absorption line in the spectrum of this atom?

A-19 $E = hc/\lambda = hc\bar{\nu}$ $\bar{\nu} = \dfrac{E}{hc}$

$\bar{\nu} = \dfrac{5.0 \times 10^{-12}\,\text{erg}}{6.63 \times 10^{-27}\,\text{erg-sec}}\left|\dfrac{\text{sec}}{3.0 \times 10^{10}\,\text{cm}}\right.$

$= 2.5 \times 10^{4}\,\text{cm}^{-1}$

R   An absorption spectrum arises from the absorption of certain wavelengths of light by an atom or molecule.

S-5   The energy that atoms and molecules can possess, according to quantum theory, is quantized. That is, in an atom or molecule, energy can have only certain discrete values.

The allowed energies are called atomic or molecular energy levels. A quantum (a distinct amount) of energy is absorbed when an atom or molecule is excited from a lower to higher energy level.

Q-20   Below is an energy diagram which represents the four lowest energy levels of an atom:

If an atom is in its lowest energy state, which level represents the energy of the atom?

A-20 E_1

Q-21   What happens to the energy of the atom as it is excited from E_1 to E_2 to E_3, etc.?

A-21   The energy increases.

Q-22   What must happen before the atom can be excited from E_1 to E_2?

A-22   The atom must absorb energy.

Q-23   Write an expression for the amount of energy necessary to excite the atom from the first to the second energy level.

A-23   First level E_1

Second level E_2

The amount of energy necessary to excite the atom would be the energy difference between the two levels.

$E_2 - E_1 = \Delta E_{2,1}$

Q-24   The energy necessary to excite the atom from one energy level to another is called a quantum of energy (a distinct amount). Why wouldn't intermediate values of energy be absorbed?

A-24   The atom has no energy levels available at intermediate energies.

Q-25   A transition from one energy level to another is indicated by use of an arrow,

Draw on the diagram of Q-20 arrows to represent the three transitions that this atom could undergo starting from its lowest energy level.

A-25

E_4

E_3

E_2

E_1

Q-26   Electromagnetic radiation can interact with atoms and molecules to supply the quantum of energy necessary to cause transitions to higher energy levels. Account for the missing wavelengths of light present in the absorption spectrum of an atom or molecule (see S-4).

A-26   An absorption spectrum is produced when an atom or molecule absorbs wavelengths of light with energy equal to the difference between two energy levels.

Q-27   Give an expression which relates the energy of absorption to the wavelength of light absorbed in the process

E_2 ──────────

E_1 ──────────

A-27

E_2

E_1

$\Delta E_{2,1} = E_2 - E_1$

$E = hc/\lambda$

Therefore,

$\Delta E_{2,1} = hc/\lambda$

Q-28   What factor determines the wavelength of light absorbed in a spectrum?

A-28   The differences between the various energy levels in the atom or molecule.

Q-29   What explanation would account for the fact that the absorption spectrum for each kind of atom and molecule is unique?

A-29   Each atom or molecule has unique differences between its energy levels.

Q-30   Consider the transitions represented in A-25. Which transition would give rise to the absorption of light of *longest* wavelength?

A-30 $\Delta E = hc/\lambda$

Wavelength is inversely proportional to transition energy. The longest wavelength absorption would be due to the $E_2 - E_1$ transition.

Q-31   For the diagram shown in A-25, which transition would cause absorption of light with the largest wave number?

A-31 $1/\lambda = \bar{\nu}$

$\Delta E = hc\bar{\nu}$

Wave number, $\bar{\nu}$, is directly proportional to the transition energy. The $E_4 - E_1$ transition would require light of the largest wave number.

Q-32   In the diagram of Q-27, assume that the difference in energy between the E_2 and E_1 levels is 6.0×10^{-11} erg.

What is the wavelength of light in Å needed to accomplish this transition?

A-32 $E_2 - E_1 = hc/\lambda \quad \lambda = hc/\Delta E_{2,1}$

$$\lambda = \frac{6.63 \times 10^{-27} \text{ erg-sec}}{6.0 \times 10^{-11} \text{ erg}} \left| \frac{3.0 \times 10^{10} \text{ cm}}{\text{sec}} \right| \frac{\text{Å}}{10^{-8} \text{ cm}}$$

$= 330\text{Å}$

R   The energy of atoms and molecules is quantized (only certain allowed energy levels). An absorption spectrum is the result of an atom or molecule being excited to a higher energy level by absorption of a quantum of energy.

$E_2 - E_1 = \Delta E_{2,1} = hc/\lambda = hc\bar{\nu}$

$E_2 - E_1 =$ transition energy.

Each different kind of atom or molecule gives its own characteristic absorption spectrum.

S-6   The energy of an atom or molecule is described in terms of its translational, rotational, vibrational, and electronic energy. Energy levels exist for each of these different types of energies.

Translational energy is the kinetic energy atoms or molecules possess due to motion from one place in space to another.

Q-33   Kinetic energy is given by the equation

$E_k = 1/2 \, mv^2$

where m is the mass of the moving body and v is its velocity. As the velocity of a molecule increases, what happens to its translational energy?

A-33   Increases. Energy is proportional to the square of the velocity.

Q-34   As temperature increases, what happens to the average velocity of atoms and molecules?

A-34   The average velocity increases with temperature.

Q-35   What happens to the kinetic energy as temperature increases?

A-35   The average kinetic energy increases as temperature increases.

Q-36   The relationship between average translational kinetic energy, E_k, for an atom or molecule and the temperature on the absolute scale, T, is given by the equation

$E_k = \frac{3}{2} k T$

where k is a constant equal to 1.38×10^{-16} erg/deg. At what temperature will the atoms or molecules be in their lowest translational energy level?

A-36 $E_k = \frac{3}{2} k T$

$E_k = 0$ at $T = 0$

Therefore, at absolute zero the atoms and molecules will be in their lowest translational energy level.

Q-37   Calculate the average translational kinetic energy of an atom or molecule at 25°C (298°K).

A-37 $E_k = \frac{3}{2} k T$

$E_k = \frac{3}{2} (1.38 \times 10^{-16} \text{erg/deg})(298 \text{ deg})$

$= 6.2 \times 10^{-14}$ erg

Q-38   Translational energy levels are so close together that they are considered to be continuous.

Draw a diagram to represent translational energy levels for an atom or molecule.

A-38

E

continuous

$E = 0$

Q-39   As the temperature increases, thermal energy is absorbed to excite the atoms or molecules into higher translational energy levels. How much energy is required to excite an atom or molecule from a given translational energy level to the next higher level?

A-39   Since the translational energy levels are very nearly continuous, a very small (infinitesimally small) amount of energy is required. It is for this reason that absorption spectra due to translational transitions are not observed.

R   The energy of an atom or molecule is made up of translational, rotational, vibrational, and electronic energy.

Translational energy is the kinetic energy atoms or molecules possess due to motion in space.

Quantum restrictions are not important in the consideration of translational energy levels (any energy is possible).

S-7   Rotational energy is the kinetic energy molecules possess due to rotation about an axis through their center of gravity.

	Q-40 As temperature increases, what should happen to the speed of rotation of a molecule?
A-40 As the temperature increases, the molecule should rotate faster.	Q-41 As the molecule rotates faster, what happens to its rotational kinetic energy?
A-41 As the molecule rotates faster, its rotational kinetic energy increases.	Q-42 The rotational energy of a molecule is quantized. Using the energy model account for the increase in rotational kinetic energy when a molecule is heated.
A-42 Thermal energy is absorbed in the amount necessary to excite the molecule to higher rotational energy levels.	Q-43 How else might a molecule be excited to higher rotational energy levels?
A-43 The molecule could absorb a quantum of light of just the right energy to excite it to higher energy levels.	Q-44 The energy difference between rotational energy levels corresponds to light in the microwave region of electromagnetic radiation. A molecule absorbs light with $\lambda = 1.0$ cm. What is the difference in energy between the rotational energy levels which gives rise to this absorption?
A-44 $\Delta E = hc/\lambda$ $\Delta E = \dfrac{6.63 \times 10^{-27}\text{erg-sec}}{}\left|\dfrac{3.0 \times 10^{10}\,\text{cm}}{\text{sec}}\right|\dfrac{}{1.0\,\text{cm}}$ $= 2.0 \times 10^{-16}$ erg	Q-45 Will there be any rotational energy at absolute zero?

A-45   Kinetic energy is proportional to absolute temperature. Therefore, at T equal to zero, E_k equals zero.

Q-46   Below is a typical rotational energy level diagram for a molecule. What does the arrow indicate? (Describe in terms of what happens to the molecule.)

E_4 ———————

E_3 ———————

E_2 ———————

E_1 ———————

A-46   The arrow indicates the excitation of the molecule from the E_2 to the E_3 rotational energy level. This requires absorption of energy. Therefore, at the E_3 energy level, the molecule will have more rotational energy, causing it to rotate faster.

Q-47   The first three rotational levels of the CO molecule have energies of 0, 7.6 x 10^{-16}, and 22.9 x 10^{-16} erg/molecule. What is the wavelength of light necessary to excite the CO molecule from the E_2 to the E_3 rotational level?

A-47 $\Delta E = E_3 - E_2 = 22.9 \times 10^{-16} - 7.6 \times 10^{-16}$

$= 15.3 \times 10^{-16}$ erg/molecule

$\Delta E = hc/\lambda \quad \lambda = hc/\Delta E$

$\lambda = \dfrac{6.63 \times 10^{-27} \text{erg-sec}}{} \left| \dfrac{3.0 \times 10^{10} \text{cm}}{\text{sec}} \right| \dfrac{}{15.3 \times 10^{-16} \text{erg}}$

$\lambda = 0.13$ cm

Q-48   The spacing between rotational energy levels is inversely proportional to the moment of inertia of a molecule. The moment of inertia is defined as

$I = \mu r^2$

where μ is the reduced mass

$\dfrac{m_1 m_2}{m_1 + m_2}$ and r is the distance between the masses. Which of the following two compounds would be expected to have the larger spacing between rotational energy levels?

Compound	μ	Bond Length
HBr	1.65×10^{-24}g	1.414Å
HI	1.66×10^{-24}g	1.604Å

A-48   HBr

$\Delta E \propto 1/I$

$I = \mu r^2 \quad \mu_{HI} \cong \mu_{HBr}$

$r^2_{HI} > r^2_{HBr}$

$I_{HI} > I_{HBr}$

Therefore, $\Delta E_{HBr} > \Delta E_{HI}$

Q-49   Which of the following two compounds would be expected to have the larger spacing between rotational energy levels?

Compound	μ	Bond Length
NO	12.4×10^{-24}g	1.151Å
NaCl	23.2×10^{-24}g	2.361Å

A-49   NO $\Delta E \propto 1/I$

$r^2_{NaCl} \cong 4r^2_{NO}$

$\mu_{NaCl} \cong 2\mu_{NO}$

$I_{NaCl} > I_{NO}$

Therefore, $\Delta E_{NO} > \Delta E_{NaCl}$

Q-50   Given two compounds, A-B and C-D, with similar reduced masses. The absorption spectra for an E_1 to E_2 transition for the two compounds gives a peak for A-B at 1 cm and for C-D at 1.5 cm. Which compound has the greater bond distance?

A-50 $E = hc/\lambda$

$\lambda_{CD} > \lambda_{AB}$

$\Delta E_{AB} > \Delta E_{CD}$

$\Delta E \propto 1/I$

$I_{CD} > I_{AB}$

$I = \mu r^2$

$r^2_{CD} > r^2_{AB}$

Therefore, compound CD would have the greater bond distance.

R   Rotational energy is the kinetic energy molecules possess due to rotation about an axis through their center of gravity. Rotational energy is quantized and gives rise to absorption spectra in the microwave region of the electromagnetic spectrum.

The difference between rotational energy levels is inversely proportional to the moment of inertia (I) of the molecule.

$\Delta E \propto 1/I$

$I = \mu r^2$

where $\mu = \dfrac{m_1 m_2}{m_1 + m_2}$ and r is the separation between masses.

S-8   Vibrational energy is the potential and kinetic energy molecules possess due to vibrational motion. The atoms in a molecule can be considered as point masses held together by bonds acting like springs. Because molecules are not rigid, their flexibility results in vibrational motion.

vibrational motion

The *force constant* (f) of a spring is a measure of the energy required to stretch the spring.

Q-51   What is the relationship expected between vibrational energy and temperature?

A-51   As the temperature increases, the amount of vibrational energy would be expected to increase.

Q-52   Using the ball and spring model (see S-8), predict what would happen to a vibrating molecule as its energy increases.

A-52   The magnitude of the displacement would increase.

Q-53   Draw a diagram to indicate the difference in the magnitude of the displacement of a ball and spring model at T_1 and T_2.

($T_1 < T_2$)

A-53

⊂⟋⟋⟋⟋⟋⟋⟋⊃

|←——— Stretching magnitude ———→| T_1

|←——————— Stretching magnitude ———————→| T_2

Q-54   What does the force or energy necessary to displace the balls depend upon?

A-54   The strength of the spring (the magnitude of the force constant).

Q-55   The magnitude of the force constant for a spring is analogous to the strength of a chemical bond. As the force constant increases, what happens to the strength of the chemical bond?

A-55   The strength of the bond increases.

A large force constant results from a strong chemical bond.

Q-56   If a stronger chemical bond requires more energy to excite a molecule from one vibrational energy level to another, what is the qualitative relationship between bond strength and vibrational energy level spacings?

A-56   As the bond strength increases, the spacing between vibrational energy levels increases.

Q-57   A typical vibrational energy level spacing is 2.0×10^{-13} erg. What wave number of light is necessary to cause a transition of 2.0×10^{-13} erg?

A-57 $\Delta E = hc\bar{\nu}$

$$\bar{\nu} = \frac{\Delta E}{hc}$$

$$\bar{\nu} = \frac{2.0 \times 10^{-13} \text{ erg}}{6.63 \times 10^{-27} \text{ erg-sec}} \left| \frac{\text{sec}}{3.0 \times 10^{10} \text{ cm}} \right.$$

$= 1.0 \times 10^3$ cm^{-1}

Q-58   In what region of the electromagnetic spectrum will vibrational energy absorption take place (refer to S-3)?

A-58   Infrared.

Q-59   Which of the three carbon to carbon bonds, C–C, C=C, or C≡C, would be expected to have the largest force constant? Why?

A-59   –C≡C–

Strengths of bonds increase single < double < triple.

Q-60   In which of the three bonds, C–C, C=C, or C≡C, would the vibrational energy level spacings be expected to be closest together? Why?

A-60   C–C. The bond strength is weakest for this interaction, thus, the vibrational energy levels are closest together.

Q-61   Draw energy level diagrams to represent the first two vibrational energy levels for the C–C, C=C, and C≡C bonds.

A-61

Q-62   On the diagram below, label the vibrational, rotational, and translational energy levels.

A-62

E

vibrational   rotational   trans-
                                         lational

R   Vibrational energy is the potential and kinetic energy molecules possess due to vibrational motion.

Vibrational energy is quantized and gives rise to absorption spectra in the infrared region of the electromagnetic spectrum.

The relative spacing between vibrational energy levels increases with increasing strength of the chemical bond between atoms.

S-9   Electronic energy is the energy molecules and atoms possess due to the potential and kinetic energy of their electrons. The kinetic energy of the electron is the result of motion, and potential energy arises from the interaction of the electron with nuclei and other electrons.

Q-63   Within an atom there are many energy levels available for the electrons. These energy levels are designated by four quantum numbers. What names are given these four quantum numbers? What values are allowed for each?

A-63 n = principal
         1,2,3, − − −
         ℓ = angular momentum,
         0,1,2, − − − − n-1
         m = magnetic,
         −ℓ − − − 0 − − +ℓ
         s = spin, ± 1/2

Q-64   The ℓ quantum number values are usually designated by letters. Give the letters that indicate the quantum values 0,1,2, and 3.

A-64

ℓ	letter
0	s
1	p
2	d
3	f

Q-65   What two quantum numbers determine the energy of an electron?

A-65 n, ℓ

Q-66   Draw an electronic energy level diagram for n = 1. Include energy level notations.

A66 n = 1 ℓ = 0

         _____ − − − − − _____

         n =1   1s

Q-67   Draw an electronic energy level diagram for n = 1 and n = 2. Include energy level notations.

A-67 $n = 1$ $\ell = 0$
$n = 2$ $\ell = 1,0$

Q-68   An atom has two electrons and is in its low-est electronic energy state. Using the diagram shown in A-67 indicate the position of the two electrons.

A-68

Each orbital can contain two electrons, one with $+1/2$ spin and one with $-1/2$ spin.

Q-69   An atom has four electrons and is in its low-est electronic energy state. Using the diagram shown in A-67 indicate the position of the four electrons.

A-69

Q-70   Using an arrow indicate on the diagram be-low an electronic transition which would give rise to an absorption spectra.

A-70

Either transition could be drawn. An arrow to any one of the 2p orbitals would be the same since each p orbital has the same energy.

Q-71   The spacing between electronic energy levels is on the order of 8.0×10^{-12} erg. Calculate the wavelength of light which would give rise to a transition of 8.0×10^{-12} erg.

A-71 $\Delta E = hc/\lambda \quad \lambda = hc/\Delta E$

$$\lambda = \frac{6.63 \times 10^{-27} \text{erg-sec}}{8.0 \times 10^{-12} \text{ erg}} \left| \frac{3.0 \times 10^{10} \text{ cm}}{\text{sec}} \right.$$

$= 2.5 \times 10^{-5}$ cm

Q-72   In what region of the electromagnetic spectrum will electronic absorption occur? (Refer to S-3.)

A-72   Ultraviolet. Electronic absorptions also give rise to spectra in the visible region.

Q-73   The spectrum of an atom shows an absorption in the ultraviolet and the visible region. Which absorption results from transition between the most widely spaced energy levels?

A-73   The absorption in the ultraviolet region.

Q-74   How does the difference between electronic energy levels compare with those of translational, rotational, and vibrational?

A-74   The difference between electronic energy levels is greater than for all the others.

R   Electronic energy is the energy molecules and atoms possess due to the potential and kinetic energy of their electrons.

Electronic energy is quantized and gives rise to absorption spectra in the visible and ultraviolet regions of the electromagnetic spectrum.

S-10   Molecules have electronic energy levels which are analogous to electronic energy levels in atoms. These molecular energy levels are called molecular orbitals. Molecular orbitals arise from the interactions of atomic orbitals of the atoms forming the molecule.

The s orbitals of atoms A and B interact with one another to produce two molecular orbitals in the molecule AB. One orbital produced is of lower energy and one of higher energy than the original s orbitals. This is illustrated in the following diagram:

The lower energy molecular orbital is called a bonding orbital, σ_S, and the higher orbital is called an antibonding orbital, σ_S^*.

Q-75 Two hydrogen atoms interact to form the H_2 molecule. Diagram the atomic and molecular orbitals and show the electrons.

A-75

Q-76 Will the H_2 system be more or less stable than two H atoms? Why?

(Hint: What is the relationship between energy and stability?)

A-76 The H_2 system will be more stable since the electrons are in a lower energy level. The lower the energy, the more stable a system is.

Q-77 Account for the fact that two hydrogen atoms will combine to form an H_2 molecule.

A-77 Bond formation occurs because the molecule H_2 results in a lower energy system.

Q-78 The *anti-bonding, σ_S**, and bonding molecular orbitals can be pictured using a charge cloud diagram.

Which diagram would represent the bonding molecular orbital and which the anti-bonding molecular orbital?

A-78 Bonding

orbitals overlap

Anti-bonding

no overlap

Q-79 Diagram the molecular orbitals which result from the interaction of a hydrogen atom ($H°$) and a hydride ion (H^-) to form the H_2^- ion. Show electrons.

A-79

Q-80   Would the H_2^- ion be expected to be more or less stable than the H_2 molecule? Why?

A-80   Less. An electron in the anti-bonding molecular orbital increases the energy of the system making it less stable.

Q-81   Draw a molecular orbital diagram to illustrate the electronic structures in the molecule He_2^+. Show the electrons in the proper orbitals.

A-81

Q-82   From an energy point of view would the molecule He_2 be expected to form? Why?

A-82   No. There would be no net stability. The stability gained by the electrons in the bonding molecular orbital would be lost by the two electrons in the anti-bonding orbital.

Therefore, there would be no net gain in stability on bond formation.

Q-83   Using the energy diagram for the H_2 molecule draw an arrow to illustrate the electronic transition to form an excited H_2 molecule.

A-83

Q-84   Molecular orbitals that are formed which are symmetrical to rotation around the bond are called σ orbitals. Molecular orbitals which are not symmetrical to rotation around the bond are called π orbitals. Below are some contour diagrams for molecular orbitals. Label them as being σ or π molecular orbitals.

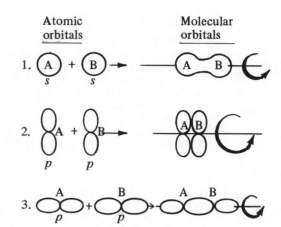

A-84   1. and 3. would be σ molecular orbitals.

2. would be a π molecular orbital.

This rotation is not symmetrical about the bond axis.

Q-85   Would the overlap of an s and a ρ orbital, as described below, give rise to a σ or π molecular orbital?

A-85 σ

Q-86   Draw an energy diagram to show the anti-bonding and bonding molecular orbitals which arise from the interaction of two p orbitals end to end. Are the molecular orbitals σ or π orbitals?

A-86

σ molecular orbitals

Q-87   Draw an energy diagram to show the molecular orbitals arising from side-to-side interaction of p orbitals. Are the molecular orbitals σ or π orbitals?

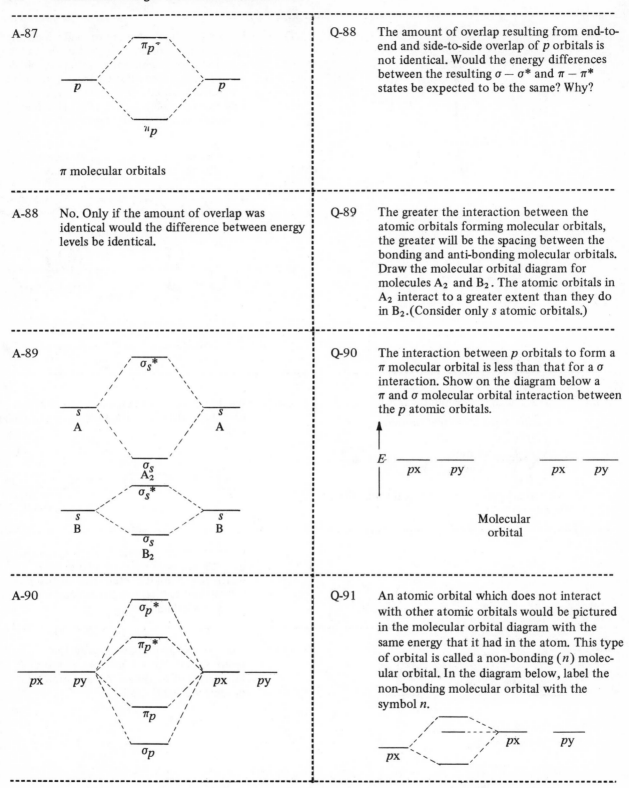

A-87

π_p^*

p p

π_p

π molecular orbitals

Q-88 The amount of overlap resulting from end-to-end and side-to-side overlap of p orbitals is not identical. Would the energy differences between the resulting $\sigma - \sigma^*$ and $\pi - \pi^*$ states be expected to be the same? Why?

A-88 No. Only if the amount of overlap was identical would the difference between energy levels be identical.

Q-89 The greater the interaction between the atomic orbitals forming molecular orbitals, the greater will be the spacing between the bonding and anti-bonding molecular orbitals. Draw the molecular orbital diagram for molecules A_2 and B_2. The atomic orbitals in A_2 interact to a greater extent than they do in B_2.(Consider only s atomic orbitals.)

A-89

σ_s^*

s s
A A

σ_s
A_2

σ_s^*

s s
B B

σ_s
B_2

Q-90 The interaction between p orbitals to form a π molecular orbital is less than that for a σ interaction. Show on the diagram below a π and σ molecular orbital interaction between the p atomic orbitals.

E ___ ___   ___ ___
      px py px py

Molecular
orbital

A-90

σ_p^*

π_p^*

px py px py

π_p

σ_p

Q-91 An atomic orbital which does not interact with other atomic orbitals would be pictured in the molecular orbital diagram with the same energy that it had in the atom. This type of orbital is called a non-bonding (n) molecular orbital. In the diagram below, label the non-bonding molecular orbital with the symbol n.

___   ___ px   ___ py

px

A-91

Q-92   Which molecular orbitals in the following diagram would be non-bonding molecular orbitals?

A-92

R   Molecules, in a manner analogous to atoms, have electronic energy levels associated with them called molecular orbitals. These arise from interaction between the atomic orbitals of the atoms forming the molecule. The interaction of atomic orbitals gives rise to a molecular orbital of low energy called a bonding orbital and one of high energy called an anti-bonding orbital. An orbital that does not interact is called a non-bonding orbital. p orbitals can interact end-to-end or side-to-side to form, respectively, σ or π molecular orbitals.

Chapter 2 | ULTRAVIOLET AND VISIBLE SPECTRA

Ultraviolet and visible spectroscopy is useful in determining structures of organic molecules and in quantitative analysis. This chapter will deal mainly with the theory of electronic transitions and with the elucidation of structure from ultraviolet spectral data.

Part I: Electronic Transitions

After completing this section you should

> a) be able to determine the types of chromophores present in a molecule and determine which chromophore gives rise to the lowest energy transition
> b) be able to predict approximate wavelength regions for different types of transitions
> c) understand why conjugated systems absorb at longer wavelength
> d) be able to predict solvent effects on $\pi \rightarrow \pi^*$ and $n \rightarrow \pi^*$ transitions
> e) be able to calculate $\mathcal{E}_{max}$ from the Lambert-Beer relationship.

Part II: Use of Ultraviolet Spectra in Structural Determinations

After completing this section you should

> a) be able to predict λ_{max}^{hexane} for conjugated dienes
> b) be able to predict $\lambda_{max}^{ethanol}$ for α, β − unsaturated ketones
> c) be able to predict structures of compounds with the aid of ultraviolet spectra.

Ultraviolet and Visible Spectra
PART I: Electronic Transitions

S-1   The electronic spectrum of a molecule results from a transition between two different molecular electronic energy levels. A transition between two states will be denoted by using the notation illustrated below:

denoted as $\sigma \rightarrow \sigma^*$

Q-1   Two atoms, each containing a single half-filled s orbital, are allowed to interact so as to form a σ bond. Draw an energy diagram for this process and label the bonding and anti-bonding molecular orbitals. Show the electrons in the lowest energy state.

A-1

Q-2   Two carbon atoms interact so as to form a π bond. Draw an energy diagram for this process showing only p orbital interactions. Label the bonding (π) and anti-bonding (π^*) molecular orbitals.

A-2

Q-3   Two atoms interact to form a bond. A p orbital of atom A interacts side-to-side with a p orbital of atom B. A second p orbital of atom B does not interact. Sketch an energy level diagram for interaction between A and B and label all the orbitals.

A-3

The second ρ orbital of atom B does not interact, therefore, its energy remains the same.

Q-4   A total of four electrons must be added to the molecular orbitals formed by the interaction described in Q-3. Show where these four electrons should be placed when the molecule is in the ground state (lowest energy state).

A-4

Q-5   The energy level diagram for ethylene is given below. What kind of electronic transitions can the highest energy electrons undergo?

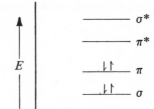

A-5 $\pi \rightarrow \pi^*$
      $\pi \rightarrow \sigma^*$

Q-6   The energy level diagram for the carbonyl group is given below. What kind of electronic transitions can the highest energy electrons undergo?

A-6 $n \rightarrow \pi^*$
      $n \rightarrow \sigma^*$

Q-7   Which of the two possible transitions for the non-bonding electrons in the carbonyl group (see Q-6) will require the greatest energy? Which transition will require the longest wavelength of light?

A-7 The $n \to \sigma^*$ transition will require the most energy. Because wavelength is inversely proportional to energy, the $n \to \pi^*$ transition will require the longer wavelength of light (lower energy).

R Electronic spectra of molecules result from transitions between two different molecular electronic energy levels. The notation used to represent a transition from a σ bonding molecular orbital to a σ^* anti-bonding molecular orbital is $\sigma \to \sigma^*$.

S-2 Systems responsible for the absorption of light are called *chromophores or chromophoric* groups. Chromophores which give rise to $\sigma \to \sigma^*$ transitions are systems which contain electrons in σ molecular orbitals. Compounds containing only σ molecular orbitals are saturated organic molecules which *do not* contain atoms with lone pair electrons. Examples of $\sigma \to \sigma^*$ type chromophores are $\geq C - C \leq$ and $\geq C - H$.

Chromophores which give rise to $n \to \sigma^*$ transitions are systems which contain electrons in non-bonding and σ molecular orbitals. Compounds containing only n and σ molecular orbitals are saturated organic molecules which contain one or more atoms with lone pair electrons. Examples of $n \to \sigma^*$ type chromophores are $\geq C - \ddot{O} -$, $\geq C - \ddot{S} -$, $\geq C - \ddot{N} -$, and $\geq C - \ddot{C}l:$.

Chromophores which give rise to $\pi \to \pi^*$ type transitions are systems which contain electrons in π molecular orbitals. Unsaturated organic compounds have π molecular orbitals. Examples of $\pi \to \pi^*$ type chromophores are $\geq C = C \leq$ and $- C \equiv C -$.

Q-8 Which of the following transitions requires the most energy?

$$\sigma \to \sigma^*, n \to \sigma^*, \pi \to \pi^*$$

A-8 $\sigma \to \sigma^*$ requires the most energy.

Q-9 What types of transitions are possible in cyclopentene (C_5H_8)?

A-9 $\sigma \to \sigma^*$
$\sigma \to \pi^*$
$\pi \to \pi^*$
$\pi \to \sigma^*$

Q-10 What *chromophore* in cyclopentene is responsible for the lowest energy transition?

A-10 $\geq C = C \leq$
The $\pi \to \pi^*$ is the lowest energy transition.

Q-11 Cyclopentene absorbs light near 190 mμ (1900Å). Absorption at higher wavelength does not occur. What type of transition is responsible for the observed absorption? Illustrate by use of an energy level diagram.

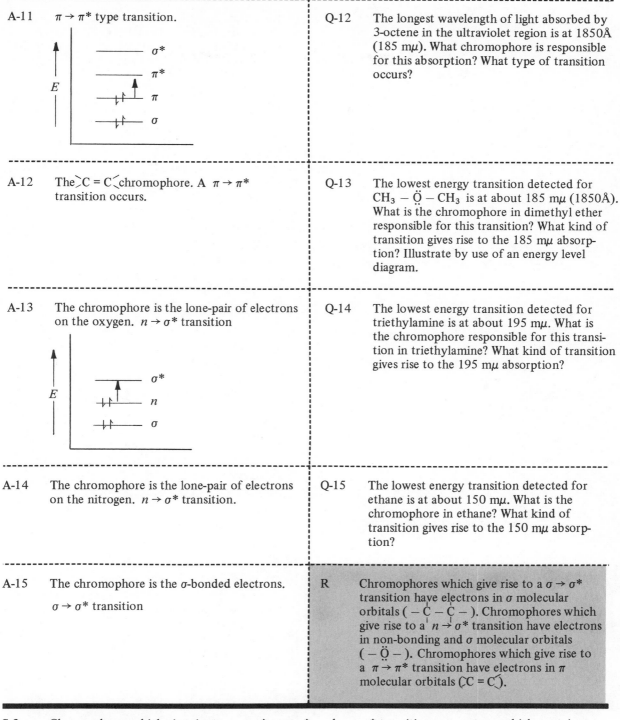

A-11 $\pi \rightarrow \pi^*$ type transition.

Q-12   The longest wavelength of light absorbed by 3-octene in the ultraviolet region is at 1850Å (185 mμ). What chromophore is responsible for this absorption? What type of transition occurs?

A-12   The $\diagup$C = C$\diagdown$ chromophore. A $\pi \rightarrow \pi^*$ transition occurs.

Q-13   The lowest energy transition detected for $CH_3 - \ddot{O} - CH_3$ is at about 185 mμ (1850Å). What is the chromophore in dimethyl ether responsible for this transition? What kind of transition gives rise to the 185 mμ absorption? Illustrate by use of an energy level diagram.

A-13   The chromophore is the lone-pair of electrons on the oxygen. $n \rightarrow \sigma^*$ transition

Q-14   The lowest energy transition detected for triethylamine is at about 195 mμ. What is the chromophore responsible for this transition in triethylamine? What kind of transition gives rise to the 195 mμ absorption?

A-14   The chromophore is the lone-pair of electrons on the nitrogen. $n \rightarrow \sigma^*$ transition.

Q-15   The lowest energy transition detected for ethane is at about 150 mμ. What is the chromophore in ethane? What kind of transition gives rise to the 150 mμ absorption?

A-15   The chromophore is the σ-bonded electrons.

       $\sigma \rightarrow \sigma^*$ transition

R   Chromophores which give rise to a $\sigma \rightarrow \sigma^*$ transition have electrons in σ molecular orbitals ($- \overset{|}{C} - \overset{|}{C} -$). Chromophores which give rise to a $n \rightarrow \sigma^*$ transition have electrons in non-bonding and σ molecular orbitals ($- \ddot{O} -$). Chromophores which give rise to a $\pi \rightarrow \pi^*$ transition have electrons in π molecular orbitals ($C = C$).

S-3   Chromophores which give rise to $n \rightarrow \pi^*, n \rightarrow \sigma^*$, and $\pi \rightarrow \pi^*$ transitions are systems which contain electrons in both non-bonded and π molecular orbitals. Compounds with both n and π molecular orbitals are those containing atoms with lone pair electrons and a π orbital *or* atoms with lone-pair electrons conjugated with other atoms containing π orbitals. Examples of these types of chromophores are $\diagup$C = $\ddot{O}$ and $\diagup$C = C $-$ $\ddot{O}$ $-$.

Q-16 The energy level diagram for the carbonyl chromophore ($>C = \ddot{O}$) is given below. Arrange the $n \rightarrow \sigma^*$, $\pi \rightarrow \pi^*$, and $n \rightarrow \pi^*$ transitions in order of decreasing energy.

A-16 $\pi \rightarrow \pi^* > n \rightarrow \sigma^* > n \rightarrow \pi^*$ highest $\rightarrow$ lowest energy.

Q-17 Acetone absorbs light at 280, 187, and 154 mμ. What chromophore is responsible for each of these absorptions? What type of transition causes each absorption?

A-17 The carbonyl group is the chromophore.

280 mμ	$n \rightarrow \pi^*$
187 mμ	$n \rightarrow \sigma^*$
154 mμ	$\pi \rightarrow \pi^*$

Q-18 What types of transitions, other than $\sigma \rightarrow \sigma^*$, would be expected for the following compounds?

a. $CH_2 = CH \ddot{O} CH_3$

b. $CH_2 = CH CH_2 CH_2 \ddot{O} CH_3$

A-18 a. $n \rightarrow \pi^*$
$n \rightarrow \sigma^*$
$\pi \rightarrow \pi^*$

b. $\pi \rightarrow \pi^*$ (isolated double bond)
$n \rightarrow \sigma^*$ (isolated $C - \ddot{O} - C$). The oxygen is not conjugated with the π orbital system.

Q-19 What is the chromophore in each of the following molecules which gives rise to the lowest energy transition?

a.

b. $CH_3 OH$

A-19 a. Chromophore $>C = C<$.
$\pi \rightarrow \pi^*$

b. Chromophore $- \ddot{O} -$.
$n \rightarrow \sigma^*$

Q-20 What types of chromophores, other than $\sigma \rightarrow \sigma^*$, do each of the following molecules have? What types of transitions will be expected to occur in each?

a. $CH_3 \overset{\overset{\displaystyle O}{\|}}{CH}$

b. $(CH_3)_2 \ddot{N} CH = CH_2$

A-20 a. Chromophore $>C = O$.
$n \rightarrow \pi^*$
$n \rightarrow \sigma^*$
$\pi \rightarrow \pi^*$

b. Chromophore $-\ddot{N} - C = C$ system.
$n \rightarrow \pi^*$
$n \rightarrow \sigma^*$
$\pi \rightarrow \pi^*$

R Chromophores containing atoms with lone-pair electrons and π orbitals *or* atoms with lone-pair electrons conjugated with other atoms containing π orbitals give rise to $n \rightarrow \pi^*$, $n \rightarrow \sigma^*$, and $\pi \rightarrow \pi^*$ transitions.

S-4   In general, compounds which have only $\sigma \to \sigma*$ transitions absorb light near 1500Å while compounds with $n \to \sigma*$ and $\pi \to \pi*$ transitions (due to unconjugated chromophores) absorb light close to 2000Å. Compounds with $n \to \pi*$ transitions absorb light in the quartz ultraviolet (2000-4000Å). The ultraviolet region below 2000Å (vacuum ultraviolet) will not be considered in detail since it is a difficult area in which to obtain spectra and yields little information regarding the structure of organic molecules.

Q-21   A compound whose energy diagram appears below showed absorptions at 1900Å and 3000Å. What type of transition is associated with each absorption?

A-21   3000Å $n \to \pi*$
        1900Å $n \to \sigma*$

Q-22   A compound whose energy diagram is shown below absorbed light at 185 mμ but had no absorption bands in the quartz ultraviolet. What type of transition was the absorption due to?

A-22 $\pi \to \pi*$

Q-23   Acetaldehyde (CH_3COH) has absorption peaks at 160, 180, and 290 mμ. What type of transition is responsible for each of these absorptions?

A-23   290 $n \to \pi*$
        180 $n \to \sigma*$
        160 $\pi \to \pi*$

Q-24   What transition is responsible for each of the three absorptions in the spectrum of acetone (CH_3COCH_3)? Will these absorptions occur in the quartz or in the vacuum region of the ultraviolet?

A-24 $n \rightarrow \pi^*$ Quartz (actual 279)

$n \rightarrow \sigma^*$ Vacuum (actual 189)

$\pi \rightarrow \pi^*$ Vacuum (actual 166)

R		Approximate region of
	Transition	absorption
	$\sigma \rightarrow \sigma^*$	150 mμ
	$n \rightarrow \sigma^*$	less than 200 mμ
	$\pi \rightarrow \pi^*$	less than 200 mμ
	(unconjugated)	
	$n \rightarrow \pi^*$	300 mμ

Vacuum ultraviolet region is below 200 mμ.
Quartz ultraviolet region is between 200 and
400 mμ.

S-5   Different electronic environments within molecules will affect the degree of interaction between orbitals. Consequently, the energy differences between similar electronic levels in two different molecules will not be identical. For example, the environments about the chromophores in compounds A and B are not the same because of the nature of the groups attached. The energy level diagrams below illustrate this effect.

Molecule A   Molecule B

$\begin{matrix} R \\ R \end{matrix} C = C \begin{matrix} R \\ R \end{matrix}$ $\begin{matrix} R \\ R' \end{matrix} C = C \begin{matrix} R' \\ R' \end{matrix}$

	Q-25 The energy diagrams for two different carbon-carbon double bonds are shown in S-5. In which compound is there the greatest interaction between p orbitals? Which bond is the longer?
A-25 Compound B has the greatest interaction between p orbitals. The π bond in compound B will be the shorter bond (see Q-89, Chapter I).	Q-26 Which of the two compounds described in S-5 will have the lower energy $\pi \rightarrow \pi^*$ transition?
A-26 The $\pi \rightarrow \pi^*$ transition in compound A will require the lower energy.	Q-27 The absorptions due to the $\pi \rightarrow \pi^*$ transitions in ethylene and 3-octene occur at 163 and 185 mμ, respectively. Why aren't the absorptions at the same wavelength?
A-27 Both absorptions are due to $\pi \rightarrow \pi^*$ transitions. Because the double bonds have different groups attached, the electronic environments of the chromophores are different. Thus, the energy difference between the π and π^* states are not the same.	Q-28 Is the interaction of p orbitals greater in ethylene or 3-octene?

A-28   The interaction is greater in ethylene. The lower wavelength absorption indicates the greater energy difference between π and π^* states.

Q-29   The $\pi \rightarrow \pi^*$ transitions for two compounds are given below. Why don't the two transitions absorb at the same wavelength?

$$CH_3 C \equiv CH \qquad 1870\text{\AA}$$

$$\underset{\displaystyle CH_3\,\overset{\textstyle \|}{\overset{\textstyle O}{C}}\,CH_3}{} \qquad 1540\text{\AA}$$

A-29   While both absorptions are due to a $\pi \rightarrow \pi^*$ type transition, the electronic environment of the carbonyl group is not identical to the environment about the triple bond. Thus, the transitions require different energy.

Q-30   For the three compounds given below, can the observed absorption bands be due to the same type of transition? Explain.

$$CH_3 - Cl \qquad 1720\text{\AA}$$

$$CH_3 - I \qquad 2580\text{\AA}$$

$$CH_3 - Br \qquad 2040\text{\AA}$$

A-30   Yes. All the absorptions are due to $n \rightarrow \sigma^*$ transitions. Because the electronegativity of each halogen is different, the electronic environment in each molecule will be different; this results in a different degree of interaction of molecular orbitals and, consequently, a difference in energy between the n and σ^* states.

R   Different electronic environments within molecules affect the degree of interaction between orbitals. As interactions between orbitals increase the length of the bond formed becomes less, and the difference in energy between the bonding and anti-bonding molecular orbitals increases.

S-6   The intensity of the absorption due to a $\pi \rightarrow \pi^*$ type transition is always 10 to 100 times more intense than $n \rightarrow \sigma^*$ or $n \rightarrow \pi^*$ type absorptions. The spectrum of a compound which has both $n \rightarrow \pi^*$ and $\pi \rightarrow \pi^*$ transitions is shown below. The position of maximum absorption of each band (called λ_{max}) corresponds to the wavelength of light necessary for the transitions. The width of the bands is, in part, due to instrumentation.

Q-31   For the following spectrum, indicate the λ_{max} for each peak.

A-31 λ_{max} = 205 mμ.
λ_{max} = 235 mμ.

Q-32   The spectrum for a compound which has both $n \rightarrow \pi^*$ and $\pi \rightarrow \pi^*$ transitions is given below. Give λ_{max} for the band resulting from each type of transition.

A-32 $n \rightarrow \pi^*$ λ_{max} = 230 mμ.
         $\pi \rightarrow \pi^*$ λ_{max} = 190 mμ.

Q-33   A compound was known to be either a saturated amine $\diagdown N - \overset{|}{C} - \overset{|}{C} - \overset{|}{C} -$ or an unsaturated amine $\diagdown N - \overset{|}{C} - \overset{|}{C} = C \diagup$. The spectrum of the compound is given below. What structure is indicated? Justify your answer.

170mμ 200mμ 250mμ

wavelength (λ)

A-33   The structure $\diagdown N - \overset{|}{C} - \overset{|}{C} = C \diagup$ is indicated. The presence of two peaks is indicative of two types of transitions. The strong λ_{max} of 185 mμ is due to a $\pi \rightarrow \pi^*$ transition while the weak λ_{max} at 220 mμ is due to the $n \rightarrow \sigma^*$ transition.

R   The intensity of $\pi \rightarrow \pi^*$ transitions is 10 to 100 times as great as the intensity of $n \rightarrow \sigma^*$ and $n \rightarrow \pi^*$ type absorptions. The position of maximum absorption of a band is denoted as λ_{max}.

S-7   In conjugated systems, such as $\diagdown C = \overset{|}{C} - \overset{|}{C} = C \diagup$, π orbitals from each double bond interact to form a new set of bonding and anti-bonding orbitals. This interaction is illustrated below.

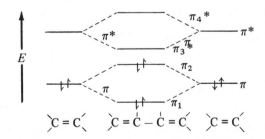

As the conjugated system in a molecule becomes longer (involves more atoms with π bonds), the difference in energy between the ground states and the excited states for the $\pi \rightarrow \pi^*$ transitions becomes less. Consequently, as the conjugated system increases in length the energy required for a $\pi \rightarrow \pi^*$ transition becomes less and absorption will occur at longer wavelength.

| | Q-34 | For the conjugated system diagrammed in S-7 what is the lowest energy transition possible? |

A-34 $\pi_2 \rightarrow \pi_3{}^*$

Q-35   The λ_{max} for ethylene is about 1850Å while λ_{max} for 1,3-butadiene ($CH_2 = CH - CH = CH_2$) is 2170Å.

Using the energy level diagram shown in S-7 explain why butadiene absorbs at longer wavelength.

A35

| ethylene type system | butadiene type system |

The $\pi \rightarrow \pi^*$ transition in ethylene requires higher energy than the $\pi_2 \rightarrow \pi_3{}^*$ transition in butadiene.

Q-36   Why doesn't 1,4-pentadiene absorb light above 2000Å in the ultraviolet region of the spectrum?

$CH_2{=}CHCH_2\,CH{=}CH_2$ λ_{max} = 1750Å

$CH_2{=}CHCH{=}CH_2$ λ_{max} = 2170Å

A-36   In 1,4-pentadiene the two double bonds are *not* conjugated and do not interact. Consequently, the $\pi \rightarrow \pi^*$ transition is of high energy. In 1,3 butadiene the double bonds are conjugated and the lower energy $\pi_2 \rightarrow \pi_3{}^*$ transition is possible.

Q-37   Predict the difference in the spectrum in the *quartz* region of the ultraviolet for the two compounds

A   and   **B**

A-37   Compound **A** has a conjugated diene system and would absorb light between 200 and 400 mμ. λ_{max} (actual) $\approx$ 235 mμ.

Compound **B** has two isolated double bonds and would have *no* absorption in the 200 – 400 mμ region.

Q-38   The spectra of compounds **C** and **D** (below) are obtained in the region 200 – 400 mμ. The concentration is such that only the high intensity $\pi \rightarrow \pi^*$ transition absorptions are detected. What difference in the spectra of the two compounds would be expected?

C   **D**

A-38   Compound **C** would have no $\pi \to \pi^*$ absorption between 200 and 400 mμ. Compound **D** would show absorption in the 200-230 mμ region. An absorption at 218 mμ is actually observed for D.

Q-39   Which of the following would be expected to absorb light of the longest and shortest wavelength? Why?

Consider only the $\pi \to \pi^*$ transition.

A-39   **B** the shortest, **C** the longest. The longer the conjugated system, the lower the energy for the $\pi \to \pi^*$ transition. **C** has the longest conjugated system. **B** has only isolated double bonds.

Q-40   Which of the following would be expected to absorb light of the longest and shortest wavelength? Why?

A $CH_3(CH_2)_5 \ CH_3$
B $(CH_3)_2 \ C = CHCH_2 CH = C \ (CH_3)_2$
C $CH_2 = CH \ CH = CHCH_3$

A-40   **C** would absorb at longest wavelength, **A** at shortest. **C** has a conjugated system.

Q-41   The $\pi \to \pi^*$ transitions for compounds **E** and **F** (below) were obtained. One compound had a $\lambda_{max} = 303$ mμ while the other had $\lambda_{max} = 263$ mμ. Which compound has the $\lambda_{max} = 303$ mμ?

$CH_3 CH=CHCH=CHC \overset{\nearrow O}{H}$ **E**

$CH_3 CH=CHCH=CHCH=CHC \overset{\nearrow O}{H}$ **F**

A-41   Compound **F** has λ_{max} 303. The longer conjugated system absorbs light of longer wavelength.

Q-42   The compound called β-carotene has eleven conjugated double bonds and absorbs light in the colored region of the spectrum. Explain.

A-42   As the length of the conjugated system increases, the energy difference between the highest occupied energy level and the lowest unoccupied energy level decreases. In β-carotene this energy difference must correspond to visible (low energy) light.

R   In conjugated systems, π orbitals interact to form a new set of bonding and anti-bonding orbitals in which the energy difference between the ground and excited states for the $\pi \to \pi^*$ transition is less. As the length of the conjugated system increases, the wavelength of absorption for the $\pi \to \pi^*$ transition becomes greater.

S-8   In most $\pi \to \pi^*$ transitions the excited states are more polar than the ground states. As a result, in the $\pi \to \pi^*$ transition, absorption will shift toward longer wavelength in polar solvents. This shift toward longer wavelength is referred to as a *bathochromic* effect (red shift).

Molecules with non-bonded electrons are able to interact with hydrogen bonding solvents to a greater extent in the ground state than in their excited state. As a result the $n \to \pi^*$ transition absorption will shift toward shorter wavelength as the hydrogen bonding ability of the solvent increases. A shift toward shorter wavelength is called a *hypochromic* effect (blue shift).

Q-43 Polar interactions of solvents with molecules result in the lowering of energy states. Will the π or $\pi*$ state be stabilized to the greater extent by a polar solvent?

A-43 The $\pi*$ state will be stabilized to a greater extent because it is more polar than the π state. As solvent interaction increases the stability of the state increases.

Q-44 On the energy level diagram below show the relative changes in energy that a polar solvent has on both the π and $\pi*$ state.

A-44

Q-45 Using the energy level diagram drawn for A-44 explain why a polar solvent causes a $\pi \rightarrow \pi*$ transition to shift to longer wavelength.

A-45 The energy required for a $\pi \rightarrow \pi*$ transition in a molecule interacting with a polar solvent is less than the energy required for the $\pi \rightarrow \pi*$ transition for the molecule in a non-polar solvent.

Q-46 A conjugated diene has a λ_{max} at 219 mμ in hexane solvent λ_{max}^{hexane} = 219 mμ. Will λ_{max} be greater or smaller than 219 mμ if the solvent is changed to ethanol?

Explain.

A-46 $\lambda_{max}^{ethanol}$ is greater than 219 mμ. Ethanol is a more polar solvent than hexane. Therefore, ethanol would stabilize the $\pi*$ state to a greater extent than the π state.

Q-47 Hydrogen bond interactions between lone-pair electrons and solvent result in the lowering of the energy state. For an $n \rightarrow \pi*$ type transition will the n or $\pi*$ state be stabilized to the greater extent by a hydrogen bonding solvent? Why?

A-47   The n state will be stabilized to the greater extent. Non-bonded electrons interact to a greater extent with hydrogen bonding solvent in their ground states than in their excited states.

Q-48   Below is the energy level diagram for a ketone. Show the effect on the $n \rightarrow \pi^*$ transition when the molecule is dissolved in a polar, hydrogen bonding solvent such as ethanol. Show the effect of the same solvent on the $\pi \rightarrow \pi^*$ transition. Explain.

A-48

no solvent   solvated with ethanol

The solvent will hydrogen bond and stabilize the n ground state to a greater extent than it will stabilize the excited (π^*) state. The energy difference for the $n \rightarrow \pi^*$ transition will become larger (blue shift). The polar solvent stabilizes the π^* state to a greater extent than it stabilizes the π state. Thus, the energy difference for the $\pi \rightarrow \pi^*$ transition becomes less (red shift).

Q-49   A certain compound dissolved in hexane had a $\lambda_{max}^{hexane} = 305$ mμ. When the same compound was dissolved in ethanol the $\lambda_{max}^{ethanol}$ was 307 mμ. Is the absorption due to an $n \rightarrow \pi^*$ or a $\pi \rightarrow \pi^*$ type transition? Give your reasoning.

A-49 $\pi \rightarrow \pi^*$

Ethanol is a more polar solvent and better hydrogen bonding solvent than hexane. The transition is of lower energy in ethanol than in hexane. Therefore, the excited state must be stabilized to a *greater* extent by ethanol than the ground state. The shift to longer wavelength with more polar solvents is characteristic of $\pi \rightarrow \pi^*$ transition.

Q-50   The following spectral data is available for a compound.

$\lambda_{max}^{ethanol} = 287$ mμ

$\lambda_{max}^{dioxane} = 295$ mμ

What type of transition gives rise to the observed peaks?

A-50   The transition must be an $n \to \pi^*$ or an $n \to \sigma^*$ since increasing the hydrogen bonding ability of the solvent causes a blue shift.

R   For $\pi \to \pi^*$ transitions the excited states are more polar. Increasing the polarity of the solvent causes a red shift (shift to longer wavelength) of the $\pi \to \pi^*$ transition. For $n \to \pi^*$ transitions the ground states interact with hydrogen bonding solvents better than do excited states. Increasing the hydrogen bonding ability of the solvent causes a blue shift (shift to shorter wavelength) of the $n \to \pi^*$ transition.

S-9   The ultraviolet spectra of compounds are usually obtained by passing light of a given wavelength (monochromatic light) through a dilute solution of the substance in a non-absorbing solvent such as water, ethanol, or hexane.

The intensity of the absorption band is measured by the percent of the incident light that passes through the sample.

$\%$ transmittance = $(100)\, I/I_0$

where I_0 is the intensity of incident light and I is the intensity of the transmitted light.

Because light absorption is a function of the concentration of the absorbing molecules, a more precise way of reporting intensity of absorption is by use of the Lambert-Beer Law

$\log I/I_0 = -\mathcal{E}c\ell = -$ Absorbance

where I and I_0 have the same meaning as before, c is the concentration of the sample in mole/l, ℓ is the length of cell through which the light passes, and $\mathcal{E}$ is a constant called the *extinction* coefficient. Extinction coefficients of absorption bands are reported as $\mathcal{E}_{max}$.

Q-51   A compound had an absorption maximum at 235 mμ (λ_{max} = 235). At 235 mμ, 20% of the incident light was transmitted by a 2.0×10^{-4} molar solution of the sample in a 1.0 cm cell. What was the extinction coefficient at 235 mμ ($\mathcal{E}_{max}$)?

A-51

$\log I/I_0 = -\mathcal{E}c\ell$

$\ell = 1.0$

$c = 2.0 \times 10^{-4}$ mole/l

$\log I/I_0 = \log 0.20 = -0.70$

$-0.70 = -\mathcal{E}\, (2.0 \times 10^{-4})\, (1.0)$

$\mathcal{E} = 3.5 \times 10^3$

Q-52   A 1.0×10^{-5} molar solution of a compound has a $\%$ transmittance of 50 at λ_{max} = 280 mμ when a 1.0 cm cell is used. Calculate $\mathcal{E}_{max}$ at 280 mμ.

A-52

$\log I/I_0 = -\mathcal{E}c\ell$

$\ell = 1.0$ cm.

$c = 1.0 \times 10^{-5}$ M

$\log I/I_0 = \log 0.50 = -0.30$

$-0.30 = -\mathcal{E}\, (1.0 \times 10^{-5})\, (1.0)$

$\mathcal{E} = 3.0 \times 10^4$

Q-53   The $\mathcal{E}_{max}$ for aniline at λ_{max} = 280 mμ is 1,430. A solution of aniline in water is to be prepared such that the $\%$ transmission of the solution in a 1.0 cm cell will be 30. How many grams of aniline will be required to prepare 100 ml of solution?

A-53 $\log I/I_0 = -\varepsilon c \ell$

$\ell = 1.0$ cm

$\varepsilon = 1,430$

$\log I/I_0 = \log 0.30 = -0.52$

$-0.52 = -(1,430)(c)(1.0)$

$c = 3.6 \times 10^{-4}$ mole/l

$MW_{C_6H_7N} = 93$

$(3.6 \times 10^{-4})(93)$ g of aniline to prepare one liter of solution.

0.0034 g of aniline to prepare 100 ml of solution.

Q-54   2-cyclohexenone (C_6H_8O) has an ε_{max} of 10,000 at $\lambda_{max} = 225$ mμ. If a solution of this compound is to be prepared such that the absorbance is 0.30 when using 1.0 cm cells, how many grams of 2-cyclohexenone will be required per liter of solution? Remember that $\log I/I_0 = -$ absorbance.

A-54 $\log I/I_0 = -\varepsilon c \ell = -$ absorbance

$\varepsilon = 10,000$

$\ell = 1.0$ cm

Absorbance = 0.30

$(10,000)(1.0)(c) = 0.30$

$c = 3.0 \times 10^{-5}$ mole/l

$MW_{C_6H_8O} = 96$

Grams of 2-cyclohexenone/l of solution = $(96)(3.0)10^{-5}$

$= 2.9 \times 10^{-3}$ g

Q-55   The λ_{max}^{hexane} and $\varepsilon_{max}^{hexane}$ for butyl nitrite are given below. Calculate the % transmission at each λ_{max} for a 1.0×10^{-4} molar solution of the compound in hexane if a 1.0 cm cell is used.

	λ_{max}^{hexane}	$\varepsilon_{max}^{hexane}$
butyl nitrite	220	14,500
	356	87

A-55 $\log I/I_0 = -\varepsilon c \ell$

$\varepsilon_{220} = 14,500$

$c = 1.0 \times 10^{-4}$

$\ell = 1.0$

$\log I/I_0 = -(14,500)(1.0 \times 10^{-4})(1.0)$

$= -1.45 = -2.0 + 0.55$

$I/I_0 = .035$

% transmittance = 3.5%

$\varepsilon_{356} = 87$

$\log I/I_0 = -(87)(1.0 \times 10^{-4})(1.0)$

$= -0.0087$

$= -1.0000 + 0.9913$

$I/I_0 = 0.98$

% transmittance = 98%

Q-56   Below is the ultraviolet spectrum of compound **A**. Give λ_{max} and ε_{max} for the compound.

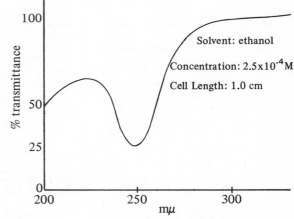

Solvent: ethanol

Concentration: 2.5×10^{-4} M

Cell Length: 1.0 cm

A-56 $\lambda_{max}^{ethanol}$ = 250 mμ

      $\mathscr{E}_{max}$ = $-$ log 0.25/ (2.5 x 10^{-4})(1.0)

          = 2,400

Q-57   Below is the ultraviolet spectrum of compound B (mole wt = 100). Give λ_{max} and $\mathscr{E}_{max}$ for the compound.

Solvent: H_2O

Concentration: 1.9 mg in 25.0 ml H_2O

Cell Length: 1.0 cm

A-57 λ_{max} = 270 mμ

Concentration:

$$\frac{1.9mg}{25.0ml} \left| \frac{1000ml}{1\ 1} \right| \frac{1g}{1000mg} \left| \frac{1\ mole}{100g} \right. = 7.6 \times 10^{-4}M$$

    $\mathscr{E}_{max}$ = 1.2/ (1.0) (7.6 x 10^{-4})

        = 1.58 x 10^3

Q-58   If the % transmission of a solution is 10% at 254 mμ what is the absorbance at that wavelength?

A-58   log I/I_0 = $-$ absorbance

    log 0.10 = $-$ absorbance

        1 = absorbance

Q-59   If the % transmission of a solution is 90% at 310 mμ what is the absorbance at that wavelength?

A-59   log I/I_0 = $-$ absorbance

    log 0.90 = $-$ absorbance

      0.05 = absorbance

R   Lambert-Beer Law:

    log I/I_0 = $-$ $\mathscr{E}c\ell$ = $-$ absorbance

    I = intensity of transmitted light

    I_0 = intensity of incident light

    ℓ = length of cell through which light passes

    c = concentration in moles/l

    $\mathscr{E}$ = molar extinction coefficient

Ultraviolet and Visible Spectra
PART II: Use of Ultraviolet Spectra in Structural Determinations

S-10   A bathochromic effect (red shift) is observed when the length of a conjugated system is increased. Bathochromic effects are also observed when conjugated systems are substituted with various groups. Some general rules have been formulated which enable λ_{max}^{hexane} to be calculated for certain conjugated systems.

The first system to be considered will be that of conjugated dienes ($\overset{|}{C} = \overset{|}{C} - \overset{|}{C} = \overset{|}{C} -$). The unsubstituted diene, butadiene, with $\lambda_{max}^{hexane} = 217$ mμ is used as the parent system. Each double bond which extends the conjugated system increases λ_{max} by 30 mμ. Each *alkyl* group attached to a carbon of the conjugated system increases λ_{max} by 5 mμ. If the diene system is within a ring (i.e., 1,3-cyclohexadiene) λ_{max} is increased by 36 mμ. For each double bond of the conjugated system which is exocyclic (i.e.,

attached to a ring ,) λ_{max} is increased by 5 mμ. The calculated values are reliable to within ±5 mμ.

A summary of these rules and red shifts caused by other groups is listed below. These rules are *not* applicable for "crossed conjugated systems" (such as **A** below) or aromatic systems.

$$\langle\!\!\!= CH_2$$

A

crossed
conjugated
system

Value assigned to parent diene system	217 mμ
Increment added for:	
diene system within a ring (homoannular diene)	36 mμ
each alkyl substituent or ring residue	5 mμ
the exocyclic nature of any double bond	5 mμ
a double bond extension	30 mμ
auxochrome — OAcyl	0 mμ
— OAlkyl	6 mμ
— SAlkyl	30 mμ
— Cl, — Br	5 mμ
— NAlkyl$_2$	60 mμ

(Reprinted with permission from A.I. Scott, *Interpretation of the Ultraviolet Spectra of Natural Products,* Pergamon Press, Oxford, 1964.)

Q-60   How many substituents are attached to double bond carbons in the molecule below? Has the basic conjugated system been extended? How many exocyclic double bonds are in the molecule?

A-60   Three substituents are attached to double bond carbons. The conjugated diene system has not been extended. There are no exocyclic double bonds.

substituents

Q-61   For the following compound how many substituents are attached to double bond carbons of the conjugated system? Are there any exocyclic double bonds?

CH$_3$

A   B

A-61   There are four substituents attached to double bond carbons of the conjugated system. There is one exocyclic double bond (the double bond is exocyclic to ring A).

Q-62   Using the values given in S-10 calculate λ_{max}^{hexane} for the following compound.

A-62
Parent system	217 mμ
Homoannular diene	36 mμ
Alkyl substituents (2x5)	10 mμ
λ_{max}^{hexane} (calc) =	263 mμ
λ_{max}^{hexane} (actual) =	258 mμ

Q-63   Using the values given in S-10 calculate λ_{max}^{hexane} for

---

A-63
Parent system	217 mμ
Exocyclic double bond	5 mμ
Alkyl substituents (3x3)	15 mμ
λ_{max}^{hexane} (calc) =	237 mμ
λ_{max}^{hexane} (actual) =	235 mμ

Q-64   Calculate λ_{max}^{hexane} for

A-64
Parent system	217 mμ
Homoannular ring diene	36 mμ
Exocyclic double bond	5 mμ
Alkyl substituents (3x5)	15 mμ
λ_{max}^{hexane} (calc) =	273 mμ
λ_{max}^{hexane} (actual) =	275 mμ

Q-65   Calculate the λ_{max}^{hexane} for

A-65	Parent system	217 mμ
	Homoannular ring system	36 mμ
	Alkyl substituents (4x5)	20 mμ
	Exocyclic double bond (1x5)	5 mμ
	Extension of conjugated system (1 x 30)	30 mμ
	λ_{max}^{hexane} (calc) =	308 mμ

Q-66 Calculate λ_{max}^{hexane} for

A-66	Parent system	217 mμ
	Homoannular ring system	36 mμ
	Alkyl substituents (3x5)	15 mμ
	Substituent ($OCOCH_3$)	0 mμ
	Exocyclic double bond (1x5)	5 mμ
	Extension of conjugated system (1 x 30)	30 mμ
	λ_{max}^{hexane} (calc) =	303 mμ
	λ_{max}^{hexane} (actual) =	304 mμ

Q-67 Calculate λ_{max}^{hexane} for the following compound.

A-67	Parent system	217 mμ
	Homoannular ring	36 mμ
	Alkyl substituents (4x5)	20 mμ
	Exocyclic double bond (0x5)	0 mμ
	Extension of conjugated system (1x30)	30 mμ
	λ_{max}^{hexane} (calc) =	303 mμ

Q-68 Calculate λ_{max}^{hexane} for the following compound.

A-68   Parent system   217 mμ

Alkyl substituents (5x5)   25 mμ

Extension of system (1x30)   30 mμ

Exocyclic double bond (2x5)   10 mμ*

λ_{max}^{hexane} (calc) =   282 mμ

*The double bond is exocyclic to two rings.

A-69   Parent system   217 mμ

Alkyl substituents (4x5)   20 mμ*

Exocyclic double bond (2x5)   10 mμ‡

Extension of system (0x30)   0 mμ

λ_{max}^{hexane} (calc) =   247 mμ

*Only substituents on double bonds conjugated with the base system are counted.

‡Only exocylic double bonds which are part of the conjugated system are counted.

A-70   Compound A:

Parent system   217 mμ

Alkyl substituents (4x5)   20 mμ

Exocyclic double bond (1x5)   5 mμ

λ_{max}^{hexane} (calc) =   242 mμ

Compound B:

Base Value   217 mμ

Alkyl substituents (3x5)   15 mμ

Exocyclic double bond (0x5)   0 mμ

λ_{max}^{hexane} (calc) =   232 mμ

Yes, the two compounds could probably be distinguished.

Q-69   Calculate λ_{max}^{hexane} for the following compound.

Q-70   Calculate λ_{max}^{hexane} for the two isomers

A   **B**

Assuming that λ_{max}^{hexane} can be predicted with a certainty of 5 mμ, could the compounds shown above be distinguished by using ultraviolet spectroscopy?

Q-71   Calculate λ_{max}^{hexane} for the following compound.

A-71

Parent system	217 mμ
Homoannular diene system	36 mμ
Alkyl substituents (4x5)	20 mμ
λ_{max}^{hexane} (calc) =	273 mμ
λ_{max}^{hexane} (actual) =	275 mμ

Q-72   Using values given in S-10 calculate λ_{max}^{hexane} for the following compound.

A-72

Parent system	217 mμ
Homoannular diene system	36 mμ
Alkyl substituents (5 x 5)	25 mμ
OAcyl substituent	0 mμ
Extension of conjugated system (2 x 30)	60 mμ
Exocyclic double bonds (3 x 5)	15 mμ
λ_{max}^{hexane} (calc) =	353 mμ
λ_{max}^{hexane} (actual) =	356 mμ

Q-73   Calculate λ_{max}^{hexane} for the following compound.

Compare the λ_{max}^{hexane} (calc) for this compound and its isomer given in Q-72.

A-73

Parent system	217 mμ
Homoannular diene system	36 mμ
Alkyl substituents (5 x 5)	25 mμ
OAcyl substituent	0 mμ
Extension of conjugated system (2 x 30)	60 mμ
Exocyclic double bonds (1 x 5)	5 mμ
λ_{max}^{hexane} (calc) =	343 mμ

R   Rules used for predicting λ_{max}^{hexane} of dienes are given in Table I of the Appendix.

S-11   The $\lambda_{max}^{ethanol}$ for the $\pi \to \pi^*$ transitions in α, β-unsaturated acyclic and cyclic ketones ($\overset{|}{\underset{}{C}} = \overset{|}{C} - \overset{|}{\underset{|}{C}} = O$) may be calculated by a method analogous to that used for the dienes. The base value used for the system is 215 mμ. For each exocyclic double bond which is part of the conjugated system, 5 mμ is added to the base value. For each $C = C$ group extending the conjugated system, 30 mμ is added to the base value. Values to be added for substituents vary with the position of the substituent and are listed below. If the compound has a homoannular diene system (both C = C in a single ring) an additional 39 mμ is added. Similar trends are followed by α, β-unsaturated acids and esters (see Table III in the Appendix for the rules regarding these compounds).

The rules given below are *not* applicable to "crossed" conjugated nor aromatic systems.

Rules for α, β-unsaturated Ketone and Aldehyde Absorption

$$\overset{\delta}{C} = \overset{\gamma}{C} - \overset{\beta}{C} = \overset{\alpha}{C} - C = O$$

ε values are usually above 10,000 and increase with the length of the conjugated system.

Value assigned to parent α, β-unsaturated six-ring or acyclic ketone	215 mμ
Value assigned to parent α, β-unsaturated five-ring ketone	202 mμ
Value assigned to parent α, β-unsaturated aldehyde	207 mμ
Increments added for:	
a double bond extending the conjugation	30 mμ
each alkyl substituent α	10 mμ
β	12 mμ
γ and higher	18 mμ
each substituent	
$-$ OH α	35 mμ
β	30 mμ
δ	50 mμ
$-$ OAc α, β, δ	6 mμ
$-$ OMe α	35 mμ
β	30 mμ
γ	17 mμ
δ	31 mμ
$-$ SAlk β	85 mμ
$-$ Cl α	15 mμ
β	12 mμ
$-$ Br α	25 mμ
β	30 mμ
$-$ NR$_2$ β	95 mμ
each exocyclic double bond	5 mμ
homoannular diene	39 mμ
λ_{max}^{EtOH} (calc) Total	

Q-74 At what positions does the following unsaturated ketone have substituents?

A-74
α : None
β : One
γ : None
δ : One

Q-75 Using the values given in S-12 calculate the $\lambda_{max}^{alcohol}$ for the compound shown in the previous question.

A-75

Parent system	215 mμ
Substituents β (1 x 12)	12 mμ
δ (1 x 18)	18 mμ
Exocyclic double bond (1 x 5)	5 mμ
Extension of system (1 x 30)	30 mμ*
$\lambda_{max}^{alcohol}$ (calc) =	280 mμ

*Remember that the basic system is

$$-\overset{\overset{\displaystyle O}{\|}}{C}-\overset{|}{C}=C\diagup$$

Q-76 Calculate the $\lambda_{max}^{alcohol}$ for

A-76

Parent system	215 mμ
Substituents β (2 x 12)	24 mμ
$\lambda_{max}^{ethanol}$ (calc) =	239 mμ

Q-77 Calculate $\lambda_{max}^{alcohol}$ for each of the compounds below. If the values predicted were within 5 mμ of the observed $\lambda_{max}^{ethanol}$, could the two compounds be distinguished by their ultraviolet spectrum?

A **B**

A-77

	A	B
Parent system	215 mμ	215 mμ
Substituents γ	18(1) mμ	18(1) mμ
δ	36(2) mμ	18(1) mμ
Homoannular diene system	39 mμ	0 mμ
Exocyclic double bond	0 mμ	5 mμ
Extension of system	30 mμ	30 mμ
$\lambda_{max}^{ethanol}$ (calc) =	338 mμ	286 mμ

The two compounds could be distinguished from their ultraviolet spectrum.

Q-78 Calculate $\lambda_{max}^{alcohol}$ for each of the following isomers.

CH_3 C_8H_{17} CH_3 OH

CH_3 CH_3

A   B

A-78

	A	B
Parent system	215 mμ	215 mμ
Substituents α		10(1) mμ
β	24(2) mμ	12(1) mμ
Exocyclic double bond	5	5
$\lambda_{max}^{alcohol}$ (calc) =	244 mμ	242 mμ
$\lambda_{max}^{alcohol}$ (actual) =	234 mμ	240 mμ

Q-79   Calculate $\lambda_{max}^{alcohol}$ for the following compounds.

A-79

	A	B
Parent system	215 mμ	215 mμ
Substituents β	12(1) mμ	
γ		18(1) mμ
δ	18(1) mμ	18(1) mμ
Exocyclic double bond	5 mμ	5 mμ
Extension of system	30 mμ	30 mμ
$\lambda_{max}^{ethanol}$(calc) =	280 mμ	286 mμ
$\lambda_{max}^{ethanol}$ (actual) =	280 mμ	290 mμ

Q-80   A compound was believed to have either structure **A** or **B**. The spectrum of the compound had $\lambda_{max}^{alcohol} = 352$ mμ. What is the most likely structure for the compound?

A-80

	A	B
Base value	215 mμ	215 mμ
Homoannular ring	39 mμ	39 mμ
Substituents α	10(1) mμ	10(1) mμ
β	12(1) mμ	12(1) mμ
γ	18(1) mμ	
δ	18(1) mμ	18(1) mμ
Exocyclic double bond	15(3) mμ	
Extension of system	30 mμ	30 mμ
$\lambda_{max}^{alcohol}$ (calc) =	357 mμ	324 mμ

The compound is more likely to have structure **A**.

Q-81   A compound known to be a substituted cyclohexanone derivative had a $\lambda_{max}^{ethanol}$ of 235 mμ. Could the compound be a conjugated dieneone (i.e., $-\overset{|}{C} = \overset{|}{C} - \overset{|}{C} = \overset{|}{C} - \overset{O}{\underset{}{C}} - $)? Explain?

A-81   No. If the compound were a conjugated dieneone, $\lambda_{max}^{ethanol}$ (calc) would be at least 245 mμ.

Parent value	215 mμ
Extension of conjugated system	30 mμ
	245 mμ

Q-82   For the compound described in Q-81 how many mμ must be accounted for by substituents?

A-82

Actual λ_{max}	235 mμ
— Parent system	215 mμ
20 mμ must be accounted for.	20 mμ

Q-83 Assume for the compound described in Q-81 that substituents attached to the conjugated system are alkyl. What are possible structures for the chromophoric system? Show alkyl substituents as R groups.

A-83

$\lambda_{max}^{ethanol}$ (calc)

One α and one β substituent A   237 mμ

Two β substituents B   239 mμ

One α substituent and an exocyclic double bond C.   230 mμ

    A   **B**   **C**

Q-84 A compound, $C_7H_{10}O$, known to be either a cyclohexenone derivative or an acyclic ketone had an observed $\lambda_{max}^{ethanol}$ of 257 mμ.

Is the compound likely to have a cyclic structure? How many carbon-carbon double bonds does the molecule have?

A-84 The compound is most likely an acyclic

dienone, $\text{C} = \text{C} - \text{C} = \text{C} - \text{C} = \text{O}$. The only possible cyclohexenone structures that fit the molecular formula are

$\lambda_{max}^{ethanol}$ (calc) = 227   237   239   230

An acyclic dienone has a minimum value for $\lambda_{max}^{ethanol}$ (calc) of 245 mμ. For the compound $CH_2 = CHCH = C(CH_3) COCH_3$

$\lambda_{max}^{ethanol}$ (calc) = 255 mμ.

Q-85 The compound $C_{10}H_{16}O$ was known to be a substituted derivative of cyclohexenone. The spectrum of the compound is shown below.

Give two structures consistent with the data.

A-85   The basic structure must be

Parent $\lambda_{max}^{ethanol}$ (calc) = 227 or

Parent $\lambda_{max}^{ethanol}$ (calc) = 230.

Extension of the conjugated system is not possible since the compound can have only two double bonds and one ring ($C_nH_{2n-4}O$).

Possible structures are

and

R   Rules for predicting $\lambda_{max}^{ethanol}$ of α, β-unsaturated aldehydes and ketones are given in Table II of Appendix. Rules for predicting $\lambda_{max}^{ethanol}$ of α, β-unsaturated acids and esters are given in Table III of the Appendix.

S-12   The ultraviolet spectrum of benzene shows several distinct bands. Substitution of the ring with groups containing non-bonded electrons or π electrons adjacent to the ring will cause shifts to longer wavelengths (*bathochromic* effect). For disubstituted benzene rings, prediction of λ_{max} is not always possible but two general rules are useful.

1. When an electron withdrawing group (i.e., $-NO_2$, $-C\overset{O}{\underset{}{\diagdown}}$) and an electron donating group (i.e., $-OH$, $-OCH_3$, $-X$) are situated *para* to each other, there is a red shift (*bathochromic* effect).

2. When an electron withdrawing and a donating group are situated *meta* or *ortho* to each other, the spectrum differs little from that of the separate monosubstituted aromatic compounds.

3. When two electron withdrawing or two electron donating groups are situated *para* to each other, the spectrum differs little from that of the separate monosubstituted aromatic compounds.

Absorption Maxima of the Substituted Benzene Rings Ph — R

R	λ_{max} mμ(ε) (solvent H_2O or MeOH)					
— H	203	(7400)	254	(204)		
— NH_3^+	203	(7500)	254	(160)		
— Me	206	(7000)	261	(225)		
— I	207	(7000)	257	(700)		
— Cl	209	(7400)	263	(190)		
— Br	210	(7900)	261	(192)		
— OH	210	(6200)	270	(1450)		
— OMe	217	(6400)	269	(1480)		
— SO_2NH_2	217	(9700)	264	(740)		
— CN	224	(13,000)	271	(1000)		
— CO_2^-	224	(8700)	268	(560)		
— CO_2H	230	(11,600)	273	(970)		
— NH_2	230	(8600)	280	(1430)		
— O^-	235	(9400)	287	(2600)		
— NHAc	238	(10,500)				
— COMe	245	(9800)				
— CH = CH	248	(14,000)	282	(750)	291	(500)
— CHO	249	(11,400)				
— Ph	251	(18,300)				
— OPh	255	(11,000)	272	(2000)	278	(1800)
— NO_2	268	(7800)				
— CH $\overset{t}{=}$ CHCO$_2$H	273	(21,000)				
— CH $\overset{t}{=}$ CHPh	295	(29,000)				

(Most values taken with permission from H.H. Jaffé and M. Orchin, *Theory and Applications of Ultraviolet Spectroscopy*, Wiley, New York, 1962.)

Some rules for predicting $\lambda_{max}^{ethanol}$ for disubstituted compounds of the type

where Z = H, OH, OAlkyl, or alkyl have been formulated.

These rules are listed in the table below and refer to the strongest band in the 200-400 $m\mu$ region.

Rules for the Principal Band of Substituted Benzene Derivatives R C_6H_4 COX

	Orientation	EtOH λ_{calc} $m\mu$
Parent Chromophore:		
X = alkyl or ring residue		246
X = H		250
X = OH or OAlkyl		230
Increment for each substituent:		
R = alkyl or ring residue	o-, m-	3
	p-	10
R = OH, OMe, OAlkyl	o-, m-	7
	p-	25
R = O⁻	o-	11
	m-	20
	p-	78
R = Cl	o-, m-	0
	p-	10
R = Br	o-, m-	2
	p-	15
R = NH₂	o-, m-	13
	p-	58
R = NHAc	o-, m-	20
	p-	45
R = NHMe	p-	73
R = NMe₂	o-, m-	20
	p-	85

(Reprinted with permission from A.I. Scott, *Interpretation of the Ultraviolet Spectra of Natural Products,* Pergamon Press, Oxford, 1964.)

Q-86   Calculate $\lambda_{max}^{ethanol}$ for

A-86	Parent value	230 $m\mu$
	Substituent	58 $m\mu$
	$\lambda_{max}^{ethanol}$ calc) =	288 $m\mu$
	$\lambda_{max}^{ethanol}$ actual) =	288 $m\mu$

Q-87   Calculate $\lambda_{max}^{ethanol}$ for

A-87   Parent value =   246 mμ

        Substituent   7

        $\lambda_{max}^{ethanol}$ (calc) =   253 mμ

Q-88   A compound, known to be a bromobenzoic acid, had a $\lambda_{max}^{ethanol}$ (actual) = 244 mμ.

What is the most likely structure for the compound?

A-88

$\lambda_{max}^{ethanol}$(calc) = 245 mμ

R   Rules for predicting $\lambda_{max}^{ethanol}$ of substituted aromatic aldehydes and acid derivatives are given in Table IV of the Appendix.

Chapter 3 | INFRARED SPECTROSCOPY

PART I: Vibrational Energy Levels

After completing this section, you should be able to

   a) determine the kinetic and potential energy and the vibrational frequency of a harmonic oscillator
   b) determine the force constants, vibrational frequencies, and spacings between vibrational energy levels for various chemical bonds
   c) determine the number of rotational, vibrational, and translational degrees of freedom for molecules
   d) determine which vibrational modes are infrared inactive.

PART II: Interpretation of Infrared Spectra

After completing this section, you should be able to

   a) locate the seven major spectral regions and identify types of bond vibrations which cause absorption in these regions
   b) distinguish between two different functional group isomers by use of infrared spectra
   c) distinguish between position isomers of alkenes, alkynes, and derivatives of benzene by use of infrared spectra
   d) determine the presence or absence of major functional groups by use of infrared spectra.

INFRARED SPECTROSCOPY
PART I: Vibrational Energy Levels

S-1   The infrared spectrum of a molecule is a result of transitions between two different *vibrational* energy levels. Vibrational motions of a molecule resemble the motions observed for a ball attached to a spring (i.e., harmonic oscillator). The ball and spring model will be used to develop the concepts for vibrational motion.

The stretching vibration of a simple ball and spring system is illustrated below. The potential energy, E_p, of the stretching vibration is a function of the force constant, k, of the spring and the displacement, d, of the ball, from the rest position.

$$E_p = 1/2\, k\, (d)^2$$

$+d$

$d = 0$ (rest position)

$-d$

The kinetic energy, E_k, of the system shown above is given by the equation

$$E_k = 1/2\, mv^2$$

where m is the mass of the ball and v is its velocity.

	Q-1 What is the potential energy of the spring system shown in S-1 when the ball is in the rest position?
A-1 $E_p = 0$. At rest position $d = 0$. Therefore, $E_p = 1/2\, k\, (d)^2 = 0$	Q-2 The ball of the spring system shown in S-1 is stretched to position $-d$ and released. At what positions will the potential energy of the system be a maximum and a minimum?
A-2 Maximum potential energy is at the position of greatest displacement, $+d$ and $-d$. Minimum potential energy is at the rest position, $d = 0$.	Q-3 At what positions will the *kinetic* energy of the ball be a maximum and a minimum for the system set in motion as described in Q-2?
A-3 Maximum kinetic energy will occur at maximum velocity which is attained at position $d = 0$. Minimum kinetic energy ($E_k = 0$) will occur at positions of maximum displacement, $+d$ and $-d$.	Q-4 Balls of equal mass are attached to two different springs. Spring A has a force constant twice as great as for spring B. Each ball is stretched 1 cm from the rest position. Which system has the greater potential energy?

A-4   Spring **A** has the greater potential energy.

$$E_p = 1/2\, k\, (d)^2$$

$$k_A > k_B$$

Q-5   Which system described in Q-4 requires the greater energy to displace the balls 5 cm?

A-5   System **A**, the system with the larger force constant.

R   For a harmonic oscillator (one vibrating ball on a spring)

$$E_p = 1/2\, k\, (d)^2$$

$$E_k = 1/2\, mv^2$$

S-2   A spring with a ball attached to it is set in vibration. The *frequency* of vibration (number of oscillations or cycles per second), ν, of the system is a function of the force constant of the spring, k, and the mass of the ball, m.

$$\nu = \frac{1}{2\pi}\sqrt{\frac{k}{m}}$$

Q-6   Spring **A** is attached to a ball with a mass of 1.0 g. The spring has a force constant of 4.0 dynes/cm. What is the frequency of this system when set into vibration? What is the unit for the frequency? (Hint: 1 dyne = $1\frac{\text{g-cm}}{\text{sec}^2}$)

A-6

$$\nu = \frac{1}{2\pi}\sqrt{\frac{4.0\ \frac{\text{g-cm}}{\text{sec}^2\text{-cm}}}{1.0\ \text{g}}}$$

$$\nu = \frac{2}{2\pi} = \frac{1}{\pi}\ \text{cycle/sec or Hertz (Hz)}$$

Q-7   Spring **B** is attached to a ball with a mass of 1.0 g. The spring has a force constant of 9.0 dynes/cm. What is the frequency of this ball when set into vibration?

A-7

$$\nu = \frac{1}{2\pi}\sqrt{\frac{9.0\ \frac{\text{g-cm}}{\text{sec}^2\text{-cm}}}{1.0\ \text{g}}}$$

$$\nu = 3/2\pi\ \text{cycle/sec or Hertz}$$

Q-8   As the force constant of a spring increases does the frequency of vibration increase or decrease?

A-8   Increase. The frequency increases with the square root of the force constant.

Q-9   Which system will vibrate with the greater frequency, spring **A** (force constant = 4.0 dynes/cm) attached to a 1.0 g ball or spring **A** attached to a 4.0 g ball?

A-9   Frequency for spring **A** attached to 1.0 g ball:

$\nu = \dfrac{1}{\pi} \text{ sec}^{-1}$

Frequency for spring **A** attached to 4.0 g ball:

$\nu = \dfrac{1}{2\pi} \sqrt{\dfrac{\dfrac{4.0 \text{ g-cm}}{\text{sec}^2\text{-cm}}}{4.0 \text{ g}}}$

$\nu = \dfrac{1}{2\pi} \text{ cycle/sec}$

The frequency of the system with a 1.0 g ball is greater.

Q-10   A spring (k = 4.0 dynes/cm) with a 1.0 g ball attached is set into vibration so that the maximum displacement of the ball from the rest position is ± 1.0 cm. A second spring (k = 4.0 dynes/cm) with a 1.0 g ball attached is set into vibration so that the maximum displacement of the ball from the rest position is ± 2.0 cm. Which vibrating system has the greater frequency? (Hint: What are the factors which determine the frequency?)

A-10   Both systems have the same frequency. The factors affecting frequency are the force constant and the mass of the ball attached.

Q-11   Which of the two spring systems described in Q-10 has the greater *potential* energy?

A-11   The potential energy of the system with the 2.0 cm displacement is greater.

$E_p = 1/2\, k\, (d)^2$

The potential energy is dependent upon the displacement and the force constant.

Q-12   As more energy is added to a vibrating spring system, will the frequency of the vibrations change? Why?

A-12   No. The frequency remains unchanged because frequency is dependent only upon the force constant and the mass of the system.

Q-13   As energy is added to a vibrating spring system, the frequency remains unchanged. What characteristic of the vibrating system does change with increasing potential energy?

A-13   The displacement or *amplitude* of the vibration.

R   Frequency of a harmonic oscillator (one ball on a spring)

$\nu = \dfrac{1}{2\pi} \sqrt{\dfrac{k}{m}}$

S-3   For a harmonic oscillator consisting of two balls of mass m_1 and m_2 connected by a spring (Figure I), the equation for the potential energy is a function of the force constant, k, and the total displacement of the two balls from the equilibrium position $(d_1 + d_2)$. The frequency of vibration for the system is a function of the force constant and the mass of each ball.

Figure I

$E_p = \dfrac{1}{2} k\, (d_1 + d_2)^2$

$\nu = \dfrac{1}{2\pi} \sqrt{\dfrac{k}{\dfrac{m_1 m_2}{m_1 + m_2}}}$

Q-14 A spring (k = 5 dynes/cm) is connected to two balls of mass 1.0 and 2.0 grams, respectively. If the 1.0 g mass is displaced 2 cm from equilibrium and the 2 g mass is displaced 1.0 cm from equilibrium, what will be the potential energy of the system? (Hint: 1 dyne cm = 1 erg)

A-14 E_p = 1/2 (5.0 dyne/cm) $(1.0 + 2.0)^2$ cm^2

= 23 dyne-cm

= 23 erg

Q-15 A spring system is stretched so that the potential energy is 36 ergs. If the force constant of the spring is 9 dynes/cm and the two balls attached to the spring each have a mass of 1.0 g, what must be the total displacement of the balls from their equilibrium position?

A-15 36 dyne-cm = 1/2 (9.0 dyne/cm)$(d_1 + d_2)^2$

8 cm^2 = $(d_1 + d_2)^2$

Total displacement = $\sqrt{8\text{cm}^2}$

$(d_1 + d_2)$ = 2.8 cm

Q-16 What is the *frequency* of vibration for the following spring system?

k = 5 dynes/cm

m = 1.0 g m = 1.0 g

A-16

$$\nu = \frac{1}{2\pi} \sqrt{\frac{5.0 \text{ dyne/cm}}{\frac{(1.0)(1.0)\text{g}^2}{(1.0 + 1.0)\text{g}}}}$$

$$= \frac{1}{2\pi} \sqrt{5.0 \text{ dyne/cm}/0.5\text{g}}$$

$$= \frac{1}{2\pi} \sqrt{10} \text{ sec}^{-1}$$

ν = 0.5 cycle/sec

Q-17 What is the frequency of vibration for the following spring system?

k = 5 dynes/cm

m = 1.0 g m = 2.0 g

A-17

$$\nu = \frac{1}{2\pi} \sqrt{5.0 \text{ dyne/cm}/\frac{(1.0)(2.0)\text{g}^2}{(1.0 + 2.0)\text{g}}}$$

$$\nu = \frac{1}{2\pi} \sqrt{7.5} \text{ sec}^{-1} = 0.43 \text{ cycle/sec}$$

Q-18 As the mass of the balls on a vibrating system increases, how does the frequency change?

A-18   As the mass of the balls increases, the frequency decreases.

Q-19   Each ball of the spring system shown below can be displaced to any value of d_1 or d_2. What are the possible values for the potential energy of this system?

k = 5.0 dynes/cm

A-19 $E_p = 1/2\ k\ (d_1 + d_2)^2$

Because d_1 and d_2 can have any value from $0 \to \infty$, the potential energy, E_p, can have any value from $0 \to \infty$.

Q-20   If two balls are connected by a spring with a force constant k, what is the potential energy of the system when $d_1 + d_2 = 0$?

A-20 $E_p = 1/2\ k\ (0)^2 = 0$

The potential energy = 0.

Q-21   If two balls are connected by a spring with a force constant k dynes/cm, what is the potential energy of the system (in terms of k) for each of the following values of $(d_1 + d_2)$?

$\pm (d_1 + d_2)$	E_p
0	0 k
1	
2	
3	
4	
5	

A-21

$\pm (d_1 + d_2)$	E_p
0	0 k
1	0.5 k
2	2 k
3	4.5 k
4	8 k
5	12.5 k

Q-22   On the graph below, plot the E_p for the $\pm (d_1 + d_2)$ values found in A-21.

A-22

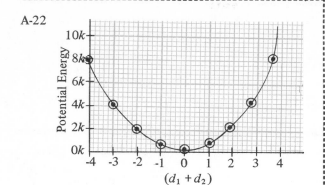

Q-23   The potential energy diagram below is for a spring system where the force constant is equal to k. Sketch on the graph the potential energy diagram for a spring system where the force constant is $2k$.

A-23

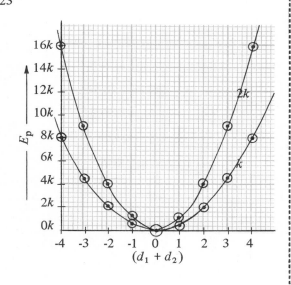

Q-24   The potential energy diagrams below are for four spring systems, each with a different force constant. Which spring system has the largest force constant? Which system has the smallest force constant?

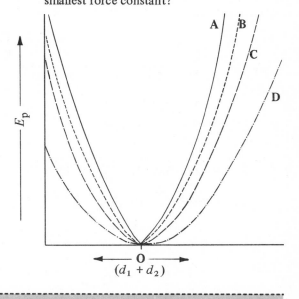

A-24   Spring system **A** has the largest force constant, and system **D** has the smallest force constant.

R   For a harmonic oscillator with two balls on a spring

$$E_p = 1/2\, k\, (d_1 + d_2)^2$$

$$E_k = 1/2\, mv^2$$

$$\nu = \frac{1}{2\pi} \sqrt{k \Big/ \left(\frac{m_1\, m_2}{m_1 + m_2} \right)}$$

S-4   In molecular systems the frequency of vibration, v, is a function of the mass of atoms, m_1 and m_2, and the strength of the bond (force constant), k.

$$v = \frac{1}{2\pi}\sqrt{k \left/ \left(\frac{m_1 m_2}{m_1 + m_2}\right)\right.}$$

The quantity $\left(\dfrac{m_1 m_2}{m_1 + m_2}\right)$ is called the reduced mass, $\mu_{m_1\text{-}m_2}$.

Q-25   If the force constant of a C-H bond is 5.0 x 10^5 dynes/cm, and the mass of carbon and hydrogen atoms are 20 x 10^{-24} g and 1.6 x 10^{-24} g, respectively, what is the vibrational frequency of the C-H bond?

A-25

$$v = \frac{1}{2\pi}\sqrt{k/\mu_{\text{C-H}}}$$

$$v = \frac{1}{2\pi}\sqrt{5.0 \times 10^5 \;\frac{\text{dyne}}{\text{cm}} \left/ \left(\frac{20 \times 1.6 \times 10^{-48}\,\text{g}^2}{20 \times 10^{-24}\text{g} + 1.6 \times 10^{-24}\text{g}}\right)\right.}$$

$$= 0.16\sqrt{5.0 \times 10^5 \;\frac{\text{dyne}}{\text{cm}}\;(6.7 \times 10^{23}\,\text{g}^{-1})}$$

$$= 0.16\sqrt{34 \times 10^{28}\;\text{sec}^{-2}}$$

$$= 9.3 \times 10^{13}\;\text{cycle/sec}$$

Q-26   If the force constant of a C-D bond is 5.0 x 10^5 dynes/cm, what is the vibrational frequency of the bond? Compare the vibrational frequency of the C-D and the C-H bond (see A-25).

A-26

$$v = \frac{1}{2\pi}\sqrt{5.0 \times 10^5 \;\frac{\text{dyne}}{\text{cm}} \left/ \left(\frac{20 \times 3.2 \times 10^{-48}\,\text{g}^2}{20 \times 10^{-24}\text{g} + 3.2 \times 10^{-24}\text{g}}\right)\right.}$$

$$= 0.16\sqrt{5.0 \times 10^5\;(3.6 \times 10^{23})\;\text{sec}^{-2}}$$

$$= 0.16\,(4.2 \times 10^{14})\;\text{sec}^{-1}$$

$$= 6.7 \times 10^{13}\;\text{cycle/sec}$$

Q-27   If the force constant of an O-H bond is 5.0 x 10^5 dynes/cm, calculate the vibrational frequency of the bond.

$(\mu_{\text{OH}} = 1.5 \times 10^{-24}\,\text{g})$

A-27

$$v = 0.16\sqrt{5.0 \times 10^5 \;\frac{\text{dyne}}{\text{cm}} \left/ (1.5 \times 10^{-24}\,\text{g})\right.}$$

$$= 0.16\sqrt{33 \times 10^{28}\;\text{sec}^{-2}}$$

$$= 9.2 \times 10^{13}\;\text{cycle/sec}$$

Q-28   If the force constant of the C = C bond is 1.0 x 10^6 dynes/cm, calculate the vibrational frequency of the bond.

$(\mu_{\text{C = C}} = 1.0 \times 10^{-23}\,\text{g})$

A-28

$$v = 0.16\sqrt{1.0 \times 10^6 \;\frac{\text{dyne}}{\text{cm}} \left/ (1.0 \times 10^{-23}\,\text{g})\right.}$$

$$= 0.16\sqrt{1.0 \times 10^{29}\;\text{sec}^{-2}}$$

$$= 5.1 \times 10^{13}\;\text{cycle/sec}$$

R   The vibrational frequency of a chemical bond is a function of the bond strength and the reduced mass.

$$v = \frac{1}{2\pi}\sqrt{k/\mu_{m_1 - m_2}}$$

$$\mu_{m_1 - m_2} = \frac{m_1 m_2}{m_1 + m_2}$$

S-5   The chemical bond *differs* from the "two balls on a spring" system in that for molecules only certain vibrational energy levels are allowed; that is, the vibrational energy is quantized.

The energy levels possible are

$$E_{\text{vibrational}} = (n + 1/2)h\nu$$

where n is a vibrational quantum number $(0, 1, 2, \ldots)$, h is Planck's constant $(6.63 \times 10^{-27}$ erg-sec), and ν is the vibrational frequency of the bond.

	Q-29 The vibrational frequency of a bond is given by $$\nu = \frac{1}{2\pi}\sqrt{k/\mu_{m_1 - m_2}}$$ Derive an expression for E_{vib} in terms of the reduced mass of the atoms and the force constant. What are the units for E_{vib}?
A-29 $E_{\text{vib}} = (n + 1/2)h\nu$ $$\nu = \frac{1}{2\pi}\sqrt{k/\mu_{m_1 - m_2}}$$ $$E_{\text{vib}} = \frac{(n + 1/2)h}{2\pi}\sqrt{k/\mu_{m_1 - m_2}}$$ Units: n and π are unitless, h is in erg-sec, μ is in gram, and k is in dyne/cm. Therefore, the unit of E_{vib} is erg.	Q-30 What is the value of E_{vib} when $n = 0$?
A-30 $E_{\text{vib}} = (n + 1/2)h\nu$ When $n = 0$ $E_{\text{vib}} = 1/2 h\nu$	Q-32 What is the difference in energy (ΔE_{vib}) between the lowest possible energy level of a bond and the next highest energy level?
A-31 $\Delta E_{\text{vib}} = E_{\text{vib}\ n=1} - E_{\text{vib}\ n=0}$ $\Delta E_{\text{vib}} = 3/2 h\nu - 1/2 h\nu$ $\qquad = h\nu$	Q-32 What is the difference in energy (ΔE_{vib}) between the energy states $n = 1$ and $n = 2$?
A-32 $\Delta E_{\text{vib}} = E_{\text{vib}\ n=2} - E_{\text{vib}\ n=1}$ $\Delta E = 5/2 h\nu - 3/2 h\nu$ $\qquad = h\nu$	Q-33 What is the difference between any two successive vibrational energy levels?
A-33 ΔE_{vib} between any two successive levels = $h\nu$	Q-34 Derive an equation which relates ΔE_{vib} to the force constant and reduced mass of the atoms.

A-34 ΔE_{vib} is directly proportional to the frequency of vibration. The frequency is dependent upon the reduced mass of the atoms and the force constant.

$$\Delta E_{vib} = h\nu = \frac{h}{2\pi}\sqrt{k/\mu_{m_1 - m_2}}$$

Q-35   How does the separation between energy levels, ΔE_{vib}, change as the force constant increases?

A-35 $\Delta E_{vib} = \frac{h}{2\pi}\sqrt{k/\mu_{m_1 - m_2}}$ As k increases ΔE_{vib} increases. The separation increases.

Q-36   Assuming the harmonic oscillator model (ball and spring) is valid for chemical bonds, sketch the potential energy and vibrational energy levels for the two bonds, $C - C$ and $C = C$. The force constant for the $C = C$ bond is greater than the force constant for the $C - C$ bond.

A-36

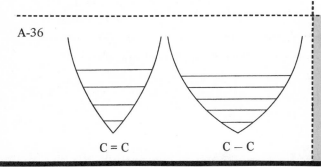

C = C   C − C

R   Vibrational energy of a chemical bond is quantized and can have the value

$E_{vib} = (n + 1/2)h\nu$.

The spacing between two successive energy levels (ΔE_{vib}) is

$\Delta E_{vib} = h\nu$

S-6   The potential energy curves for chemical bonds are *not* symmetrical like those for harmonic oscillators. For molecular vibrations the potential energy curves are distorted as shown below.

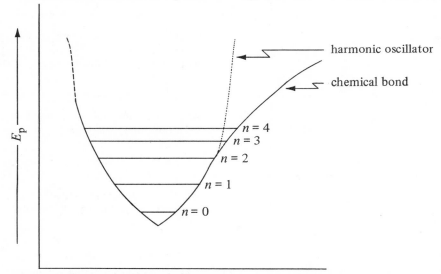

At ordinary temperatures, where molecules are in their lowest vibrational levels, the harmonic oscillator model is a good approximation of the chemical bond.

Absorption of light with energy equal to the difference in energy between two vibrational energy levels (ΔE_{vib}) will cause a vibrational transition to occur. Light with this energy is found in the infrared region of the electromagnetic spectrum.

Transitions from the ground state ($n = 0$) to the first excited state ($n = 1$) absorb light strongly giving rise to intense fundamental spectral bands. Transitions from the ground state to the second excited state ($n = 2$) absorb light and give rise to weak *overtone* bands.

Q-37   The molecule A-B has the potential energy curve shown in S-6. Are the energy levels equally spaced in the molecule?

A-37   No. As the quantum number increases, the energy levels become more closely spaced.

Q-38   At what energy level does the potential energy diagram of the molecule A-B (S-6) deviate appreciably from the harmonic oscillator curve?

A-38 $n = 3$ or 4

Q-39   Derive an equation which relates the *wavelength* of light absorbed in causing a transition between two energy levels in molecule **A-B**, the force constant of **A-B**, $k_{A\text{-}B}$, and the reduced mass of atoms **A** and **B**, $\mu_{A\text{-}B}$.

A-39 $\lambda = c/\nu$

$$\nu_{AB} = \frac{1}{2\pi}\sqrt{k_{AB}/\mu_{AB}}$$

$$\lambda = \frac{c}{\frac{1}{2\pi}\sqrt{k_{AB}/\mu_{AB}}}$$

Q-40   Derive an equation relating the *wave number* of light required to cause a transition between two adjacent energy levels in the molecule **AB**, k_{AB}, and the reduced mass, μ_{AB}.

A-40 $$\lambda = \frac{c}{\frac{1}{2\pi}\sqrt{k_{AB}/\mu_{AB}}}$$

$$\bar{\nu} = 1/\lambda$$

$$\bar{\nu} = \frac{1}{2\pi c}\sqrt{k_{AB}/\mu_{AB}}$$

Q-41   The frequency for the $C - H$ bond was calculated from the force constant and mass of the atoms and found to be 9.3×10^{13} sec^{-1}. What is the wavelength (in Å) and wave number (in cm^{-1}) of this fundamental ($n = 0$ to $n = 1$ transition) absorption band for the $C - H$ bond?

A-41 $\nu = 9.3 \times 10^{13}$ sec^{-1}

$$\lambda = c/\nu = \frac{3.0 \times 10^{10} \text{ cm} - \text{sec}^{-1}}{9.3 \times 10^{13} \text{ sec}^{-1}}$$

$\lambda = 3.2 \times 10^{-4}$ cm or $32,000$Å

$\bar{\nu} = 1/\lambda = 3.1 \times 10^{3}$ cm^{-1} or $3,100$ cm^{-1}.

Q-42   Assuming that the $n = 0$, $n = 1$, and $n = 2$ energy levels are equally spaced, what would the wavelength (in Å) and wave number (in cm^{-1}) be for the first overtone band ($n = 0$ to $n = 2$) of the $C - H$ bond?

A-42 $h\nu_{light} = 2h\nu_{vib}$

$\nu_{light} = 2\nu_{vib} = 2(9.3 \times 10^{13})$ sec^{-1}

$$\lambda = \frac{c}{\nu_{light}} = \frac{3.0 \times 10^{10} \text{ cm-sec}^{-1}}{2(9.3 \times 10^{13} \text{ sec}^{-1})}$$

$\lambda = 16,000$Å $\bar{\nu} = 6,200$ cm^{-1}

Q-43   Calculate the wavelength and wave number of the fundamental absorption band for the $C = O$ vibration. Assume a force constant of 1.0×10^{6} dynes/cm ($\mu_{C = O} = 1.2 \times 10^{-23}$ g).

A-43 $k = 1.0 \times 10^6$ dyne/cm

$$\nu_{\text{light}} = \nu_{\text{vib}} = \frac{1}{2\pi} \sqrt{1.0 \times 10^6 \frac{\text{dyne}}{\text{cm}} \bigg/ 1.2 \times 10^{-23}\,\text{g}}$$

$$= 0.16 \sqrt{8.3 \times 10^{28}\,\text{sec}^{-2}}$$

$$= 4.6 \times 10^{13}\,\text{sec}^{-1}$$

$$\lambda_{\text{light}} = c/\nu = \frac{3.0 \times 10^{10}\,\text{cm-sec}^{-1}}{4.6 \times 10^{13}\,\text{sec}^{-1}} = 6.5 \times 10^{-4}\,\text{cm}$$

$$= 65{,}000\text{Å}$$

$$\bar{\nu} = 1/\lambda = 1/6.5 \times 10^{-4} = 1{,}500\,\text{cm}^{-1}$$

Q-44   Cyclopentanone has an intense absorption band at $\bar{\nu} = 1750$ cm^{-1} due to the $\rangle C = O$. Assuming that this is the fundamental band, calculate the force constant for the $\rangle C = O$ in cyclopentanone ($\mu_{C=O} = 1.2 \times 10^{-23}$ g).

A-44 $\bar{\nu} = 1750$ cm^{-1}

$\lambda = 1/\bar{\nu}$ $\lambda = c/\nu$

$$\bar{\nu} = \nu/c = \frac{1}{2\pi c} \sqrt{k/\mu_{C=O}}$$

$$1750\,\text{cm}^{-1} = 5.3 \times 10^{-12} \frac{\text{sec}}{\text{cm}} \sqrt{k/1.2 \times 10^{-23}\,\text{g}}$$

$$(3.3 \times 10^{14})^2\,\text{sec}^{-2} = 8.3 \times 10^{22}\,\text{g}^{-1}\,k$$

$$\frac{11 \times 10^{28}}{8.3 \times 10^{22}}\,\text{sec}^{-2}\,\text{g} = k = 1.3 \times 10^6\,\frac{\text{g}}{\text{sec}^2}$$

$$= 1.3 \times 10^6\,\frac{\text{dyne}}{\text{cm}}$$

Q-45   Carbon to carbon bond stretch vibrations give rise to absorptions in the following wavelength regions.

$\rangle C - C \langle$	7.0μ
$\rangle C = C \langle$	6.0μ
$- C \equiv C -$	4.5μ

Arrange the three bonds in order of increasing force constant.

A-45   Wavelengths are inversely proportional to the square root of force constants.

$$\lambda = \frac{c}{\frac{1}{2\pi} \sqrt{k\mu_{cc}}}$$

smallest → largest force constant

$$\rangle C - C \langle \; < \; \rangle C = C \langle \; < \; - C \equiv C -$$

Q-46   What is the relationship between force constant and the strength of a chemical bond?

A-46   The force constant is directly proportional to the strength of a bond.

Q-47   Fundamental stretching vibrations of $\rangle C - C \langle$, $\rangle C - N -$, and $\rangle C - O -$ give rise to absorptions in the following regions.

	λ, μ	$\bar{\nu}$, cm^{-1}
C – C	7.0	1,430
C – N	7.5	1,330
C – O	7.8	1,280

Compare the relative differences between the $n = 0$ and $n = 1$ vibrational energy levels for the C – C, C – N, and C – O bonds.

A-47

$\bar{\nu} - cm^{-1}$ 1,430   1,330   1,280

R   At ordinary temperatures, the potential energy diagram of a molecule approximates that of a harmonic oscillator. For fundamental absorptions ($n = 0$ to $n = 1$)

$$h\nu_{light} = h\nu_{vibration}$$

S-7   Polyatomic molecules may exhibit more than one fundamental vibrational absorption band. The number of these fundamental bands is related to the *degrees of freedom* in a molecule. The number of *degrees of freedom* is equal to the sum of the coordinates necessary to locate all the atoms of the molecule in space.

Q-48   Consider a single atom at position P_1 in *space*.

How many *coordinates* are required to describe the position of the atom P_1?

A-48   Three coordinates are required, the X, Y, and Z.

Q-49   How many degrees of freedom does the single atom **P** have?

A-49   Three. Because three coordinates are required to locate the atom in space.

Q-50   Consider a single atom restricted to movement in a plane. How many *translational* degrees of freedom would such an atom have? Why?

A-50   Two translational degrees of freedom, because only two coordinates (X, Y) would be required to fix the position of the atom in the plane.

Q-51   If there were two atoms in space, how many *total* translational degrees of freedom would the two atoms have? Why?

A-51   Six. Each atom would have three translational degrees of freedom because three coordinates would be required to fix the position of *each* atom.

Q-52   If there were n atoms in *space*, how many total translational degrees of freedom would the n atoms have? Why?

A-52   There would be $3n$ translational degrees of freedom. Three coordinates would be required to fix the position of *each* atom.

Q-53   An atom is located at position X, Y, Z in space. The atom rotates 180° about its internal axis. Are any new coordinates required to describe the rotation of the atom? Why?

A-53   No. The new orientation of the atom is identical to the original orientation because of the symmetry of the atom.

Q-54   An atom moving in space has three translational degrees of freedom. Are any additional degrees of freedom necessary to describe the rotational motion of the atom?

A-54   No, because no coordinates are necessary to specify the rotational orientation.

R   The number of degrees of freedom equals the number of coordinates necessary to fix position in space.

S-8   Atoms have three degrees of freedom, all of which are translational. When atoms combine to form molecules, no degrees of freedom are lost. That is, the total number of degrees of freedom of the molecule will be $3n$ where n is the number of atoms in the molecule. The $3n$ degrees of freedom of the molecule will be made up of *rotational, vibrational,* and *translational* degrees of freedom.

Rotational degrees of freedom result from the rotation of a molecule about an axis through the center of gravity. These rotations result in a degree of freedom *only if* the positions of the atoms in space change during the rotation.

All degrees of freedom not accounted for by translational and rotational are vibrational degrees of freedom.

$3n$ degrees of freedom = translational + rotational + vibrational.

Q-55   How many coordinates are necessary to locate the diatomic *molecule* in space? How many translational degrees of freedom does a diatomic molecule have?

A-55   Three coordinates. A diatomic molecule has three translational degrees of freedom.

Q-56   Rotation of a diatomic molecule around the X, Y, and Z axes is illustrated below. Which of these rotations will result in rotational degrees of freedom?

A-56   Y and Z.

Rotation about the Y and Z axes will result in a change in position of the atoms; rotation about the X axis will not.

Q-57   Give the number of translational, rotational, and vibrational degrees of freedom in a diatomic molecule.

A-57   Total degrees of freedom = 3 (n) = 6

Translational = 3 (A-55)

Rotational = 2 (A-56)

Vibrational = $3n-5$ = 1

Q-58   What motion is associated with the one vibrational degree of freedom in the diatomic molecule?

A-58

Q-59   Give the number of translational, rotational, and vibrational degrees of freedom for CO_2.

O = C = O

A-59   Total degrees of freedom = $3n$ = 9

Translational = 3

Rotational = 2

Vibrational = $3n-5$ = 4

Q-60   Give the number of translational, rotational, and vibrational degrees of freedom for acetylene.

$H - C \equiv C - H$

A-60   Total degrees of freedom = $3n$ = 12

Translational = 3

Rotational = 2

Vibrational = $3n-5$ = 7

Q-61   Rotations of a non-linear molecule (H_2O) around the X, Y, and Z axes are illustrated below. Which of these rotations will result in rotational degrees of freedom?

A-61   X, Y, and Z.

Rotation about all axes will result in a change in the position of the atoms.

Q-62   Give the number of translational, rotational, and vibrational degrees of freedom for the non-linear molecule, water.

A-62   Total degrees of freedom = $3n$ = 9

Translational = 3

Rotational = 3

Vibrational = $3n-6$ = 3

Q-63   Give the number of translational, rotational, and vibrational degrees of freedom for the non-linear molecule, CH_4.

A-63   Total degrees of freedom = $3n$ = 15

Translational = 3

Rotational = 3

Vibrational = $3n-6$ = 9

Q-64   Give the number of translational, rotational, and vibrational degrees of freedom for benzene, C_6H_6.

A-64	Total degrees of freedom $= 3n = 36$
	Translational $= 3$
	Rotational $= 3$
	Vibrational $= 3n-6 = 30$

R A molecule with n atoms has $3n$ degrees of freedom.

$3n$ degrees of freedom = translational + rotational + vibrational.

For linear molecules:
Vibrational degrees of freedom $= 3n-5$.

For non-linear molecules:
Vibrational degrees of freedom $= 3n-6$.

S-9 An infrared absorption band will be observed for each vibrational degree of freedom provided:

1. A change in the dipole moment of the molecule occurs during the vibration.

2. The band does not coincide in frequency with some other fundamental vibration (the energy levels are degenerate).

3. The absorption falls within the infrared region.

4. The intensity of the absorption is strong enough to be detected.

Additional bands may appear in the spectrum due to overtones and *combination* tones (combinations of two or more fundamental vibrations).

Q-65 In the following diagram, the arrows represent the direction and magnitude of the dipole moment of each bond during various stages of a vibration. The dotted arrow represents the resultant dipole of the molecule. Does the dipole moment of the molecule change during the vibration illustrated? Will the vibration be infrared active?

Symmetrical stretching

A-65   Yes, the dipole changes. The vibration will be infrared active.

Q-66   The two other fundamental vibrational modes of water are shown below. The arrows represent the motion of the atoms. Does the dipole moment of the molecule change during the vibrations illustrated? Will the vibrations be infrared active?

Unsymmetrical stretching

Bending vibration

A-66   Both unsymmetrical stretching and bending vibrations will result in a change in dipole of the molecule. Both vibrations are infrared active.

Q-67   How many bands would be expected in the infrared spectrum of water?

A-67   Three. The infrared spectrum of water is shown below.

Q-68   The fundamental vibrational modes for CO_2 are given below. Which of the vibrations illustrated will be infrared active?

$$\overset{\leftarrow}{O} = C = \vec{O}$$
Symmetrical stretching

$$\vec{O} = \overset{\leftarrow}{C} = \vec{O}$$
Unsymmetrical stretching

$\uparrow O = C = O \uparrow$
$\downarrow$
Bending X, Y plane

$\overset{\nearrow}{O} = C = \overset{\nearrow}{O}$
$\swarrow$
Bending Y, Z plane

A-68
Symmetrical stretch	inactive
Unsymmetrical stretch	active
Bending X, Y plane	active
Bending Y, Z plane	active

Q-69   The two fundamental bending modes for CO_2 are degenerate. How many bands would be expected in the infrared spectrum of CO_2?

A-69   Two bands would be expected.

R   Vibrational modes are infrared active if a change in dipole moment occurs during the vibration.

INFRARED SPECTROSCOPY
PART II: Interpretation of Infrared Spectra

S-1   Identification of characteristic absorption bands caused by different functional groups is the basis for the interpretation of infrared spectra. Thus, $O - H$ stretching frequencies give rise to strong absorption bands in the 3350 cm^{-1} region. The presence of a strong band in the 3350 cm^{-1} region of the infrared spectrum of a compound is strongly suggestive that the molecules contain the $O - H$ functional group. The following section will demonstrate the technique used in interpreting infrared spectra.

The eight most important and well-defined areas used in a preliminary examination of the spectra are given below.

Spectral region		Bond causing absorption
Wavelength mμ	Wave number $\bar{\nu} - $ cm^{-1}	
2.7 — 3.3	3750 — 3000	$O - H, N - H$ stretching
3.0 — 3.4	3300 — 2900	$-C \equiv C - H, >C = C<^H, Ar - H, (C - H$ stretch)
3.3 — 3.7	3000 — 2700	$CH_3-, -CH_2-, \gtreqqless C - H, C \overset{O}{\diagup} - H$ ($C - H$ stretch)
4.2 — 4.9	2400 — 2100	$C \equiv C, C \equiv N$ stretching
5.3 — 6.1	1900 — 1650	$C = O$ (acids, aldehydes, ketones, amides, esters, anhydride) stretching
5.9 — 6.2	1675 — 1500	$>C = C<$ (aliphatic and aromatic) $>C = N<$ stretching
6.8 — 7.7	1475 — 1300	$-C - H$ bending
10.0 — 15.4	1000 — 650	$>C = C<^H, Ar - H$ bending (out of plane)

Q-1   In which of the eight infrared spectral regions listed above would the following compound be expected to absorb light? What bond gives rise to each absorption?

$$CH_3 \; CH_2 \; C \overset{O}{\diagup} - H$$

A-1   **Region $\bar{\nu} - $ cm^{-1}**

3000 — 2700	$C - H$ stretch of CH_3, CH_2 and aldehyde proton
1900 — 1650	$C = O$ stretch
1475 — 1300	$C - H$ bending of $CH_3-, -CH_2-$

Q-2   In which of the eight spectral regions would the following compound be expected to absorb light?

A-2   **Region $\bar{\nu} - $ cm^{-1}**

3750 — 3000	$N - H$ stretch
3000 — 2700	$C - H$ stretch
1900 — 1650	$C = O$ stretch
1475 — 1300	$C - H$ bending

Q-3   In which of the eight spectral regions would the following compound be expected to absorb light? To what type of vibration would each absorption be due?

$$HO-\langle \bigcirc \rangle - C \overset{O}{\diagup} - H$$

A-3 | **Region $\bar{\nu}$ — cm^{-1}**

3750 — 3000	O — H stretch
3300 — 3000	C — H stretch of Ar — H
3000 — 2700	aldehyde hydrogen
1900 — 1650	C = O stretch
1675 — 1500	C = C stretch (Ar)
1000 — 650	Ar — H bending (out of plane)

Q-4 In which of the eight spectral regions would the following compound be expected to absorb light? To what type of vibration would the absorptions be due?

$$CH_3 \overset{O}{\overset{\|}{C}} OCH_2 C \equiv CH$$

A-4 | **Region $\bar{\nu}$ — cm^{-1}**

3300 — 2900	C $\equiv$ C — H stretch
3000 — 2700	C — H stretch of CH$_3$— and —CH$_2$—
2400 — 2100	C $\equiv$ C stretch
1900 — 1650	C = O stretch

Q-5 In which of the eight spectral regions would the following compound be expected to absorb light? To what type of vibration would each absorption be due?

— CH$_2$ NHCH$_3$

A-5 | **Region $\bar{\nu}$ — cm^{-1}**

3750 — 3000	N — H stretch
3300 — 3000	C = C — H (C — H stretch)
3000 — 2700	CH$_3$—, —CH$_2$— C — H (C — H stretch)
1475 — 1300	C — H bending
1675 — 1625	C = C stretch
1000 — 650	C = C — H bending

Q-6 Below is a portion of the infrared spectrum of a compound. What types of groups are possible? What types of groups are known to be absent?

A-6

Region $\bar{\nu}$ – cm^{-1}	
3750 – 3000	NH or OH stretch
3300 – 2700	C – H stretch of CH$_3$ –, –CH$_2$ –, $\geq$C – H, Ar – H, $\geq$C = C$\overset{}{-}$H, – C ≡ C – H or aldehyde hydrogen
2400 – 2100	C ≡ C or C ≡ N stretch
1475 – 1300	C – H bending
Absent	
1900 – 1650	C = O stretch
1675 – 1625	C = C stretch

Q-7   Below is a partial spectrum of a compound which is known to have either structure I or II. Which structure is *not* consistent with the spectrum? Why?

A-7   Structure I is not consistent with the spectrum because of the lack of bands in the 3750 – 3300 cm^{-1} (O – H stretch) region and the 1675 – 1625 cm^{-1} (C = C stretch) region. Absorption in the 1900 – 1650 cm^{-1} region (C = O stretch) is consistent with structure II.

Q-8   Below is a partial spectrum of a compound which is known to have either structure I or II. Which structure is *not* consistent with the spectrum? Why?

A-8 Structure II is *not* consistent with the spectrum because of the lack of C = O stretch (1900 − 1650 cm⁻¹) and the presence of absorption in the 2400 − 2100 cm⁻¹ region (C ≡ N stretch).

Q-9 A portion of the infrared spectrum of a molecule known to have either structure I or II is given below. Which structure *is consistent* with the spectrum? Why?

A-9 Structure I. The $\overset{\frown}{C} = \overset{\frown}{C} - H$ absorption at 3080 cm⁻¹ is consistent with structure I but not structure II.

Q-10 A portion of the infrared spectrum of a molecule known to have structure I, II, or III is given below. Which structure is consistent with the spectrum? Why?

A-10   Structure II. The presence of the 3300 cm⁻¹ ($-C \equiv C - H$) band eliminates III. Lack of $C = O$ stretch $1900 - 1650$ cm⁻¹ eliminates I and III. Note the very weak $- C \equiv C -$ stretch band (2200 cm⁻¹) in the spectrum.

Q-11   A portion of the infrared spectrum of a molecule known to have structure I, II, or III is given below. Which structure is consistent with the spectrum? Why?

A-11   Structure III. The presence of both aromatic $C - H$ stretch (above 3000 cm⁻¹) and aliphatic $C - H$ stretch ($3000 - 2700$ cm⁻¹) is consistent with only structure III.

Q-12   A compound whose spectrum appears below was thought to have structure I, II, III, or IV. Which structure is most nearly consistent with the spectrum?

A-12   Structure II. The presence of $C - H$ stretch above 3000 cm⁻¹ eliminates I. The presence of $C = O$ stretch at 1700 cm⁻¹ eliminates structures III and IV.

S-2   Certain important distinctions can be made in the $O - H$, $N - H$ stretching region of the spectrum $(3750 - 3000$ cm^{-1}).

Free (non-hydrogen bonded) $O - H$ stretching vibrations are in the $3700 - 3500$ cm^{-1} range. Free phenol OH vibrations will tend to have absorption at the low (3500) end of this range. The free OH bands have lower intensity than bonded OH bands and will be evident in only dilute solutions (or in gas phase).

A hydrogen bonded OH absorption appears in the range $3450 - 3200$ cm^{-1} as a rather broad and intense band.

Non-bonded amines exhibit bands in the $3500 - 3300$ cm^{-1} region while bonded amines give bands in the $3500 - 3100$ region; these bands are weaker than the bonded OH bands but much sharper. Primary amines show two bands, 2° amines and imines show only one band and 3° amines show no bands. Amides and lactams also show $N - H$ absorption in the $3500 - 3300$ region.

Carboxylic acids in the solid state and even in relatively dilute solutions exist as dimers and show no OH absorption in the expected region. Instead, strong broad absorptions in the $3000 - 2500$ cm^{-1} region occur.

Q-13   Indicate the absorptions expected in the spectrum of the following compound. The spectrum was obtained of a *neat* sample (i.e., no solvent was present).

$CH_3 - CH_2 - OH$

A-13   A strong band in the bonded OH stretching region ($3450 - 3200$ cm^{-1}) and bands in the $C - H$ stretch region ($3000 - 2700$ cm^{-1}) characteristic of $CH_{\overline{3}}$ and $-CH_{\overline{2}}$.

Q-14   Indicate the absorption expected for the following compound.

$$CH_3 - \overset{O}{\overset{\|}{C}} - \overset{H}{\overset{|}{N}} - CH_2 - CH_3$$

A-14   A weak but sharp $N - H$ absorption in the $3500 - 3300$ cm^{-1} region. Absorption in the $C - H$ region ($3000 - 2700$ cm^{-1}) due to $CH_{\overline{3}}$ and $-CH_{\overline{2}}$ stretch and a $\rangle C = O$ absorption in the carbonyl region ($1900 - 1650$ cm^{-1}).

Q-15   A very dilute solution of *cis*-cyclopentane $-1,2$-diol in CCl$_4$ shows bands at 3620 and 3455 cm^{-1}. Explain.

A-15   The absorption at 3620 cm^{-1} is due to free OH stretch. Absorption at 3485 cm^{-1} is due to bonded OH stretch. The bonded stretch in a dilute solution is indicative of intramolecular hydrogen bonding, i.e.,

Q-16   How would the infrared spectra of the following compounds differ?

$C_6 H_5 CH_2 NH_2$

$$CH_3 \overset{O}{\overset{\|}{C}} N (CH_3)_2$$

A-16   The benzylamine would have two peaks in the $3500 - 3100$ cm^{-1} region and no $C = O$ stretch, while N,N-dimethylacetamide would have no H$-$N stretch at $3500 - 3100$ cm^{-1} but would have a $C = O$ stretch near 1650 cm^{-1}.

Q-17   How would the infrared spectra of the following compounds differ?

$(t-C_4 H_9)_2 N-H$ $(C_2 H_5)_3 N$

A-17   Di-*t*-butylamine would have an H–N stretch in the 3500 – 3100 cm^{-1} region while trimethylamine would have no N–H stretch.

Q-18   How would the infrared spectra of the following compounds differ (neat samples)?

OH
|
CH_3CHCH_3

$(CH_3CH_2CH_2CH_2)_2NH$

A-18   *i*-propyl alcohol would have a strong broad OH stretch (3400 – 3200 cm^{-1}) and C–H stretch bands characteristic of CH_3– and $\underset{/}{\overset{\frown}{\underset{}{}}}$C–H, while *n*-dibutylamine would have a weak, sharp single band in the N–H stretch region (3500 – 3100 cm^{-1}) and bands characteristic of CH_3– and $–CH_2–$.

Q-19   How would the infrared spectra of the following compounds differ (neat samples)?

$CH_3(CH_2)_6COOH$ $(CH_3)_3CCHOHCH_2CH_3$

A   B

$(CH_3)_3CCH(CH_2CH_3)N(CH_3)_2$
C

A-19   **A** would show no OH absorption in the 3500 – 3100 cm^{-1} region but would absorb in the 3000 – 2500 cm^{-1} region as well as in the C = O region (1900 – 1650 cm^{-1}). **B** would give a strong OH band in the 3450 – 3200 cm^{-1} region and no C = O absorption while **C** would give neither an absorption in the 3400 – 3100 cm^{-1} region nor in the C = O region (1900 – 1650 cm^{-1}).

Q-20   How would the infrared spectra of the following compounds differ (neat samples)?

A-20   Both would exhibit OH stretching in the 3450 – 3200 cm^{-1} region (the phenol at lower wave numbers). However, the phenol would show Ar–H absorption and cyclohexanol would give $–CH_2–$ and $\underset{/}{\overset{\frown}{\underset{}{}}}$C–H absorption. Also, phenol would give some aromatic C–H bending in the 1000 – 650 cm^{-1} region while cyclohexanol would not.

R

Non-bonded	OH	3700 – 3500 cm^{-1}
Bonded	OH	3450 – 3300 cm^{-1}
Non-bonded	NH	3500 – 3300 cm^{-1}
Bonded	NH	3500 – 3100 cm^{-1}
Carboxylic Acids		3000 – 2500 cm^{-1}

S-3   Different types of C—H bonds show absorption within well-defined areas of the C—H stretching region (3300 − 2700 cm^{-1}). The *approximate* positions of the C—H bands for different types of groups are shown below.

Type H	$\bar{\nu} - $ cm^{-1}	Band intensity
Ar—H	3030	moderate intensity
C≡C—H	3300	high intensity
C=C—H	3040 − 3010	moderate intensity
—CH$_3$	2960 & 2870	high intensity
—CH$_2$—	2930 & 2850	high intensity
$>$CH	2890	low intensity
—C—H ‖ O	2720	low intensity

Note that C≡C—H, C=C—H and Ar—H absorb **above** 3000 cm^{-1} while aliphatic and aldehydic C—H absorb below 3000 cm^{-1}.

Also note that —CH$_3$ and —CH$_2$— give rise to **two bands**.

Q-21   At approximately what positions in the C—H stretch portion of the spectrum would the following absorb?

$CH_3 CH_2 CH = CH_2$

A-21   A band in the region 3040 − 3010 cm^{-1} due to the ethylenic hydrogens. Two bands in the region 2960 − 2870 cm^{-1} due to CH$_3$ and two bands in the region 2930 − 2850 cm^{-1} due to —CH$_2$—.

Q-22   At approximately what positions in the C—H stretch portion of the infrared spectrum would the following be expected to absorb light?

$$CH_3 CH_2 \overset{\overset{O}{\|}}{C} C \equiv CH$$

A-22   A band in the 3300 cm^{-1} region due to C≡CH stretch, two bands (2960 − 2870 cm^{-1} region) due to CH$_3$ —, and two bands (2930 − 2850 cm^{-1} region) due to —CH$_2$—.

Q-23   At approximately what positions in the C—H stretch portion of the infrared spectrum would the following be expected to absorb?

A-23   A weak band in the 2720 cm^{-1} region due to
O
‖
C—H stretch, two bands near 2930 and 2850 cm^{-1} due to —CH$_2$—, and a weak band near 2890 cm^{-1} due to $>$C—H.

Q-24   At approximately what positions in the C—H stretch portion of the infrared spectrum would the following be expected to absorb?

A-24   A band near 3030 cm^{-1} due to aromatic C—H stretch along with a band in the 3040 − 3010 cm^{-1} region due to H—C = C. (These bands may overlap and not be resolved as separate peaks.) A weak band near 2720 cm^{-1} due to —C—H stretch.
$$\overset{\text{O}}{\underset{\|}{}}$$

Q-25   At approximately what positions in the C—H stretch portion of the infrared spectrum would the following be expected to absorb?

A-25   A band near 3030 cm^{-1} due to Ar—H stretch, a weak band near 2890 cm^{-1} due to $>$C—H, and two bands near 2960 and 2870 cm^{-1} due to CH$_3$— stretch.

Q-26   At approximately what positions in the C—H stretch portion of the infrared spectrum would the following be expected to absorb?

$CH_3CH_2CH(CH_3)_2$

A-26   A weak band near 2890 cm^{-1} due to $>$C—H, two bands near 2960 and 2870 cm^{-1} due to CH$_3$— stretch, and two bands near 2930 and 2850 cm^{-1} due to —CH$_2$— stretch.

Q-27   How would the C—H stretch region of the following compounds differ?

$$\mathbf{A}\ \ C_6H_5\overset{\text{O}}{\underset{\|}{C}}H \qquad \mathbf{B}\ \ (CH_3)_3C\overset{\text{O}}{\underset{\|}{C}}H$$

A-27   **A** would have Ar—H stretch near 3030 cm^{-1} and $\overset{\text{O}}{\underset{\|}{C}}$ — H stretch near 2720 cm^{-1}, while **B** would have no C — H stretch above 3000 cm^{-1}. **B** would have two bands near 2960 and 2870 cm^{-1} due to CH$_3$— and a $\overset{\text{O}}{\underset{\|}{}}$ C—H stretch close to 2720 cm^{-1}.

R

—C ≡ C—H		3300 cm^{-1}
Ar—H		3030 cm^{-1}
$>$C = C$<^H$		3040 − 3010 cm^{-1}
CH$_3$—		2960 and 2870 cm^{-1}
—CH$_2$—		2930 and 2850 cm^{-1}
$\geqslant$CH		2890 cm^{-1}
$-\overset{\text{O}}{\underset{\|}{C}}-$H		2720 cm^{-1}

S-4   The triple bond symmetrical stretch region is summarized below:

Type triple bond	$\bar{v}$—cm^{-1}	Intensity of bond
H—C ≡ C—R	2140 − 2100	strong
R—C ≡ C—R′	2260 − 2190	variable intensity
RC ≡ CR	no absorption	
RC ≡ N	2260 − 2240	strong

Conjugation will cause a small shift of these values to **lower** wave number, e.g., aryl cyanides absorb in the 2240 − 2190 cm^{-1} region. The symmetrical acetylenes show no absorption because **symmetrical vibration causes no change in dipole.**

Q-28   What infrared absorptions would be expected for the following compound?

$CH_3CH_2C ≡ CH$

A-28   A band near 3300 cm^{-1} (C ≡ C—H), two bands near 2960 − 2870 cm^{-1} (CH$_3$), two bands near 2930 − 2850 cm^{-1} (CH$_2$), one band near 2140 − 2100 cm^{-1} (symmetrical — C ≡ C — stretch) and aliphatic C — H bending, 1475 − 1300 cm^{-1}.

Q-29   What infrared absorptions would be expected for the following compound (neat sample)?

$HC ≡ CCH_2OH$

A-29   A strong broad band in the 3450 – 3300 cm^{-1} region due to OH, which might cover up the 3300 cm^{-1} band of the C≡CH stretch. Two bands in the 2930 – 2850 cm^{-1} regions due to – CH$_2$ – stretch, a band near 2140 – 2100 cm^{-1} due to symmetrical C≡C stretch and aliphatic C – H bending near 1475 – 1300 cm^{-1}.

Q-30   What infrared absorptions would be expected for the following compound?

A-30   A band near 3030 cm^{-1} due to Ar–H stretch but **no** band near 2260 – 2190 cm^{-1} because the symmetrical C≡C stretch does not give rise to a change in dipole. Aromatic C = C stretch in the 1675 – 1500 cm^{-1} region and Ar–H bending in the 1000 – 650 cm^{-1} region.

Q-31   What infrared absorptions would be expected for the following compound (neat sample)?

$CH_3C≡CCH_2CH_2NH_2$

A-31   Two sharp but not very strong bands in the 3500 – 3100 cm^{-1} region due to H–N stretch, two bands in the 2960 – 2870 cm^{-1} region (CH$_3$), at least two bands in the 2930 – 2850 cm^{-1} region (CH$_2$), a band (probably low intensity) in the 2260 – 2190 cm^{-1} region due to C≡C stretch, and aliphatic C–H bending, 1475 – 1300 cm^{-1}.

Q-32   What infrared absorptions would be expected for the following compound (saturated CCl$_4$ solution)?

A-32   A band (strong, wide) in the 3450 – 3300 cm^{-1} region due to OH (bonded) stretch. A band near 3030 cm^{-1} due to Ar–H stretch, two bands in the 2960 – 2870 cm^{-1} region (CH$_3$), one band (weak) near 2890 cm^{-1} (>C–H), a band in the 2260 – 2190 cm^{-1} region (although it may be very weak) due to symmetrical C≡C stretch, aromatic C = C stretch 1675 – 1500 cm^{-1} region, aliphatic C–H bending 1475 – 1300 cm^{-1} region, and aromatic C–H bending 1000 – 650 cm^{-1} region.

Q-33   What infrared absorptions would be expected for the following compound?

A-33   A band in the 3030 cm^{-1} region due to Ar–H stretch. This may be masked by a rather wide diffuse band in the 3000 – 2500 cm^{-1} region due to COOH. The C≡N would give a band in the 2260 – 2240 cm^{-1} region. There would be aromatic C = C stretch, 1675 – 1500 cm^{-1}, and bending, 1000 – 650 cm^{-1}.

R		
HC≡CR	2140 – 2100 cm^{-1}
RC≡CR′	2260 – 2190 cm^{-1}
RC≡CR	no absorption
RC≡N	2260 – 2240 cm^{-1}

S-5   Many important bands appear in the carbonyl region of the spectra.

Type carbonyl	$\bar{\nu} - cm^{-1}$	Intensity of band
$\overset{O}{\overset{\|}{R-C}}H$ (saturated)	1740 — 1720	strong
COOH (saturated)	1705 — 1725	strong
$R-\overset{O}{\overset{\|}{C}}-R$ (saturated)	1705 — 1725	strong
$R-\overset{O}{\overset{\|}{C}}-OR$ (6 and 7 membered lactones)	1750 — 1730	strong
5 membered lactones	1780 — 1760	strong
Esters (non-cyclic)	1740 — 1710	strong
Acid halides	1815 — 1720	strong
Anhydrides	Two bands separated by approximately 60 cm^{-1} at 1850 — 1800 cm^{-1} and 1780 — 1740 cm^{-1}	
Amides	1700 — 1640 cm^{-1}	strong

Conjugation will shift all the absorption bands to smaller wave numbers (note that strain on lactone rings shifts absorptions to higher frequencies).

Q-34   How would the absorption spectra of the following differ in the region 4000 — 1650 cm^{-1}?

$$CH_3CH_2COOH \qquad CH_3CH_2\overset{O}{\overset{\|}{C}}H$$

$$CH_3\overset{}{\underset{O}{\overset{\|}{C}}}CH_3$$

A-34   All would have a strong absorption in the 1740 — 1700 cm^{-1} region. The acid would have a wide diffuse band in the 3000 — 2500 cm^{-1} region due to —OH, while the aldehyde would have a weak absorption in the 2720 cm^{-1} region due to CH stretch.

Q-35   How would the absorption spectra of the following differ in the region 4000 — 1650 cm^{-1}?

A-35   All three compounds would have Ar—H stretch in the 3030 cm^{-1} region. A would have two N—H stretch peaks in the 3500 — 3100 cm^{-1} region, while B would have only one N—H stretch peak in that region, and C would have none. A would have a C = O stretch peak in the 1700 — 1640 cm^{-1} region while B would have none. C would have the C = O stretch at approximately 1700 cm^{-1}. C would have a wide diffuse band in the 3000 — 2500 cm^{-1} region due to OH.

Q-36   How would the absorption spectra of the following differ in the region 4000 — 1650 cm^{-1}?

$$CH_3\overset{O}{\overset{\|}{C}}O\overset{O}{\overset{\|}{C}}CH_3 \qquad A$$

$$CH_3\overset{O}{\overset{\|}{C}}OCH_3 \qquad B$$

$$CH_3\overset{O}{\overset{\|}{C}}N(CH_3)_2 \qquad C$$

A-36   All three compounds would have at least two bands (2960 − 2870 cm^{-1} region) due to CH$_3$ − stretch. **A** would have two C = O stretch bands separated by approximately 60 cm^{-1} in the 1850 − 1740 cm^{-1} region, while **B** would have a single C = O band in the 1740 − 1710 cm^{-1} region, and **C** would have a single C = O stretch in the 1700 − 1640 cm^{-1} region.

A-37   Compound **A** would have a single HN stretch peak in the 3500 − 3100 cm^{-1} region, **B** would have two NH stretch peaks, and **C** would have none. **A** and **B** would have absorption in the 1640 cm^{-1} region (low because of conjugation). Certainly the surest way of distinguishing between these compounds is the inspection of the NH stretch region.

A-38   **B** would show an OH stretch absorption in the 3450 − 3300 cm^{-1} range while **A** and **C** would show none. **A** would have a carbonyl stretch absorption in the 1740 − 1720 cm^{-1} region. **C** would also have a weak absorption at 2720 cm^{-1} due to the C−H stretch of the aldehyde.

Q-37   How would the absorption spectra of the following (concentrated solutions) differ in the 4000 − 1650 cm^{-1} region?

Q-38   How would the absorption spectra of the following (concentrated solutions) differ in the 4000 − 1650 cm^{-1} region?

Q-39   How would the absorption spectra of the following (concentrated solutions) differ in the 4000 − 1650 cm^{-1} region?

A-39   **A** would show *no* $C \equiv C$ stretch (no change in dipole) and no $C = O$ stretch. **B** would have a weak $C \equiv C$ absorption in the $2260 - 2190 \text{ cm}^{-1}$ region as well as a $C = O$ stretch in the 1700 cm^{-1} region and a $C-H$ stretch near 2720 cm^{-1}. The $C = O$ stretch and aldehyde $C-H$ stretch in **C** would be like those in **B**, but **C** would have *no* $C \equiv C$ stretch in the $2260 - 2190 \text{ cm}^{-1}$ region. **C** would have absorption in the 2930 and 2850 cm^{-1} region due to $-CH_2-$.

R		
	COOH (saturated)	$1705 - 1725 \text{ cm}^{-1}$
	RCOR (saturated)	$1705 - 1725 \text{ cm}^{-1}$
	RCHO (saturated)	$1720 - 1740 \text{ cm}^{-1}$
	Lactones (6 and 7 membered)	$1730 - 1750 \text{ cm}^{-1}$
	Lactones (5 membered)	$1760 - 1780 \text{ cm}^{-1}$
	R COOR	$1710 - 1740 \text{ cm}^{-1}$
	RCOX	$1720 - 1815 \text{ cm}^{-1}$
	RCOOCOR	$1800 - 1850$ and $1740 - 1780 \text{ cm}^{-1}$
	$RCONH_2$	$1680 - 1700 \text{ cm}^{-1}$ (free) $1640 - 1660 \text{ cm}^{-1}$ (bonded)

Conjugation shifts bands to lower wave numbers.

S-6   The symmetrical double bond stretch region from $1680 - 1600 \text{ cm}^{-1}$ contains bands due to the following groups.

Type Double Bond	$\bar{\nu}-\text{cm}^{-1}$	Intensity of Band
$C = C$	$1680 - 1620$	variable
$C = N-$	$1690 - 1640$	variable
$-N = N-$	$1630 - 1575$	variable

The $C = C$ band will be quite weak for a relatively symmetrical molecule. Aromatic systems have one or more strong bands in the $1400 - 1500 \text{ cm}^{-1}$ region.

Q-40   How would the spectra of the following compounds differ?

    A   **B**

A-40   Only **A** would have a band in the $3040 - 3010 \text{ cm}^{-1}$ region ($C = CH$) and a band in the $1680 - 1620 \text{ cm}^{-1}$ region ($C = C$).

Q-41   How would the spectra of the following compounds differ?

$$CH_3 CH = CH \ CH_2 \overset{\overset{O}{\|}}{C}H$$

          A

B

A-41   **A** would have a band in the $3040 - 3010 \text{ cm}^{-1}$ region ($CH = C$), two bands in the $2960 - 2870 \text{ cm}^{-1}$ region (CH_3), one weak band in the 2720 cm^{-1} region (CHO), and a $C = C$ stretch in the $1680 - 1620 \text{ cm}^{-1}$ region which would not be present in the spectrum of **B**.

Q-42   How would the spectra of the following compounds differ?

    A   **B**

A-42 Both **A** and **B** would have C = CH stretch ($3040 - 3010$ cm^{-1}). **A** would have $-CH_2-$ stretch ($2930 - 2850$ cm^{-1}) which **B** would not have. **A** would have a single C = O stretch in the $1725 - 1705$ cm^{-1} region while **B** would have two C = O stretch bands about 60 cm^{-1} apart in the $1850 - 1740$ cm^{-1} region. Both **A** and **B** would have **very** weak C = C stretch in the $1690 - 1620$ cm^{-1} region.

R		
$\overset{>}{\underset{}{}}C = C\overset{<}{\underset{}{}}$	$1620 - 1680$ cm^{-1}	
$\overset{>}{\underset{}{}}C = N-$	$1640 - 1690$ cm^{-1}	
$-N = N-$	$1575 - 1630$ cm^{-1}	

S-7 The C—H bending region ($1000 - 650$ cm^{-1}) yields information useful in characterizing olefins and substitution positions on aromatic rings. A list of useful characteristic absorptions in this region is given below:

Ethylenic C—H Bending:

Type Olefin	$\bar{\nu} -$cm^{-1}	Intensity of Band
RCH = CH$_2$	990 and 910	strong
RCH = CRH (*cis*)	690	moderate to strong
RCH = CRH (*trans*)	970	moderate to strong
R$_2$C = CH$_2$	890	moderate to strong
R$_2$C = CHR	$840 - 790$	moderate to strong

Substituted Benzene:

Type Substitution	$\bar{\nu} -$cm^{-1}	Intensity of Band
monosubstituted aromatic (5 adjacent H)	750 and 700	usually moderate to strong
ortho aromatic (4 adjacent H)	750	usually moderate to strong
meta aromatic (3 adjacent H)	$780 - 810$	usually moderate to strong
para aromatic (2 adjacent H)	$850 - 800$	usually moderate to strong

Q-43 In what regions of the infrared spectrum would the following compounds exhibit different characteristic absorptions?

A CH$_3$CH = CHCH$_3$ **B** CH$_3$CH = CH$_2$

A-43 **A** would have a weaker C = C stretch in the $1680 - 1620$ cm^{-1} region than would **B**. **B** would have bands at 910 and 990 cm^{-1} characteristic of the $\overset{>}{\underset{}{}}C = CH_2$, while **A** would have a band at 970 cm^{-1} (if *trans*) or 690 cm^{-1} if *cis*.

Q-44 In what regions of the infrared spectrum would the following compounds exhibit different characteristic absorptions?

(CH$_3$)$_2$C = CHCH$_3$	**A**
CH$_3$(CH$_2$)$_2$CH = CH$_2$	**B**

A-44   While both compounds would show some absorption in the $1680 - 1620$ cm^{-1} region, **B** would have two bands, 990 and 910 cm^{-1} (characteristic of RCH = CH$_2$) while **A** would have a single band in the $840 - 790$ cm^{-1} region.

Q-45   In what regions of the infrared spectrum would the following compounds exhibit different characteristic absorptions?

A-45   *m*-xylene has three adjacent H and would show a single band in the $780 - 810$ cm^{-1} region. *p*-xylene has only two adjacent H and would show a single peak in the $800 - 850$ cm^{-1} region.

Q-46   In what regions of the infrared spectrum would the following compounds exhibit different characteristic absorptions?

A   *p*-tolunitrile

B   *o*-tolunitrile

A-46   While both **A** and **B** would have a C $\equiv$ N stretch band in the $2260 - 2240$ cm^{-1} region, **B** has 4 adjacent H and would have a band in the 750 cm^{-1} region. **A** has only 2 adjacent H and would have a band in the $850 - 800$ cm^{-1} region.

Q-47   In what regions of the infrared spectrum would the following compounds exhibit different characteristic absorptions?

ethylbenzene   *o*-xylene

A-47   Ethylbenzene has 5 adjacent H and would have two bands in the 750 and 700 cm^{-1} region. *o*-xylene has only 4 adjacent H and would have but one band near 750 cm^{-1}. Ethylbenzene would have two peaks in the $2930 - 2850$ cm^{-1} region ($-$CH$_2-$) which would not be present in *o*-xylene.

Q-48   In what regions of the infrared spectrum would the following compounds exhibit different characteristic absorptions?

cis-2-butene   *trans*-2-butene

A-48   The *cis*-compound would have a strong absorption in the 690 cm^{-1} region, while the *trans* isomer would have an absorption in the 970 cm^{-1} region.

Q-49   In what regions of the infrared spectrum would the following compounds exhibit different characteristic absorptions?

A-49   **A** would have a single band in the $840 - 790$ cm^{-1} region and a rather weak double bond stretch band ($1680 - 1620$ cm^{-1} region). **B** would have two bands near 910 and 990 cm^{-1} and a strong double bond stretch ($1680 - 1620$ cm^{-1} region).

Q-50   In what regions of the infrared spectrum would the following compounds exhibit different characteristic absorptions?

A-50   **A** would have a single strong band in the 840 − 790 cm⁻¹ region, while **B** would have a single strong band in the 690 cm⁻¹ region.

Q-51   Below is the spectrum of an organic compound containing only C, H, and O. Is the compound aromatic or aliphatic? Is the compound an alcohol?

A-51   The lack of any C−H stretch bands above 3000 cm⁻¹ would indicate the compound is not aromatic. The C−H stretch at 2960 and 2930 cm⁻¹ indicate aliphatic CH. The lack of any strong bands in the 3500 − 3300 cm⁻¹ region indicates the compound is not an alcohol.

Q-52   Is the compound whose spectrum is shown above an aldehyde, ketone, ester, anhydride, or acid? Does the compound contain a double or triple bond?

A-52   The compound has absorption in the carbonyl region (1718 cm^{-1}) at the frequency typical of aldehydes, ketones, or acids. The lack of any strong, broad bands in the 3000 cm^{-1} region due to OH would indicate the compound is not an acid. The lack of any C—H stretch at 2720 cm^{-1} suggests that the compound is not an aldehyde. The lack of any absorption in the 1650 and 2200 cm^{-1} regions indicates that if double or triple bonds are present they must be symmetrical.

Q-53   Below is the infrared spectrum of a compound. Is the compound aromatic or aliphatic?

A-53   The sharp peaks in the C—H stretch region indicate either C = CH, C≡CH, or aromatic hydrogen.

Q-54   Does the compound whose spectrum was shown in Q-53 contain the C = CH or C≡CH group?

A-54   A band in the 2200 cm^{-1} region would be present if the compound had a C≡CH group. The presence of a double bond is confirmed by the 1650 cm^{-1} band and strong bands at 910 and 990 cm^{-1} (indicating CH$_2$ = C$\bar{\ }$).

Q-55   Methyl groups have a characteristic band at 1375 cm^{-1}. Methyl and methylene groups absorb at 1450 cm^{-1}. Does the compound whose spectrum appeared in Q-53 have a CH$_3$ group?

A-55   No. The 1375 cm^{-1} band is absent, but the 1450 cm^{-1} band is present.

Q-56   Does the compound described in Q-53 contain OH, NH, or C = O?

A-56   No. There is no strong absorption in the 3500 —|3300 or 1960 — 1650 cm^{-1} regions which could be associated with OH, NH, or C = O.

Q-57   Below is the infrared spectrum of a compound. What indications are there that the compound is *not* aromatic?

A-57   There is no C—H stretch above 3000 cm^{-1}, no aromatic absorption between 1650 and 1450 cm^{-1}, and no strong absorption in the 850 — 700 cm^{-1} region.

Q-58   For the compound described in Q-57, what groups are indicated in the spectral region 4000 — 2000 cm^{-1}? What groups are known to be absent from the trace shown in this region?

A-58   The strong, wide band at 3350 cm^{-1} is indicative of OH. The absorption in the 2850 — 3000 cm^{-1} region indicates —CH$_2$—, and/or —CH$_3$, and/or$\geqslant$CH. At least two of these C—H type stretchings are indicated by the three bands. The sharp 2970 cm^{-1} band is very suggestive of —CH$_3$. The C=CH, C≡CH, Ar—H, C≡N, and unsymmetrical C≡C groups are *not* indicated.

Q-59   From the spectrum of the compound described in Q-57, what groups are indicated in the 2000 — 1200 cm^{-1} region? What groups are known to be absent?

A-59   The bands at 1380 and 1470 cm^{-1} are indications that CH$_3$– and perhaps –CH$_2$– are present. The groups obviously absent are carbonyl, unsymmetrical C = C, and aromatic rings.

Q-60   Below is the spectrum of a compound. Is the compound aromatic or aliphatic?

A-60   Several things indicate the presence of an aromatic ring. All C–H stretch absorption is above 3000 cm^{-1} indicating the possible presence of AR–H, C = C–H or C ≡ C–H, and the absence of –CH$_3$, –CH$_2$–, and $\geq$CH. The strong bands at 1620, 1500, and 700 are all characteristic of aromatic compounds.

Q-61   What functional groups are indicated in the spectrum between 4000 and 1000 cm^{-1}? What groups are known to be absent?

A-61   The two sharp bands of medium strength in the 3500 region are suggestive of NH$_2$. The groups known to be absent are OH, C = O, C ≡ N, and unsymmetrical C ≡ C.

Q-62   Following is the spectrum of a compound whose formula is C$_8$H$_8$O. Indicate the type functional group with which the oxygen is associated.

A-62   The lack of any strong band at 3500 − 3300 cm^{-1} indicates the lack of OH. The carbonyl band at 1690 is suggestive of aldehyde, ketone, or amide. Because there is no N in the compound, amide is eliminated. The oxygen must be in a carbonyl of an aldehyde or ketone. The lack of absorption near 2720 cm^{-1} (−COH) suggest the compound is ketone.

Q-63   Is the compound described in Q-62 aromatic? Are any aliphatic carbons indicated?

A-63   The absorption in the C−H stretch region above 3000 cm^{-1} is very suggestive of an aromatic ring. The strong bands at 1600, 1580, and 680 cm^{-1} are also suggestive of an aromatic ring. The absorptions at 2920, 2960 and 1360 cm^{-1} are indicative of CH_3.

Q-64   What type of aromatic substitution does the compound described in Q-62 most likely have?

A-64   The two bands near 700 and 750 cm^{-1} are indicative of a monosubstituted aromatic ring.

R   A complete list of characteristic infrared absorption bands is given in Table V of the Appendix.

Chapter 4

NUCLEAR MAGNETIC RESONANCE SPECTROSCOPY

Nuclear magnetic resonance (NMR) spectroscopy is a powerful tool in determining the structure of organic molecules. This technique provides information about the different kinds of hydrogen atoms in a molecule. The NMR spectrum yields information about the chemical environment of hydrogen atoms, the number of hydrogens in each different kind of environment, and the structure of groups adjacent to each hydrogen atom.

This chapter will develop the theory of nuclear magnetic resonance spectroscopy and the way it is employed in structure elucidation.

After completing this chapter, you should

a) understand the type of energy transitions giving rise to nuclear magnetic resonance spectroscopy
b) understand the relationship between energy, precession frequency, magnetic field, and oscillator frequency
c) understand what conditions are necessary to produce nuclear resonance and how resonance is detected
d) understand what factors determine nuclear shielding and how these affect chemical shifts
e) understand spin-spin coupling and the interaction of neighboring nuclei
f) understand anisotropy effects
g) understand why the rapid exchange of protons gives rise to an average resonance signal
h) be able to use chemical shifts and coupling constants in determining structural features of molecules
i) be able to recognize and calculate types of splitting patterns produced by spin-spin interaction
j) be able to estimate the value for various chemical shifts and coupling constants.

S-1   Nuclear spin angular momentum results from the spinning of a nucleus about its axis. This angular momentum is quantized and is designated by the nuclear spin quantum number **I**. The nuclear spin quantum number may have a value of 0, 1/2, 1, 1½, . . . depending on the nucleus involved. Only certain nuclei possess a spin angular momentum. If the mass number (**A**) is odd, then the spin quantum number **I** is a half integer (n+1/2, where n is a whole number or zero). If the mass number (**A**) and the atomic number (**Z**) are both **even**, the spin quantum number **I** is zero. If the mass number (**A**) is **even** and the atomic number (**Z**) is **odd**, the spin quantum number **I** is an integer (1, 2, 3, etc.). Only those nuclei with an **I** value greater than zero have a spin angular momentum.

	Q-1 Indicate which of the following nuclei will have a non-zero **I** value (**I** $\neq$ 0). Will the **I** value be a half integer or an integer value? F_9^{19} C_6^{12}
A-1 F_9^{19} has an odd mass number (19) and odd atomic number (9). Therefore, **I** is a half integer. C_6^{12} has an even mass number (12) and an even atomic number (6). Therefore, **I** is zero.	Q-2 Indicate which of the following nuclei will have a non-zero **I** value. Will the **I** value be a half integer or an integer value? P_{15}^{31} O_8^{16} H_1^1 N_7^{14}
A-2 P_{15}^{31}: **A** = odd, **Z** = odd, **I** is a half integer. O_8^{16}: **A** = even, **Z** = even, **I** is 0. H_1^1: **A** = odd, **Z** = odd, **I** is a half integer. N_7^{14}: **A** = even, **Z** = odd, **I** is an integer.	Q-3 Which of the following nuclei do not have a spin angular momentum? Li_3^7, He_2^4, C_6^{12}
A-3 Nuclei with an **I** value of zero do not have a spin angular momentum. He_2^4 : **A** = even, **Z** = even, **I** = 0. C_6^{12} : **I** = 0.	R Certain nuclei possess angular momentum which is quantized. Angular momentum is designated by the nuclear spin quantum number **I**.

S-2   When placed in a magnetic field, nuclei with an angular momentum may assume only 2**I** + 1 orientations relative to the applied field. Each of these orientations corresponds to a given energy state for the nucleus.

	Q-4 How many different orientations relative to the applied magnetic field will a nucleus with a value of **I** = 0 be able to assume when in a magnetic field?
A-4 Number of orientations = 2**I** + 1, **I** = 0. Therefore, 2(0) + 1 = 1 orientation.	Q-5 How many different energy states will a nucleus with a value of **I** = 1 have in a magnetic field?
A-5 Number of orientations = 2**I** + 1, **I** = 1. Therefore, 2(1) + 1 = 3 orientations.	Q-6 How many different orientations relative to the applied magnetic field will a proton (H_1^1) with a value of **I** = 1/2 be able to assume when in a magnetic field?

A-6   Number of orientations = $2I + 1$, $I = 1/2$.
       Therefore, $2(1/2) + 1 = 2$ orientations.

R   The number of orientations of a nucleus in an applied magnetic field = $2I + 1$. Each orientation corresponds to a given energy state of the nucleus.

S-3   For a proton (H_1^1) the energy of the orientation corresponds to $\pm \mu_H H_0$ where μ_H is the magnetic moment of the proton and H_0 is the strength of the applied magnetic field. The magnetic moment is a constant for a given type of nucleus. The higher energy level for the proton is the $+\mu_H H_0$ state.

Q-7   Draw an energy level diagram to represent the two energy levels of the proton in a magnetic field H_0. Label the energy levels.

A-7

$+ \mu_H H_0$

$- \mu_H H_0$

Q-8   A diagram is drawn below which shows the variation in the energy levels as a function of the strength of the applied magnetic field.

$+\mu_H H_0$

$- \mu_H H_0$

H_0

What are the relative values of the two energy levels for a proton in a magnetic field of zero strength?

A-8   At zero magnetic field the two energy levels are equal.

Q-9   Below is an energy diagram for the energy levels of the proton in a magnetic field equal to H_0.

$+ \mu_H H_0$

$-\mu_H H_0$

Draw the energy levels for the proton in a magnetic field equal to H_0' and H_0'' where $H_0'' > H_0 > H_0'$.

A-9

Q-10   The energy transition that is important in nuclear magnetic resonance is the transition of a nucleus from the lower energy level to the higher one. The difference between the two energy levels is ΔE. In terms of the applied magnetic field and magnetic moment, what is the energy necessary to cause a proton to be excited from the lower energy state (E_1) to the higher state (E_2)? The proton has a magnetic moment of μ_H and is in a magnetic field of strength H_0.

A-10

$$\Delta E = E_2 - E_1 = +\mu_H H_0 - (-\mu_H H_0)$$
$$\Delta E = 2\mu_H H_0$$

Q-11   If the strength of the applied magnetic field H_0 is increased, will more or less energy be required to cause a transition from energy level E_1 to E_2?

A-11   More
$$\Delta E = 2\mu_H H_0$$
ΔE increases as H_0 increases.

Q-12   The magnetic moment for a fluorine nucleus μ_F is smaller than that for a proton. Fluorine has an **I** value of 1/2.

Compare the energy required for the nuclear transition of the fluorine and hydrogen nuclei in an applied magnetic field of the same strength.

A-12   The hydrogen nucleus requires the greater energy.
$$\Delta E = \mu H_0$$
ΔE increases as μ increases.

R   The energy of a given orientation for a nucleus is given by $\pm \mu H_0$ where μ is the magnetic moment of the nucleus in question and H_0 is the strength of the applied magnetic field.

S-4   A physical picture will be developed for the energy levels of a nucleus. Consider a spinning top whose spin axis does not correspond to the direction of the gravitational field. The top will precess; that is, rotate in a circle perpendicular to the gravitational field.

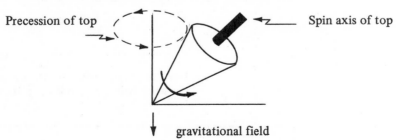

A nucleus with a spin 1/2 is similar to a top precessing about a point. The magnetic moment of the spinning nucleus lines up with or against the applied magnetic field. Because the magnetic moment cannot exactly parallel the applied magnetic field, it will precess about the field. The stronger the applied magnetic field, the faster will be the precession frequency of the magnetic moment.

| | Q-13 | The hydrogen nucleus having its magnetic moment aligned with the applied magnetic field is in the lower of the two possible energy states. Draw and give the energy for this orientation (spin state). |

A-13

$E = - \mu_H H_0$

Q-14   Draw and give the energy for the high energy spin state of the hydrogen nucleus.

A-14

$E = + \mu_H H_0$

Q-15   In terms of the nuclear spin states, what happens when the nucleus undergoes a transition from its low energy level to its higher energy level?

A-15   The nucleus flips from its spin state where the magnetic moment is aligned with the applied field to the spin state where the magnetic moment is opposed to the applied field.

Q-16   What is meant by *the frequency of precession* of the magnetic moment vector around the applied magnetic field?

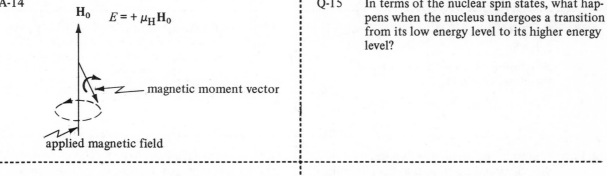

A-16   The frequency of precession is the number of complete revolutions the magnetic moment vector makes around the applied magnetic field in one second.

R   A hydrogen nucleus can exist in two different spin states, one in which the magnetic moment is aligned with the applied magnetic field and one in which the magnetic moment is opposed to the applied field. The applied magnetic field causes the magnetic moment vector to precess around the applied field.

S-5   A transition of a hydrogen nucleus from one spin state to another requires an amount of energy equal to $2\mu H_0$. This energy can be supplied by electromagnetic radiation applied in such a way that the radiation's magnetic vector component is oscillating in a plane perpendicular to that of the applied field.

precessing magnetic moment of nucleus

oscillating magnetic vector component of electromagnetic radiation

H_0

When the frequency of the oscillating magnetic vector component of the electromagnetic radiation is equal to the precessing frequency of the magnetic moment of the nucleus, the two are said to be in *resonance,* and energy can be transferred from the electromagnetic radiation to the hydrogen nucleus. When resonance occurs, the proton is transformed from one spin state to the other.

| | Q-17 | What is the relationship between energy of a transition, $\triangle E$, and frequency of electromagnetic radiation, ν? |

A-17 $\triangle E = h\nu$, where h is Planck's constant.

Q-18   Derive a relationship between the frequency of electromagnetic radiation necessary to cause resonance and the strength of the applied magnetic field, H_0.

A-18 $\triangle E = 2\mu H_0$

$\triangle E = h\nu$

At resonance the two $\triangle E$'s are equal; therefore, $h\nu = 2\mu H_0$

$$\nu = \frac{2\mu}{h} H_0$$

Q-19   As the strength of the applied field (H_0) is increased, how must the frequency of electromagnetic radiation (ν) be changed in order to cause resonance?

A-19   It must be increased. The frequency is directly proportional to the strength of the applied magnetic field.

$$\nu = \frac{2\mu}{h} H_0$$

Q-20   Using a constant frequency electromagnetic radiation, will fluorine or hydrogen nuclei require the greater applied magnetic field for resonance to occur? Why?

$$\mu_F < \mu_H$$

A-20   Fluorine. A frequency of precession equal to that of the electromagnetic radiation is necessary for resonance to occur.

$$\nu_H = \frac{2\mu_H}{h} H_0 \; ; \nu_F = \frac{2\mu_F}{h} H_0$$

Since $\mu_F < \mu_H$, H_0 for fluorine systems must be larger than H_0 for hydrogen systems in order to make the two frequencies equal to the electromagnetic radiation.

R   Resonance occurs when the frequency of the oscillating magnetic vector component of electromagnetic radiation is equal to the precession frequency of the magnetic moment of the nucleus. Resonance allows energy to be transferred from electromagnetic radiation to the nucleus thus causing the nucleus to be transferred from one spin state to another. The resonance condition for a proton is

$$\nu = \frac{2\mu}{h} H_0$$

S-6   To cause the transition of a proton from one spin state to another the sample can be placed in a fixed applied magnetic field, H_0, and the frequency of the oscillating magnetic vector component of the electromagnetic radiation, ν, varied until the resonance situation is reached. Alternatively, a fixed electromagnetic radiation frequency may be imposed and the magnetic field varied until the resonance situation is reached. The latter procedure is experimentally more satisfactory. A fixed oscillator frequency is utilized and the magnetic field is slowly varied until the resonance situation is reached.

With a fixed oscillator frequency of 60 megahertz (megacycles per second) a magnetic field of approximately 14,000 gauss is required for proton resonance. Very large magnetic fields (H_0) are used to assure a measurable separation of energy levels.

Q-21   What is the expression for the resonance frequency of a proton in an applied magnetic field of H_0?

A-21 $\nu = \frac{2\mu}{h} H_0$

Q-22   The magnetic moment for hydrogen, fluorine, and phosphorus decreases as $\mu_H > \mu_F > \mu_P$. Using a constant oscillator frequency, which nuclei would require the largest applied magnetic field for resonance to occur?

A-22 μ_P is smaller than μ_F and μ_H. Therefore, a larger value of H_0 would be necessary for phosphorus to obtain the precession frequency required for resonance.

Q-23   How does the electron density about the hydrogen nuclei in the following species differ?

a) CH_4

b) H^+

A-23   In methane each hydrogen nucleus will be surrounded by an electron cloud. The hydrogen ion has no electron cloud.

Q-24   Electrons surrounding a nucleus produce a secondary magnetic field which opposes the applied field. What effect would the electrons surrounding a nucleus be expected to have on the magnetic field felt by that nucleus?

A-24 The electrons act as a shield for the nucleus from the applied magnetic field so that the magnetic field felt by the nucleus would be slightly less.

Q-25 For a nucleus surrounded by electrons, the *shielding effect* of the electrons is directly proportional to the applied magnetic field. If σ is the proportionality constant between the shielding effect and the applied magnetic field, write an equation for the shielding effect.

A-25 *Shielding effect* = σH_0, where σ is called the shielding constant.

Q-26 The constant, σ, is directly proportional to the density of the electron cloud around the nucleus. As the density of an electron cloud increases, will the magnitude of the magnetic field felt by the nucleus increase or decrease? Why?

A-26 Decrease. As the magnitude of σ increases, the shielding effect increases, reducing the magnetic field felt by the nucleus.

Q-27 The shielding effects on the protons indicated below are different. Explain.

$$\begin{array}{c} \text{H} \\ | \\ \text{H--C--O--H} \longleftarrow \\ | \\ \text{H} \longleftarrow \end{array}$$

A-27 The electron withdrawing effect of oxygen is greater than that for carbon. Therefore, the electron density about the C-H protons will be greater than about the O-H proton; the C-H protons will be shielded to a greater extent than the O-H proton.

Q-28 Would the value for σ be expected to be the same for every proton in an organic compound such as

$$CH_3\text{-}CH_2\text{-}Cl \ ?$$

A-28 No. The value of σ is dependent upon the electron density about a proton. In ethyl chloride there are two types of protons (methyl and methylene). The electron density would be different because the methylene group has a chloro and a methyl group attached to it while the methyl group has a -CH_2Cl group attached.

Q-29 What factor will affect the electron density about a hydrogen nucleus?

A-29 The relative electron pulling or donating power (polar or inductive effect) of the atoms or groups attached to the atom bearing the hydrogen nuclei under consideration.

Q-30 If H_N represents the magnitude of the magnetic field felt by the nucleus, derive an expression for the magnitude of the field felt by the nucleus in terms of the applied field, H_0, and the shielding constant, σ.

A-30 H_0 = applied magnetic field

σH_0 = shielding effect

The shielding effect acts to reduce the applied magnetic field.

$H_N = H_0 - \sigma H_0 = H_0 (1 - \sigma)$

Q-31   Below is an energy diagram for an unshielded proton in an applied magnetic field H_0. Show the effect of electronic shielding on the nuclear energy levels.

A-31

E

no field

+ $\mu_H H_0$

+ $\mu_H H_N$

- $\mu_H H_0$

- $\mu_H H_N$
Shielded proton in field

Unshielded proton in field.

Q-32   The transition energy between nuclear energy levels for an unshielded proton was determined earlier to be $2\mu_H H_0$. What is the transition energy for the shielded proton?

A-32

+ $\mu_H H_N$

- $\mu_H H_N$

$\Delta E = \mu_H H_N - (-\mu_H H_N)$
    $= 2\mu_H H_N$

Q-33   What is the transition energy for the shielded proton in terms of the applied magnetic field, H_0, and the shielding constant, σ?

A-33 $H_N = H_0 (1 - \sigma)$

$\Delta E = 2\mu_H H_N = 2\mu_H H_0 (1 - \sigma)$

Q-34   For an unshielded proton (H^+), the relationship between the frequency of the oscillating magnetic vector component of electromagnetic radiation and the applied magnetic field when resonance occurs is

$$\nu = \frac{\mu_H}{h} H_0$$

Rewrite this equation for a shielded proton in terms of H_0 and σ.

A-34   For an unshielded proton the field felt by the nucleus (H_N) is identical to H_0.

$$\nu = \frac{2\mu_H}{h} H_0 = \frac{2\mu_H}{h} H_N$$

For a shielded proton

$$H_N = H_0 (1 - \sigma)$$

Therefore,

$$\nu = \frac{2\mu_H}{h} H_0 (1 - \sigma)$$

Q-35   In nuclear magnetic resonance the frequency is held constant. Rearrange the equation derived in A-34 to show the applied field necessary for any proton to undergo resonance.

A-35

$$\nu = \frac{2\mu_H}{h} H_0 (1 - \sigma)$$

$$H_0 = \frac{\nu h}{2\mu_H(1 - \sigma)}$$

Q-36   Which of the circled protons in the systems A and B below would be expected to have the greatest shielding? The greatest shielding constant, σ? Why?

$$R-\overset{\displaystyle \textstyle \textcircled{H}}{\underset{\displaystyle R}{C}}-CH_3 \qquad R-\overset{\displaystyle \textstyle \textcircled{H}}{\underset{\displaystyle R}{C}}-H$$

A   B

A-36   The proton in system A would be surrounded by an electron cloud of higher density than the proton in B (H is a better electron withdrawing group than -CH_3). Therefore, the proton in A would be shielded better and would have a higher σ value.

Q-37   How does the value of σ affect the magnitude of the applied field required for resonance?

A-37

$$H_0 = \frac{\nu h}{2\mu_H (1 - \sigma)}$$

If σ is increased, then the value of $\nu h/[2\mu_H (1 - \sigma)]$ will become larger. Therefore, as σ increases, H_0 required for resonance increases.

Q-38   Which of the circled protons in A and B below would be expected to show nuclear resonance with the higher applied field? Why?

$$R-\overset{\displaystyle \textstyle \textcircled{H}}{\underset{\displaystyle R}{C}}-CH_3 \qquad R-\overset{\displaystyle \textstyle \textcircled{H}}{\underset{\displaystyle R}{C}}-H$$

A   B

A-38   Since -CH_3 is a better electron donating group than H, the shielding constant for the proton in A would be expected to be larger. Therefore, the term $\nu h/2\mu_H (1 - \sigma)$ would be larger for the proton in A than in B. H_0 for system A would be higher.

Q-39   Which of the circled protons in A and B would be expected to show nuclear resonance at the lower applied field? Why?

$$R-\overset{\displaystyle \textstyle \textcircled{H}}{\underset{\displaystyle R}{C}}-OH \qquad R-\overset{\displaystyle \textstyle \textcircled{H}}{\underset{\displaystyle R}{C}}-CH_2 OH$$

A   B

A-39   Because OH is a strong electron withdrawing group, one would expect the shielding constant for the proton in A to be smaller than the shielding constant for the proton in B. Therefore, the applied magnetic field at resonance will be lower for the proton in A.

R   Shielding effect = σH_0, where σ is the shielding constant. The magnitude of σ depends upon the electron density about a hydrogen nucleus.

$H_N = H_0 (1 - \sigma)$, where H_N is the magnetic field felt by the nucleus. The resonance condition for a shielded proton is

$$\nu = \frac{2\mu_H}{h} H_0 (1 - \sigma)$$

S-7   In practice, the absolute value of H_0 cannot be determined very accurately; therefore, it is convenient to compare the H_0 required for resonance of a certain chemical system to that required of a standard. The difference is referred to as the *chemical shift*. The chemical shift parameter δ is defined as

$$\delta = \frac{H_0 - H_0 \text{ (reference)}}{H_0 \text{ (reference)}}$$

where H_0 is the magnetic field required for resonance of the proton in question.

Q-40   Derive an expression for the chemical shift between a certain proton and a reference proton in terms of their shielding constants. Remember that the precession frequencies of the sample and the reference are identical at resonance.

A-40

$$\delta = \frac{H_0 - H_0 \text{ (ref)}}{H_0 \text{ (ref)}}$$

$$H_0 = \frac{h\nu}{2\mu_H (1 - \sigma)}$$

$$H_0 \text{ (ref)} = \frac{h\nu}{2\mu_H (1 - \sigma \text{ (ref)})}$$

$$\delta = \frac{\dfrac{1}{1 - \sigma} - \dfrac{1}{1 - \sigma \text{ (ref)}}}{\dfrac{1}{1 - \sigma \text{ (ref)}}}$$

$$\delta = \frac{\sigma - \sigma \text{ (ref)}}{1 - \sigma} \quad \text{Since } \sigma \ll 1,$$

$$\delta = \sigma - \sigma \text{ (ref)}$$

Q-41   As the difference in the shielding constants of the proton in question and the reference proton increases, what happens to the chemical shift value?

A-41

$\delta = \sigma - \sigma \text{ (ref)}$

δ increases

Q-42   In the measurement of a resonance signal, the magnetic field is varied while the oscillator frequency is held constant. In determining chemical shift values, the magnetic field is most conveniently and accurately measured in frequency units and is reported in Hertz (Hz) or cycles/sec units. From the relationship, $H_0 = \kappa\nu$, where κ is a proportionality constant, derive an equation for δ in frequency units.

A-42 $H_{0(ref)} = \kappa \nu_{(ref)}$

Therefore,

$$\delta = \frac{\kappa \nu - \kappa \nu_{(ref)}}{\kappa \nu_{(ref)}}$$

$$\delta = \frac{\nu - \nu_{(ref)}}{\nu_{(ref)}}$$

R $\delta = \dfrac{H_0 - H_{0\,(ref)}}{H_{0\,(ref)}}$

$\delta = \sigma - \sigma_{(ref)}$

S-8   The quantities ν and $\nu_{(reference)}$ are very large values which are only slightly different from the fixed oscillator frequency, ν_0, used in the nuclear magnetic resonance spectrometer (usually 40, 60, or 100 megahertz for proton resonance). For convenience, therefore, the equation for the chemical shift is re-written as

$$\delta = \frac{\nu - \nu_{(reference)}}{\nu_0} \times 10^6$$

where ν_0 is substituted for $\nu_{(reference)}$ in the denominator. Chemical shift defined in this manner is dimensionless and is expressed in parts per million (ppm).

The compound usually used as a reference standard is tetramethylsilane, $(CH_3)_4 Si$, which is abbreviated TMS. TMS makes a convenient reference substance because its protons reach resonance at a higher field than all common types of organic protons. The frequency of TMS, ν_{TMS}, is arbitrarily assigned a value of zero. By convention, any proton which is in resonance at a lower field is assigned a positive chemical shift relative to that of TMS.

Q-43   Using a 60.0 MHz (megahertz = 10^6 Hertz) instrument, the difference in frequency between TMS absorption and a certain proton in a compound was found to be 120 Hz. What is the chemical shift value for this absorption in parts per million?

A-43 $\delta = \dfrac{\Delta \nu \times 10^6}{\text{oscillator frequency (Hz)}}$

$\delta = \dfrac{120 \times 10^6}{60.0 \times 10^6} = 2.00$ ppm

Q-44   Using a 60.0 MHz instrument, the difference in frequency between TMS absorption and a certain proton in a compound was found to be 430 Hz. What is the chemical shift value for this absorption in ppm?

A-44 $\delta = \dfrac{\Delta \nu \times 10^6}{\text{oscillator frequency (Hz)}}$

$\delta = \dfrac{430 \times 10^6}{60.0 \times 10^6} = 7.17$ ppm

Q-45   Using a 60.0 MHz instrument, the difference in frequency between TMS absorption and a certain proton in a compound was found to be 180 Hz. What would be the frequency difference between these same protons if a 40 MHz instrument were used?

A-45 $\delta = \dfrac{180 \times 10^6}{60.0 \times 10^6} = 3.00$ ppm

$\Delta \nu = \dfrac{\delta \ (\text{oscillator frequency})}{10^6}$

$\Delta \nu = \dfrac{3.0 \ (40 \times 10^6)}{10^6}$

$\Delta \nu = 120$ Hz

Q-46   Three different protons, A, B, and C, have shielding constants in the order

$$\sigma_B > \sigma_A > \sigma_C.$$

Arrange the three protons in order of applied field necessary for resonance.

A-46 $H_{0(B)} > H_{0(A)} > H_{0(C)}$

Q-47   The applied field necessary for resonance for three protons decreases in the following order

$$H_{0(D)} > H_{0(E)} > H_{0(F)}.$$

Arrange the protons in order of decreasing chemical shift relative to TMS.

(Hint: Any proton which has resonance at a field below that of TMS has a positive chemical shift.)

A-47 $\delta_F > \delta_E > \delta_D$

Q-48   As σ increases, does δ increase or decrease?

A-48 δ will decrease.

Q-49   Two absorption peaks are shown on the graph below. Which proton has the greater shielding constant?

Proton Proton
A   B
TMS

4   3   2   1   0

δ ppm

A-49   Proton B has the larger shielding constant. As σ becomes larger, δ (relative to TMS) becomes smaller.

Q-50   Which of the protons described in Q-49 resonates at the higher field?

A-50   Proton B resonates at the higher field. The larger the shielding constant, the higher the field necessary for resonance.

R $$\delta = \frac{\nu \text{ (sample)} - \nu \text{ (ref)}}{\nu_0} \times 10^6$$

ν (ref) is usually tetramethylsilane (TMS). By convention, any proton which reaches resonance at a lower field than TMS is assigned a positive chemical shift.

S-9   When TMS is used as a reference, the chemical shfits are often reported as τ values where

$\tau = 10.00 - \delta$

and δ is the chemical shift relative to TMS in parts per million.

Q-51   What is τ for tetramethylsilane (TMS)?

A-51 $\delta_{TMS} = 0$

$\tau = 10.00 - \delta = 10.00$

Q-52   What are the τ values for the following chemical shifts relative to TMS?

2.00 ppm

7.17 ppm

A-52 $\tau = 10 - \delta$

$\delta = 2.0$

$\tau = 10 - 2.0 = 8.0$

$\delta = 7.17$

$\tau = 10 - 7.17 = 2.83$

Q-53   As δ increases, will τ increase or decrease?

A-53   Decrease.

Q-54   As σ decreases, will τ increase or decrease?

A-54   Decrease. As σ decreases, δ increases.

Q-55   As H_0 required for proton resonance increases, will τ increase or decrease?

A-55   Increase. As H_0 increases, δ decreases.

Q-56   For the compound $CH_3 CH_2 Br$, which protons would be expected to have the lowest σ values? Why?

A-56   Because of the strong electron pulling power of the bromine, the shielding effect (σ) on the $-CH_2-$ should be lower than the shielding effect of the CH_3-.

Q-57   For the compound $CH_3 CH_2 Br$, which protons would be expected to have the lowest τ values? Why?

A-57   Since the shielding effect on the $-CH_2-$ is lower than that of its CH_3-, the chemical shift relative to TMS of the $-CH_2-$ will be larger than that of CH_3-. Therefore, τ ($\tau = 10 - \delta$) will be smaller for $-CH_2-$ and larger for CH_3-. The actual values are:

$\tau_{CH_2} = 6.60$ and $\tau_{CH_3} = 8.35$

Q-58   Qualitatively, what generalization can be made about the relationship between σ, δ, and τ?

A-58   Large shielding effects result in small chemical shifts and large τ values. $\sigma \approx 1/\delta \approx \tau$.

Q-59   As protons become more acidic, what happens to the τ values?

A-59   As the electron density about a proton decreases, it becomes more acidic. Consequently, the chemical shift becomes greater and the τ value becomes less. (This generalization is only valid when comparing the same general type of protons, i.e., O-H protons.)

Q-60   In the following compound, predict which proton will have the largest τ values. Explain.

$$\begin{array}{ccc} CH_3 & CH_3 & (b) \\ | & | & \\ H-C-O-C-H & & (a) \\ | & | & \\ CH_3 & CH_3 & \end{array}$$

A-60   Since the H_a proton is just one atom removed from the strongly electronegative oxygen, it should have a smaller shielding constant than the H_b proton which is two atoms removed from the oxygen. Consequently, τ for H_a should be smaller than τ for H_b. Actual values:

$\tau(a) = 6.44$

$\tau(b) = 8.95$

Q-61   In the following compound, which proton would be expected to have the largest τ value? Why?

$$\begin{array}{ccc} & H & H \\ & | & | \\ Cl - & C - & C - Br \\ & | & | \\ & H & H \end{array}$$

(a)   (b)

A-61   Chlorine is more electronegative than bromine; therefore, the shielding for the H_a proton would be smaller than the shielding for the H_b proton. Consequently, τ for H_a should be less than τ for H_b. Actual values:

$\tau_{(a)} = 6.23$

$\tau_{(b)} = 6.43$

Q-62   Given below is the low resolution spectrum for

CH_3CH_2Cl
(a) (b)

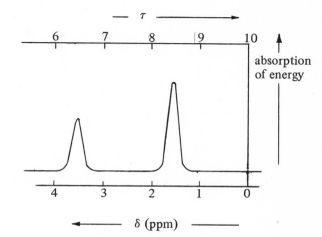

Which absorption peak corresponds to the H_a protons and which to the H_b protons? Explain.

A-62   The chlorine atom should decrease the shielding effect on H_b more than on H_a. Consequently, H_b would correspond to the absorption peak with the larger value of δ, while H_a would correspond to the absorption peak with the smaller value of δ.

Q-63   Given below is the low resolution spectrum for

$CH_3CH_2CH_2I$
(a) (b) (c)

Identify each absorption peak and justify the assignment made.

A-63   The iodine atom should decrease the shielding effect in the order, H_c more than H_b more than H_a. Therefore, H_c should have the smallest τ value.

Assignments:

$H_a = 8.8\ \tau$

$H_b = 8.0\ \tau$

$H_c = 6.9\ \tau$

R $\tau = 10 - \delta$ when TMS is used as reference.

Large σ values result in small values for δ and large values for τ.

S-10   The ratio of the areas under absorption bands is related directly to the number of equivalent protons causing the absorption. A low resolution spectrum of ethyl chloride is given below.

The ratio of areas is 3:2.

	Q-64 What should the ratio of peak areas be for the spectrum of ethanol (CH_3CH_2OH)?
A-64 CH_3 peak: CH_2 peak: OH peak = 3:2:1.	Q-65 How many different kinds of protons are there in the compound $CH_3CH_2CH_3$?
A-65 Two. The CH_3 groups are equivalent.	Q-66 What should the ratio of peak areas be for the compound $CH_3CH_2CH_3$?
A-66 CH_3 peak: CH_2 peak = 3:1.	Q-67 What should the ratio of peak areas be for the compound $(CH_3)_2CHCH_2CH(CH_3)_2$?
A-67 CH_3 peak: CH_2 peak: CH peak = 6:1:1.	Q-68 What should the ratio of peak areas be for the compound $HOCH_2CHOHCH_2OH$?
A-68 CH_2 peak: CH peak: CH_2OH peak: CHOH peak = 4:1:2:1.	Q-69 What is the ratio of peak areas for the compound:
A-69 Because all protons are equivalent, there is only one absorption peak in the spectrum. Consequently, no ratio can be determined.	R The areas under the peaks in an NMR spectrum are directly proportional to the number of equivalent protons.

S-11   In the *high* resolution spectrum of ethyl chloride, the peaks corresponding to the methyl and methylene protons are "split".

The fine structure in the high resolution spectrum arises from the phenomenon called *spin-spin splitting*. *Spin-spin splitting* is due to the various spin orientations of one nucleus with respect to the spin orientations of a neighboring proton. The magnetic field felt by a proton is affected by the various spin orientations of the neighboring protons.

	Q-70 In the molecule HF, both H and F have magnetic moments. The spin quantum number, I, for fluorine is ½. How many different orientations relative to the applied magnetic field will a F_9^{19} nucleus be able to assume?
A-70 Number of orientations = $2I + 1$ $I = ½$ Number of orientations = 2	Q-71 The orientation of the fluorine nucleus with spin = −½ is aligned with the applied magnetic field and the orientation with spin = +½ is aligned against the applied magnetic field. Will the magnetic moment resulting from the spin = −½ orientation augment or oppose the applied magnetic field? Why?
A-71 Augment. Spin = −½ is oriented with the applied field. Therefore, the magnetic moment resulting from this orientation will augment the applied magnetic field. The spin = +½ orientation will produce a magnetic field which opposes the applied magnetic field.	Q-72 Depending upon the orientation of the fluorine nucleus in HF, the magnetic moment of fluorine will either augment or oppose the applied magnetic field. Because of the close proximity, the magnetic field felt by the proton will be affected by the orientation of the fluorine nucleus. If the spin of the fluorine nucleus is −½, will the magnetic field felt by the proton in HF be larger or smaller than the applied field? Will a larger or smaller applied field be necessary to produce proton resonance?

A-72   Field where resonance occurs = applied field + field transmitted from fluorine nucleus. The magnetic moment of fluorine, with spin = $-\frac{1}{2}$, augments the applied field. Therefore, the field transmitted to the proton from the fluorine nucleus is positive, causing the proton resonance to occur at a lower applied field.

Q-73   If the spin of the fluorine nucleus is $+\frac{1}{2}$, what effect will this have on the applied magnetic field at which the proton resonance occurs?

A-73   The magnetic moment for fluorine with spin = $+\frac{1}{2}$ opposes the applied field. Therefore, the field transmitted by fluorine to the proton will be negative, causing the proton resonance to occur at a higher applied field.

Q-74   The probability of fluorine having spin = $+\frac{1}{2}$ and spin = $-\frac{1}{2}$ is practically the same. The proton resonance spectrum of HF is shown below.

Label the peaks in the spectrum arising from the interaction of the proton with the two different spin states of fluorine.

A-74   Interaction with fluorine spin state

Q-75   Why are the two peaks in the proton resonance spectrum for HF of equal intensity?

A-75   The two peaks are of equal intensity because there is practically equal probability that the fluorine will have $-\frac{1}{2}$ and $+\frac{1}{2}$ spin states.

Q-76   On the graph below, sketch the position and relative intensity of the proton resonance for HF if there were no interaction between the hydrogen and fluorine nuclei.

A-76 H_1^1 resonance

no inter-
action

with
inter-
action

— increasing H_0 ⟶

The sum of the area under the two "split"
peaks would equal the area under the
single peak.

A-77

$-\frac{1}{2}$ $+\frac{1}{2}$ F_9^{19}

resonance

⟶H_0⟶

Q-77   Sketch the fluorine resonance spectrum
for the molecule HF. The hydrogen nucleus,
with $I = \frac{1}{2}$, interacts with the fluorine
nucleus.

R   Spin-spin splitting of a nucleus (observed in
high resolution spectra) is caused by the
nuclear spin interaction of neighboring
nuclei. Neighbors with a nuclear spin of $-\frac{1}{2}$
augment, while those with spin of $+\frac{1}{2}$
oppose the applied magnetic field imposed
on a nucleus. The position of observed
resonance for a nucleus will depend upon
the spin arrangement of neighboring nuclei.
A nucleus with $I = \frac{1}{2}$ has equal probability
of being in the $+\frac{1}{2}$ and $-\frac{1}{2}$ spin states.

S-12   The distance (in ppm or Hz) between the fine structure of a resonance signal is called the *spin-spin
coupling constant, J.* The value of the spin-spin coupling constant is dependent on the nuclei interacting
and is independent of the strength of the applied magnetic field. The effect of changing the strength
of the applied field for the proton resonance in the molecule HF is illustrated below.

strength of field = 14,000 gauss J_{HF} = 615 Hertz

strength of field = 20,000 gauss J_{HF} = 615 Hertz

Even though the proton and fluorine resonance occurs at different applied fields, the distance between
the fine structure in each absorption band will be the same ($J_{HF} = J_{FH}$).

H_1^1

F_9^{19}

In certain cases, nuclei with spin-spin interaction have such small coupling constants that the interactions
may be ignored. Thus, in compounds containing Cl, Br, or I, J_{HCl}, J_{HBr}, and J_{HI} are so small that
the spin-spin interactions are not observed.

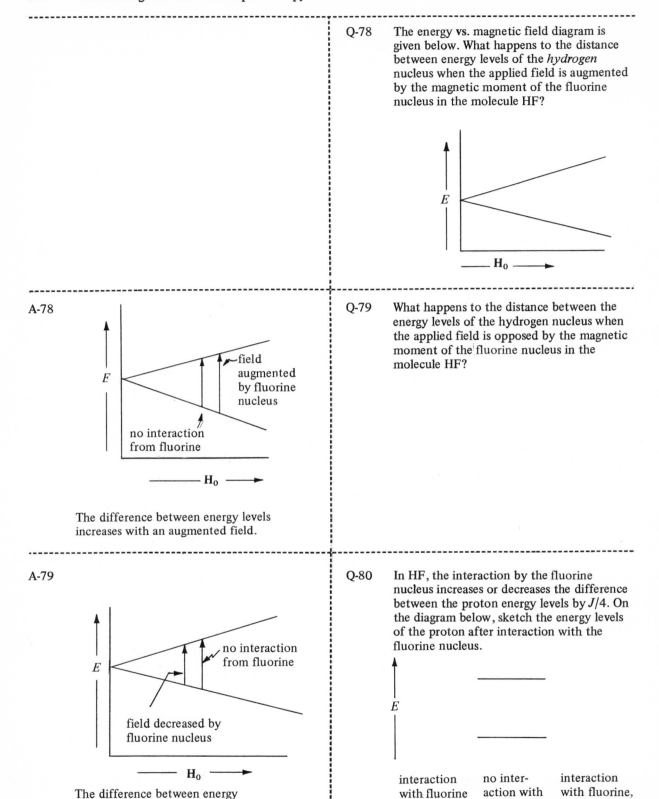

Q-78   The energy **vs.** magnetic field diagram is given below. What happens to the distance between energy levels of the *hydrogen* nucleus when the applied field is augmented by the magnetic moment of the fluorine nucleus in the molecule HF?

A-78

field augmented by fluorine nucleus

no interaction from fluorine

H_0

The difference between energy levels increases with an augmented field.

Q-79   What happens to the distance between the energy levels of the hydrogen nucleus when the applied field is opposed by the magnetic moment of the fluorine nucleus in the molecule HF?

A-79

no interaction from fluorine

field decreased by fluorine nucleus

H_0

The difference between energy levels decreases.

Q-80   In HF, the interaction by the fluorine nucleus increases or decreases the difference between the proton energy levels by $J/4$. On the diagram below, sketch the energy levels of the proton after interaction with the fluorine nucleus.

E

interaction with fluorine spin = $+\frac{1}{2}$ no interaction with fluorine   interaction with fluorine, spin = $-\frac{1}{2}$

A-80

Q-81   By what energy has the difference between the energy levels of the proton been increased or decreased by the interaction with the fluorine nucleus?

A-81 $\pm J/2$

Q-82   For the proton in HF, how many nuclear transitions are possible? What is the difference in energy between these two transitions?

A-82   Two transitions. One transition increases in energy by $J/2$; the other transition decreases in energy by $J/2$. Therefore, the difference is J.

Q-83   For the proton resonance spectrum in the HF molecule, how many peaks should result from the spin-spin interaction with fluorine?

A-83   Two peaks.

Q-84   By what distance will the two peaks in the proton resonance of HF be separated? What will be the relative areas under each peak?

A-84   Separation will be J. The areas under the two peaks will be identical. The probabilities of the fluorine having a $+\frac{1}{2}$ or $-\frac{1}{2}$ spin state are equal.

Q-85   Sketch the proton resonance spectrum for the HF molecule with and without spin-spin interaction.

A-85

Two peaks of equal intensity but half as intense as the "no-interaction" peak. (Notice that the spectrum is identical with that given in Q-74.)

Q-86   For the system given below, will there be any spin-spin interaction between the proton and the carbon -12 nucleus? Why?

$$-\overset{|}{\underset{/}{C}}{}^{12}_6 - H^1_1$$

A-86   No. The carbon — 12 nucleus has an **I** value of zero and does not have a magnetic moment.

Q-87   In which of the following systems will there be spin-spin interaction between the proton and the other atom?

$O^{16} - H$

$Cl^{35} - H$

$Br^{79} - H$

$D \quad - H$

A-87 $O^{16} - H$:
For O^{16}, **I** = 0. Therefore, no spin-spin interaction is observed.

$Cl^{35} - H$
$Br^{79} - H$:
For Cl^{35}, **I** = 3/2 and for Br^{79}, **I** = 3/2. Therefore, spin-spin interaction would be expected. However, the very large electric quadrapole moments of Cl and Br (and I), cause spin decoupling of adjacent protons and *no splitting is observed in HBr or HCl (or HI)*. In compounds containing Cl, Br, or I, no proton-halogen or halogen-halogen splitting is observed.

$D - H$:
For D, **I** = 1. Therefore, spin-spin interaction is expected. The J_{HD} value is very small and when these nuclei are separated by one atom (i.e., H — C — D) H — D splitting is not usually observed.

Q-88   In the spectrum of the following compound, the absorption for the indicated proton is split into two peaks. Indicate the other atom which gives rise to the spin-spin interaction.

$$Cl - \overset{\textcircled{H}}{\underset{Cl}{C}} - \overset{H}{\underset{Br}{C}} - Br$$

A-88   The other proton. J_{HBr} and J_{HCl} are so small that the interactions between Cl and H or Br and H are not observed.

R   The separation between fine structure peaks is called the spin-spin coupling constant, J, and is expressed in cycles/sec or Hertz. The coupling constant is independent of the applied magnetic field.

S-13   The number of peaks observed in the fine structure of the absorption for a nucleus will depend on the number of ways the spins of interacting nuclei can be arranged to give different magnetic moments. In the illustration below a +½ spin state will be denoted by the symbol ↑ while a —½ spin state will be indicated by ↓. For the molecule given below, the neighboring interacting protons H_1 and H_2 (neighbors to H_A) can have spin states arranged in the manner shown in the table.

$$Cl - \overset{H_A}{\underset{Cl}{C}} - \overset{H_1}{\underset{Cl}{C}} - H_2$$

H_1	H_2
↑	↑
↑	↓
↓	↓
↓	↑

(four possible combinations of spin states)

Q-89   If each spin interaction of H_1 and H_2 with H_A is ± $J/2$, show the total effect on the H_A resonance resulting from each of the four possible spin combinations.

A-89

Spin Combination		Total Effect
H_1	H_2	
↑	↑	$J/2 + J/2 = J$
↓	↓	$-J/2 - J/2 = -J$
↑	↓	$J/2 - J/2 = 0$
↓	↑	$-J/2 + J/2 = 0$

Q-90 For the molecule given in S-13, how many *different* magnetic moments result from the various spin combinations of H_1 and H_2?

A-90 Three. The ↑↓ and ↓↑ combinations give the same total effect.

Q-91 How many peaks will be present in the fine structure for the proton resonance of H_A in the molecule shown in S-13?

(Hint: Remember that J_{HCl} will not be observed.)

A-91 Three. There are three different spin arrangements for the neighboring protons H_1 and H_2.

Q-92 The probability of $+\frac{1}{2}$ and $-\frac{1}{2}$ spin states is equal. Predict the area under the three peaks in the fine structure of H_A.

A-92 1 : 2 : 1.
The area under the peaks resulting from the total spin interaction of zero (↑↓ and ↓↑) will be twice as probable as the other two interactions (↓↓ and ↑↑).

Q-93 Sketch on the graph below the positions of the three peaks in the fine structure of H_A. Label the distance between peaks and their relative areas. The arrow on the graph indicates the position of the H_A resonance if no spin-spin interactions occur.

A-93 Ratio of peak areas 1 : 2 : 1.

Q-94 Now consider the fine structure of the identical protons H_1 and H_2 (S-13) due to the spin-spin interaction with their neighbor, H_A. If each spin interaction of H_A with H_1 and H_2 is $\pm J/2$, show the various spin combinations of H_A and the total effect on the H_1 and H_2 resonance.

A-94

Spin Combination	Total Effect
H_A	
↑	$+J/2$
↓	$-J/2$

Identical protons (such as H_1 and H_2 in the molecule shown in S-13) do not **appear** to interact with one another.

Q-95 Sketch on the graph below the positions of the fine structure of the H_1 and H_2 protons. Label the distance between peaks and their relative areas. The arrow on the graph indicates the position of the H_1 and H_2 resonance if no spin-spin interaction occurs.

(Hint: Remember that J_{HCl} will not be observed.)

A-95   Ratio of peak areas 1 : 1.

Q-96 The chemical shift for the H_A protons is 4.23 τ while the chemical shift for $H_1 = H_2$ = 6.05 τ. The coupling constant is equal to 0.10 ppm. Sketch the proton spectrum for the molecule given in S-13 on the graph below.

A-96

Chemical shifts are measured from the center of the fine structure. The relative areas of H_A : $H_1 + H_2$ proton resonance are 1 : 2. The relative areas of the fine structure peaks are:

H_A	1 : 2 : 1
H_1 and H_2	1 : 1

Q-97 Consider the fine structure for the H_A protons in the molecule below.

$$H_A - \underset{\underset{H_A}{|}}{\overset{\overset{H_A}{|}}{C}} - \underset{\underset{H_B}{|}}{\overset{\overset{H_B}{|}}{C}} - Cl$$

If each spin interaction of H_B with H_A is $\pm J/2$, show the various spin combinations of the H_B protons and the total effect on the H_A proton resonance.

A-97

Spin Combination		Total Effect
H_B	H_B	
↑	↑	$J/2 +J/2 = +J$
↓	↓	$-J/2 -J/2 = -J$
↓	↑	$-J/2 +J/2 = 0$
↑	↓	$J/2 -J/2 = 0$

Q-98 Consider the fine structure for the H_B protons in the molecule given in Q-97. If each spin interaction of H_A with H_B is $\pm J/2$, show the various spin combinations of the H_A protons and the total effect on the H_B resonance.

A-98

Spin Combination			Total Effect
H_A	H_A	H_A	
↑	↑	↑	$J/2 +J/2 +J/2 = 3/2J$
↓	↓	↓	$-J/2 -J/2 -J/2 = -3/2J$
↑	↑	↓	$+J/2 +J/2 -J/2 = J/2$
↑	↓	↓	$+J/2 -J/2 -J/2 = -J/2$
↑	↓	↑	$+J/2 -J/2 +J/2 = J/2$
↓	↑	↑	$-J/2 +J/2 +J/2 = J/2$
↓	↑	↓	$-J/2 +J/2 -J/2 = -J/2$
↓	↓	↑	$-J/2 -J/2 +J/2 = -J/2$

Q-99 How many peaks should the H_B fine structure have? What should the relative areas under these peaks be?

A-99 Four peaks ($3/2J$, $+J/2$, $-J/2$, $-3/2J$. Relative areas 1 : 3 : 3 : 1.

Q-100 For the molecule described in Q-97, the chemical shifts for the protons are

$\delta\ H_A = 1.48$ ppm

$\delta\ H_B = 3.57$ ppm

$J_{AB} = 0.15$ ppm

Sketch the proton spectrum for $CH_3 CH_2 Cl$ on the graph below. Label the distance between fine structure peaks and give relative areas.

A-100

Relative areas of $H_A : H_B = 3 : 2$. The relative areas of fine structure peaks are: H_A 1:2:1; H_B 1:3:3:1.

R The number of peaks in the fine structure depends on the number of ways the spin of neighboring nuclei can be arranged to give different magnetic moments.

The area under the peaks for fine structure is relative to the number of ways the spin of neighboring nuclei can be arranged to give the same magnetic moments.

The chemical shift between two different types of hydrogens is measured from their centers of fine structure.

S-14   Spin-spin splitting occurs through the bonds separating the interacting nuclei. Usually this interaction will occur only between nuclei that are separated by three or fewer bonds. In general the number of peaks (#) in the fine structure of an absorption band will be given by the formula

$$\# = 2n\mathbf{I} + 1$$

where $\mathbf{I}$ is the nucleus spin quantum number of the nuclei causing the splitting and n is the number of nuclei causing the splitting.

The relative areas under peaks in the fine structure of an absorption band are given by the coefficients preceding each term in the expansion formula of:

$$(x + 1)^m$$

where m equals the number of peaks minus one ($\# - 1$). These rules can be illustrated by using

$$CH_3 - CH_2 - Cl$$
$$\quad\;\;(a)\quad\;\;(b)$$

$\#_{(a)} = 2n\mathbf{I} + 1 = 2\,(2)\,(1/2) + 1 = 3$

$\#_{(b)} = 2n\mathbf{I} + 1 = 2\,(3)\,(1/2) + 1 = 4$

Area Ratio for (a):
$(x + 1)^2 = x^2 + 2x + 1$
Peak area ratios 1 : 2 : 1
Area Ratio for (b):
$(x + 1)^3 = x^3 + 3x^2 + 3x + 1$
Peak area ratios 1 : 3 : 3 : 1

	Q-101 Will there be any spin-spin splitting in the spectrum of the molecule $Cl\,CH_2 - CH_2\,Cl$? (a)　　　　(b) Why?
A-101 No. All the protons are equivalent.	**Q-102** Will there be any spin-spin interaction observed in the molecule $CH_3 - CCl_2 - CH_2\,Cl$? (a)　　　　　　(b) Why?
A-102 No. The nonequivalent protons are more than three bonds removed from one another and J_{HCl} is too small to be observed.	**Q-103** Predict the fine structure and intensity of peaks for the (a) and (b) protons in $CHCl_2 - CH_2\,Cl$. (a)　　　(b)

A-103

Protons being split	Interacting neighbors	n	$\# = 2n\,\mathbf{I} + 1$	$(x+1)^m$
$CHCl_2 -$	$-CH_2\,Cl$	2	3	1:2:1
$-CH_2\,Cl$	$-CHCl_2$	1	2	1:1

Q-104 Predict the fine structure and intensity of peaks for the (a) and (b) protons in

$$CH_3 - CH_2 - \overset{\displaystyle O}{\overset{\|}{C}} - Cl.$$
(a)　　(b)

A-104

Protons being split	Interacting neighbors	n	$\# = 2n\,\mathbf{I} + 1$	$(x+1)^m$
$CH_3 -$	$-CH_2 -$	2	3	1:2:1
$-CH_2 -$	$-CH_3Cl_2$	3	4	1:3:3:1

Q-105 Predict the fine structure and intensity of peaks for the (a) and (b) protons in

$Cl - CH_2 - O - CH_3$.
(a)　　　　(b)

A-105 No splitting. The protons are more than three bonds apart. Each proton would give a single peak (singlet). The ratio of a:b peaks is 2:3.

Q-106 Predict the fine structure and intensity of peaks for the (a), (b), and (c) protons in

$$CH_3 - O - CH_2 - CH_3.$$
(a)   (b)   (c)

A-106

Protons being split	Interacting neighbors	n	$\# = 2n\,I + 1$	$(x+1)^m$
$CH_{3\,(a)}$	No splitting			
$-CH_{2\,(b)}-$	$-CH_3$	3	4	1:3:3:1
$-CH_{3\,(c)}$	$-CH_2-$	2	3	1:2:1

Q-107 Predict the fine structure and intensity of peaks for the equivalent protons of ammonia, NH_3.

(Hint: $I_{N^{14}} = 1$)

A-107

Protons being split	Interacting neighbor	n	$\# = 2n\,I + 1$	Intensity
H_3N	N	1	3	1:2:1

Q-108 Predict the fine structure and intensity of peaks for the protons of difluoromethane,

$$H - \overset{\overset{\displaystyle H}{|}}{\underset{\underset{\displaystyle F}{|}}{C}} - F$$

(Hint: $I_{F^{19}} = 1/2$)

A-108

Protons being split	Interacting neighbor	n	$\# = 2n\,I + 1$	Intensity
$-CH_2-$	$-CF_2-$	2	3	1:2:1

Q-109 Predict the fine structure and intensity of peaks for the methylene protons of propane,

$$CH_3 - CH_2 - CH_3 .$$

A-109

Protons being split	Interacting neighbor	n	$\# = 2n\,I + 1$	Intensity
$-CH_2-$	$(CH_3 -)_2$	6	7	
			(1:6:15:20:15:6:1)	

Q-110 For a hydrocarbon, the absorption spectrum of a proton (H_A) is split into three peaks with relative areas of 1:2:1. How many equivalent neighboring protons interact with H_A?

A-110 There must be only two equivalent protons no more than three bonds removed from the given proton.

Q-111 Give possible structures for the system which gives rise to the absorption spectrum described in Q-110. Label proton H_A and the two interacting protons H_X.

A-111

$$-\overset{\diagdown}{\underset{\underset{\displaystyle H_A}{|}}{C}} - \overset{\overset{\displaystyle H_X}{}}{\underset{\underset{\displaystyle H_X}{|}}{C}} -$$

or

$$-\overset{\overset{\displaystyle H_X}{|}}{\underset{|}{C}} - \overset{\overset{\displaystyle }{|}}{\underset{\underset{\displaystyle H_A}{|}}{C}} - \overset{\overset{\displaystyle H_X}{|}}{\underset{|}{C}} -$$

Q-112 The fine structure for proton H_A in a molecule is shown below. How many equivalent neighboring protons interact with H_A? Give possible structures for systems which could give rise to the absorption spectrum below. Label proton H_A and the interacting proton H_X.

Area ratio 1:3:3:1

Proton H_A

A-112 H_A must have only three equivalent protons, no more than three bonds removed. Possible structure is:

$$H_X - \underset{\underset{H_X}{|}}{\overset{\overset{H_X}{|}}{C}} - \underset{|}{\overset{\overset{H_A}{|}}{C}} - \qquad \mathrm{I}$$

Structure II below is not a possibility since the shielding around H_X & H_X' would not be identical.

$$- \underset{|}{\overset{\overset{H_X'}{|}}{C}} - \underset{|}{\overset{\overset{H_A}{|}}{C}} - \underset{\underset{H_X}{|}}{\overset{\overset{H_X}{|}}{C}} - \qquad \mathrm{II}$$

Q-113   The partial spectrum of a compound is given below.

Ratio $H_X : H_M : H_A = 1:1:3$

Select a partial structure from the following which is consistent with the above spectrum.

a. $CH_3 - \overset{\overset{\textstyle O}{\|}}{C} - CH_2 - \overset{\diagup}{CH}$

b. $CH_3 - CH_2 - O -$

c. $CH_3 - O - \overset{\diagup}{CH} - \overset{\diagup}{CH}$

d. $CH_3 - \underset{\underset{|}{}}{\overset{\overset{H}{|}}{C}} - O -$

A-113   Structure C

$$CH_3 - O - \underset{\underset{(H_M\ or\ H_X)}{\overset{|}{H}}}{\overset{|}{C}} - \underset{|}{\overset{|}{C}} - H\,(H_M\ or\ H_X)$$

(H_A)

R   Spin-spin coupling usually will occur only between atoms that are three or fewer bonds removed from each other. The number of peaks in fine structure of an absorption band $= 2n\mathbf{I} + 1$. The relative intensities of fine structure peaks are obtained from coefficients resulting from the expansion of $(x+1)^m$ where m = number of peaks in fine structure $- 1$.

S-15   Another way of analyzing a spectrum is by use of spin-spin coupling diagrams. The technique used in this method is illustrated for the molecule 1,1,2-trichloroethane.

$$Cl - \underset{\underset{Cl}{|}}{\overset{\overset{H_A}{|}}{C}} - \underset{\underset{Cl}{|}}{\overset{\overset{H_X}{|}}{C}} - H_X$$

The two different protons, A and X, interact and have a coupling constant of J_{AX}. The splitting of the X protons into a doublet by the A proton is diagramed below.

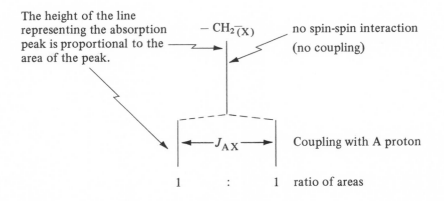

The height of the line representing the absorption peak is proportional to the area of the peak.

$- CH_2\overline{(X)}$ no spin-spin interaction (no coupling)

J_{AX} Coupling with A proton

1   :   1   ratio of areas

The splitting of the A proton by each of the equivalent X protons can be diagramed in two ways.

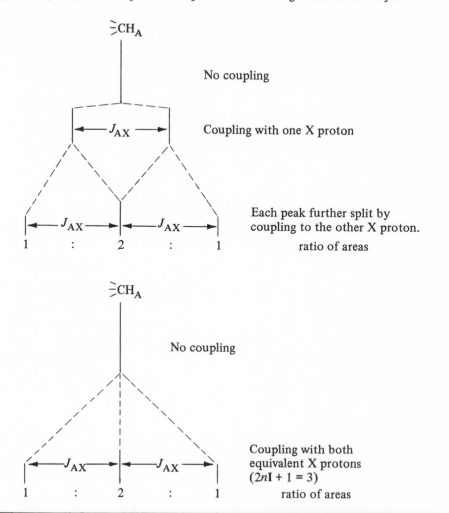

$\gtrsim$CH$_A$

No coupling

J_{AX} — Coupling with one X proton

J_{AX} J_{AX}

1 : 2 : 1

Each peak further split by coupling to the other X proton.

ratio of areas

$\gtrsim$CH$_A$

No coupling

J_{AX} J_{AX}

1 : 2 : 1

Coupling with both equivalent X protons
($2nI + 1 = 3$)

ratio of areas

Q-114   Diagram and label the splitting pattern for H$_X$ in the system shown below.

$J_{AX} = 10$ Hz

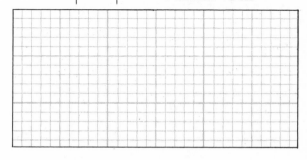

H$_A$ H$_X$
— C — — C —

1 division = 1 Hz

A-114

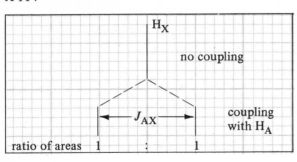

Q-115 Diagram and label the splitting pattern for H_A in the system described in Q-114.

A-115

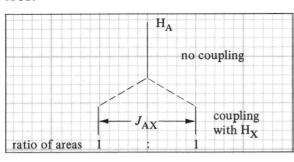

Q-116 Diagram and label the splitting pattern for H_X in the system shown below.

J_{AX} = 15 Hz

$$\begin{array}{ccc} H_X & H_A & \\ | & | & \\ -C- & C- & H_A \\ | & | & \end{array}$$

A-116

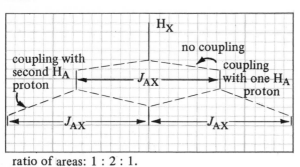

ratio of areas: 1 : 2 : 1.

Q-117 Diagram and label the splitting pattern for H_A in the system described in Q-116.

A-117

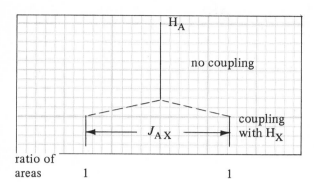

ratio of
areas   1   1

Q-118 Diagram and label the splitting pattern for H_X in the system shown below.

J_{AX} = 7 Hz

A-118

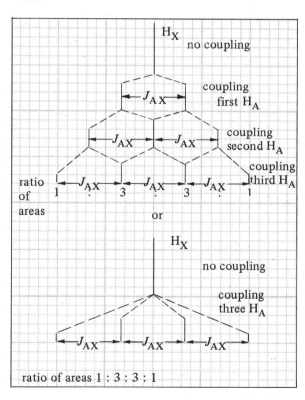

Q-119 For the system described in Q-118, diagram and label the splitting pattern for the H_A proton.

A-119

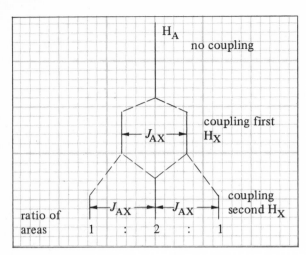

Q-120   Diagram and label the splitting pattern for the H_M proton in the system shown below.

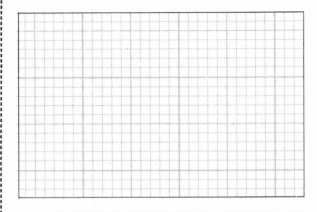

$$H_A \quad H_M \quad H_X$$
$$-\,\overset{|}{C}\,-\,\overset{|}{C}\,-\,\overset{|}{C}\,-$$

$J_{MX} = 5$ Hz $J_{AM} = 10$ Hz

A-120

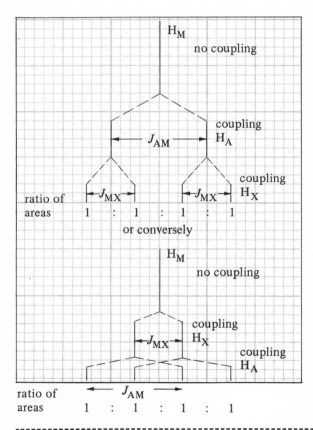

Q-121   Diagram and label the splitting pattern for the H_A and the H_X proton in the system given in Q-120.

A-121

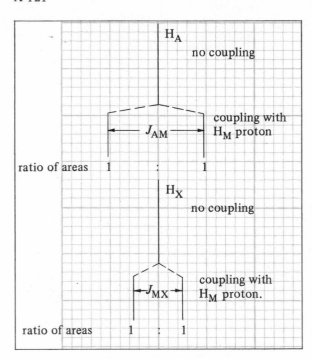

Q-122 Diagram and label the splitting pattern for the H_M proton in the system shown below.

$$J_{AM} = 4 \text{ Hz}$$

and

$$J_{MX} = 10 \text{ Hz}$$

A-122

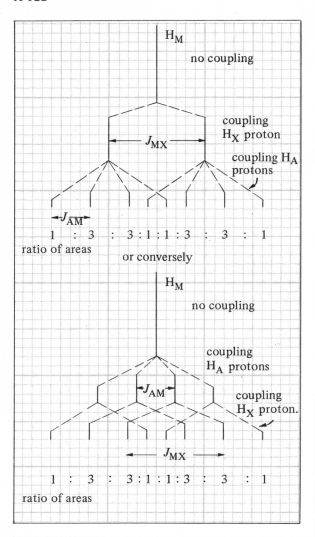

ratio of areas

or conversely

ratio of areas

Q-123   Following is the fine structure for a proton H_M. Diagram and label the splitting pattern and give the values for the coupling constants. Give the structure of the system producing the spectrum and indicate the protons interacting with H_M.

A-123

$$
\begin{array}{ccc}
H_X & H_M & H_A \\
| & | & | \\
-C - & C - & C - \\
| & | & | \\
\end{array}
$$

J_{MX} = 5 Hz

J_{AX} = 2 Hz

Q-124 Following is the fine spectrum for a proton H_M. Diagram and label the splitting pattern and give the value for the coupling constants. Give the structure of the system producing the spectrum and indicate the protons interacting with H_M.

A-124

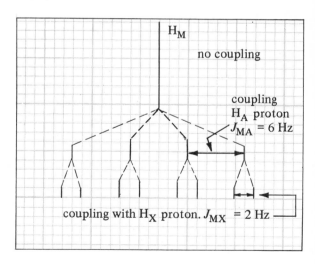

R The splitting diagram for the H_M proton in the system

$$
\begin{array}{ccc}
H_A & H_M & H_X \\
| & | & | \\
-C - & C - & C - \\
| & | & | \\
\end{array}
$$

is shown as

S-16   Interacting systems of protons are characterized by using the notation given in the table below. The letters A, M, and X are used to designate chemically different protons whose chemical shift values are very different. The term multiplicity is used to indicate the fine structure.

System	Example	No. of protons giving rise to absorption peak	Multiplicity of absorption peak
A	H_A $ns - C - ns$ ns (ns = non-splitting group)	1	singlet
A_2	H_A $ns - C - ns$ H_A	2	singlet (identical protons do not appear to "split" each other)
AX	$H_A \; H_X$ $ns - C - C - ns$ $ns \; ns$	1 (H_A) 1 (H_X)	doublet doublet
AX_2	$H_A \; H_X$ $ns - C - C - H_X$ $ns \; ns$	1 (H_A) 2 (H_X)	triplet doublet
AMX	$H_A \; H_M \; H_X$ $ns - C - C - C - ns$ $ns \; ns \; ns$	1 (H_A) 1 (H_M) 1 (H_X)	doublet four peaks (two doublets) doublet

---

	Q-125 Characterize the system of protons and give the multiplicity for each proton in the following molecule. $Cl_2 CHCHCl_2$
A-125 A_2 case. A **two** proton singlet.	**Q-126** Characterize the system of protons and give the multiplicity for each proton in the following molecule. $\overset{O}{\overset{\|}{Cl_2 CHCH}}$
A-126 AX case. Two **one** proton doublets. The A proton splits into a doublet, and the X proton splits into a doublet.	**Q-127** Characterize the system of protons and give the multiplicity for each proton in the following molecule. $Cl_2 CHCH_2 Cl$
A-127 AX_2 case. A **one** proton triplet (A proton) and a **two** proton doublet (X protons).	**Q-128** Characterize the system of protons and give the multiplicity for each proton in the following molecule. $\overset{O}{\overset{\|}{Cl_2 CHCHClCH}}$

A-128   AMX case. A **one** proton doublet (A proton), a **one** proton doublet (X proton), and **one** proton (M proton) with four peaks (two doublets).

Q-129   Characterize the system of protons and give the multiplicity for each proton in the following molecule.

$CH_3OCHClCH_2Cl$

A-129   The CH_3- protons do not couple with any others. Therefore, they are an A_3 case. The other protons couple together to form an AX_2 case. The spectrum would consist of a **three** proton singlet (A_3 case), a **one** proton triplet (A proton), and a **two** proton doublet (X_2 protons).

Q-130   Characterize the system of protons and give the multiplicity for each proton in the following molecule.

$$CHCl_2CH_2\overset{\overset{\displaystyle O}{\|}}{C}H$$

A-130   An AM_2X case. A **one** proton triplet (A proton), a **one** proton triplet (X proton), and a **two** proton pattern consisting of four peaks (two doublets).

R   Systems of protons are characterized by using the notations given in S-16. Each particular system has a characteristic multiplicity (fine structure) for the absorption peaks.

S-17   The chemical shift parameter, δ, has been shown to be a function of the electron density around the proton. The electron density about a proton is affected by the inductive effect of various groups operating through the chemical bonds attached to the proton. In addition to inductive effects, chemical shift parameters are also influenced by magnetic fields operating through space. Chemical bonds produce small magnetic fields which can operate through space. The magnetic fields produced by chemical bonds are anisotropic, that is, unsymmetrical about the bond. This anisotropic effect may result in a magnetic field in the area of the proton which either opposes or augments the applied field. An anisotropic effect which opposes the applied field will result in the proton resonance shifting to a higher field (a shielding effect). An anisotropic effect which augments the applied field results in the proton resonance shifting to lower fields (deshielding effect). The anisotropic effect becomes very important in molecules containing π bonds, such as aromatic systems and carbonyl groups.

The magnetic anisotropic effect produced by the π electron system of benzene in a uniform magnetic field, H_0, is diagramed below. The arrows indicate that the anisotropic effect opposes the applied field in the region above and below the ring while it augments the applied field in the region outside the perimeter of the ring.

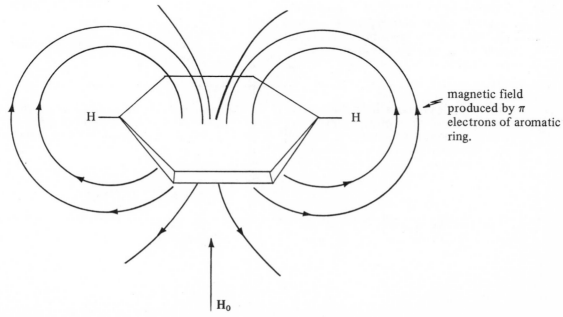

magnetic field produced by π electrons of aromatic ring.

H_0

The magnetic anisotropic effect produced by the π — electrons of the carbonyl group in a uniform magnetic field, H_0, is diagramed below.

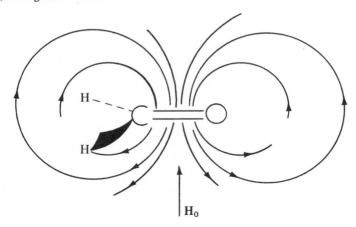

	Q-131	In an area where a secondary magnetic field augments the applied field, will proton resonance be shifted to a higher or a lower field?
A-131 When the magnetic field is augmented in the vicinity of a proton, the proton resonance will be shifted to a lower field (deshielding effect).	Q-132	In the vicinity where the applied magnetic field is opposed by a secondary field, will shielding or deshielding of the proton occur? Which way will the resonance peak shift?
A-132 The proton will be more shielded, which causes the proton resonance peak to shift to higher magnetic fields.	Q-133	Explain the fact that aromatic proton resonance occurs at low τ values $(1.0 - 4.0)$.
A-133 The protons on the benzene ring are in a region where the anisotropic effect of the ring augments the applied field. Thus, the protons have resonance at lower fields (are deshielded).	Q-134	The resonance of aldehyde protons $\overset{O}{\overset{\|}{(C}} - H)$ occurs at very low τ values $(0 - 0.6\tau)$. Explain.
A-134 The aldehyde proton is in a region where the anisotropic effect of the carbonyl group augments the applied field. Thus, the protons have resonance at lower fields (are deshielded).	Q-135	The resonance of ethylenic protons occurs at relatively low τ values $(4.0 - 5.5\tau)$. Explain the large deshielding shown by these protons.

A-135   The ethylenic protons are in a region where the anisotropic effect of the π bond augments the applied field. Thus, the protons have resonance at lower fields (are de-shielded).

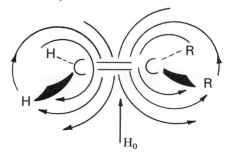

A-136   The (a) protons would be expected to have less shielding than the other two because of the inductive effect of the ethenyl group; thus, (a) protons would be expected further "down field" (lower τ) than the other two. The (c) protons would be above the π-electron cloud of the double bond, and thus be *shielded* by the anisotropic effect. The (c) protons would be expected to be found further "up field" (higher τ) than the (b) protons which are not in the proximity of the double bond.

A-137   The (a) proton lies close to the $C = O$ and is in a position in which the applied field is augmented by the anisotropic effect of the carbonyl. Thus, the (a) proton would have a lower τ value than the (b) proton which is remote from the carbonyl.

Q-136   The τ values for the methyl protons in α-pinene are given below.

$(a) = 8.37 \; \tau$

$(b) = 8.73 \; \tau$

$(c) = 9.15 \; \tau$

Explain the differences in chemical shift of the (a), (b), and (c) protons.

Q-137   Account for the τ values for the protons indicated in the compounds below.

$(a) = 3.14 \; \tau$ $(b) = 4.02 \; \tau$

Q-138   Explain the differences in τ values for the indicated protons in the following compound.

$(a) = 2.28 \; \tau$

$(b) = 2.60 \; \tau$

A-138   All of the aromatic protons are deshielded by the anisotropic effect of the benzene ring. Because of its position, proton (a) is also deshielded by the inductive and the anisotropic effect of the carbonyl group.

Q-139   The τ values for various methylene groups in the following compound are given. Explain the observed order.

$$CH_2-CH_2 \ (e)$$

(a) = 6.19 τ

(b) = 7.50 τ

(c) = 8.70 τ

(d) = 9.10 τ

(e) = 9.70 τ

A-139   The deshielding at position (a) is caused by the strong polar effects of the two phenyl groups as well as the anisotropic effect of two benzene rings. The (b) protons are deshielded by the polar and anisotropic effects of a single phenyl ring. The (c), (d), and (e) protons are lying above the electron cloud of the benzene rings; thus, a shielding effect is observed.

R   The magnetically anisotropic character of a π bond system produces an unsymmetrical magnetic field operating through space which either opposes or augments the applied field in the vicinity of neighboring protons. Protons in a region where the anisotropic effect augments the applied field will be deshielded (lower τ values) while protons in a region where the anisotropic effect opposes the applied field are shielded (higher τ values).

S-18   The positions of certain proton absorption peaks are also affected by exchange reactions. Acidic hydrogens (i.e., those attached to oxygen, nitrogen, and sulfur) undergo rapid exchange reactions such as the one shown below.

$$ROH_{(a)} + R'OH_{(b)} \rightleftharpoons ROH_{(b)} + R'OH_{(a)}$$

When such a rapid exchange occurs, separate absorption peaks for the (a) and (b) protons are not observed. Rather, a single peak is observed whose chemical shift is a weighted average of the δ values of the two types of protons. The observed chemical shift, δ_{obs}, is given by the expression

$$\delta_{obs} = N_a \delta_a + N_b \delta_b$$

where N_a and N_b are the mole fractions of the (a) and (b) protons, respectively.

Q-140   In a solution of acetic acid in H_2O, very rapid exchange occurs between the OH proton of acetic acid and the protons of water. How many peaks would be expected for the spectrum of this solution?

A-140   Two. One for the CH_3 protons of acetic acid and one for the weighted average of the OH proton of acetic acid and the H_2O protons of water.

Q-141   In the solution described in Q-140, the mole fraction of acetic acid is 0.5 and that of water is 0.5. The chemical shifts of H_2O protons in pure water and the OH proton of acetic acid in pure acetic acid are $4.8\,\tau$ and -1.6τ, respectively. What is the observed chemical shift for these protons in the solution? (Hint: Both protons in water take part in the exchange reaction.)

A-141 $\delta_{obs} = N_a\delta_a + N_b\delta_b$

Mole fraction of H_2O protons

$= \dfrac{2(0.5)}{1.5}$

Mole fraction of OH protons

$= \dfrac{0.5}{1.5}$

$\delta_{obs} = \dfrac{2(0.5)\,(4.8\tau)}{1.5} + \dfrac{0.5(-1.6\tau)}{1.5}$

$\delta_{obs} = 2.7\tau$

Q-142   What is the observed chemical shift for the OH protons in a solution containing 4.0 moles of acetic acid and 2.0 moles of H_2O?

A-142   Mole fraction of H_2O protons $= \dfrac{2(2.0)}{8.0}$

Mole fraction of OH protons of acetic acid $= 4.0/8.0$

$\delta_{obs} = \dfrac{2(2.0)\,(4.8\tau)}{8.0} + \dfrac{4.0\,(-1.6\tau)}{8.0}$

$\delta_{obs} = 1.6\tau$

R   Observed chemical shifts, δ_{obs}, for rapidly exchanging protons are given by

$\delta_{obs} = N_a\delta_a + N_b\delta_b$

S-19   Protons involved in rapid exchange reactions do not show fine structure (are unsplit) and do not cause splitting of neighboring protons. Coupling does not occur because only the *average* effect of the spin states is felt by the neighboring nuclei. Occasions may be encountered when the time required for the exchange reaction to occur is approximately the same time necessary for the nuclear transition. In these cases of slower exchange rates a broad resonance peak is observed.

Q-143   In a very pure sample of methyl alcohol, the rate of exchange of OH protons is nearly zero. What would be expected for the spectrum of pure methyl alcohol?

A-143   A three proton doublet for the CH_3 proton and a one proton quartet for the OH proton.

Q-144   Acids and bases catalyze the rate of exchange of the OH protons in methyl alcohol so that the exchange rate becomes extremely fast. Will any splitting occur in the methyl and OH resonance peaks in a solution of methyl alcohol and acid?

A-144   No. When rapid exchange occurs, only the average effect of the spin states is felt by the OH and methyl protons.

Q-145   In a very pure ethanol sample, how much splitting of the OH proton peak would be expected?

A-145   In pure ethanol the exchange rate is very slow (nearly zero). Therefore, the OH proton would appear as a triplet. This is actually the case.

Q-146   In an acidic sample of ethanol, how much splitting of the $-CH_2-$ protons would be expected?

A-146   Since fast exchange would be occurring in the acid solution, the $-CH_2-$ protons would be split only by the methyl protons. Therefore, a quartet would result.

Q-147   Besides adding acids or bases to an alcohol solution, how can the rate of exchange between OH protons be increased?

A-147   By increasing the temperature. An increase in temperature speeds up the exchange of protons.

Q-148   At room temperature the OH absorption peak of very pure methanol is a quartet. What would happen to the fine structure as the temperature of the sample is raised?

A-148   At a higher temperature the exchange rate may be rapid enough to result in a single peak for the OH proton.

Q-149   The following spectra are for OH protons undergoing exchange reactions at fast, slow, and intermediate rates. Identify each spectrum.

a)

b)

c)

A-149   a) Slow exchange, the signal for both exchanging protons is observed.
c) Fast exchange, the weighted average of the signals for the two exchanging protons is observed.
b) Intermediate, a broad signal is observed.

R   The spectrum of a molecule where proton exchange is possible is dependent upon the rate at which the protons are exchanging. When rapid exchange occurs, no spin-spin coupling between the exchanging protons and any neighbors is observed. Exchange rates intermediate between fast and slow result in broad resonance signals.

S-20   A hydrogen bonded proton is less shielded and absorbs at lower fields (smaller τ values) than non-bonded protons. Rapid equilibrium between protons in their hydrogen bonded and non-hydrogen bonded form results in a single resonance peak.

Q-150   In methanol the following equilibrium exists.

$$CH_3OH \rightleftharpoons CH_3OH \cdots \overset{\overset{\displaystyle H}{|}}{O}CH_3$$

Non-bonded   bonded

Dilution with an inert solvent will shift the equilibrium toward the non-bonded form. As methanol is diluted with CCl_4, will the OH proton resonance shift to a higher or lower field? Why?

A-150   Higher field. The hydroxyl protons in pure methanol are largely in the hydrogen bonded form. When an inert solvent is added, the equilibrium is shifted in the direction of the non-hydrogen bonded form. Since the non-hydrogen bonded chemical shift is at a higher field, the observed chemical shift moves in this direction.

Q-151   In acetic acid, an equilibrium exists between the acid proton in hydrogen bonded form and free form. As acetic acid is diluted with an inert solvent, in which direction should the acid proton resonance peak shift?

A-151   Higher field.

Q-152   Explain the down field shift of the chloroform proton when diluted with triethylamine.

A-152   The proton of chloroform forms a hydrogen bond with the nitrogen of triethylamine. This deshields the chloroform proton, shifting the resonance signal to a lower field.

Q-153   The following reaction is exothermic (gives off heat). In which direction will the equilibrium shift as the temperature is raised?

$$ROH \rightleftharpoons ROH \cdots \overset{\overset{\displaystyle H}{|}}{O} - R$$

Non-bonded   bonded

A-153   The equilibrium is shifted toward the non-hydrogen bonded form.

Q-154   What happens to the OH resonance signal for phenol as the temperature is increased?

A-154   The OH proton of phenol is hydrogen bonded. The equilibrium is shifted to the unassociated form as the temperature is increased, causing the resonance signal to shift up-field.

Q-155   Chloroform forms a hydrogen bond with the π electrons of benzene in the manner shown below.

In which direction would the C-H proton of chloroform be expected to shift in forming the hydrogen bond with benzene? Why? (Hint: Remember the anisotropic effect of benzene.)

A-155   Up-field shift (larger τ) is actually observed. A proton in the vicinity above or below a benzene ring will experience a shielding anisotropic effect. The anisotropic effect is larger than the ordinary deshielding effect observed on hydrogen bond formation.

R   A hydrogen bonded proton is deshielded, causing the resonance to shift down-field. The position of the resonance signals of a proton that can form a hydrogen bond is concentration and temperature dependent.

S-21   The position of proton resonance signals has been shown to be dependent on shielding and deshielding arising from inductive effects, anisotropic effects, hydrogen bonding, and rapid exchange of protons. However, proton resonance in certain regions of the NMR spectrum is indicative of certain *types* of protons. For example:

Aliphatic $-$ C-H protons, which do not have any adjacent atoms except hydrogen and sp^3 hybridized carbons, absorb in the region $8.2 - 10\tau$.

Aliphatic $-$ C-H protons, which have adjacent halogen, O, or N atoms (Cl-C-H, O-C-H, N-C-H) or sp^2 or sp hybridized carbons ($>$C=C-C-H,$-$C≡C-C-H), absorb in the region $5.0 - 8.5\ \tau$

Acetylenic $-$ C ≡ C-H protons absorb in the region $7.0 - 8.2\tau$.

Olefinic $-$ C=C-H protons absorb in the region $2.5 - 5.5\tau$.

Aromatic $-$ (Benzenoid and heterocyclic) protons absorb in the region $0.5 - 4.0\tau$.

Aldehydic $-$ $\overset{\overset{\displaystyle O}{\|}}{C}$ $-$ H protons absorb in the region $0.0 - 1.0\tau$.

Even though considerable overlap of the regions exists, the generalizations delineated above are very useful.

Q-156   A compound was believed to be either an aliphatic aldehyde or a ketone. The NMR spectrum showed an absorption at 0.10τ. What conclusion could be drawn?

A-156   The compound was an aldehyde.

A $\overset{\overset{\displaystyle O}{\|}}{C}$-H proton absorbs in the region $0.0 - 1.0\tau$.

Q-157   A compound was believed to be either diphenyl ether or diphenylmethane. Could the NMR spectrum be used to distinguish between these two compounds? How?

A-157 Yes. Diphenylmethane would have a two proton peak in the region $5-8.5\tau$, while diphenyl ether would have absorption in the $0.5-4.0\tau$ region only.

Q-158 A hydrocarbon was known to be either an alkene or alkane. The NMR spectrum showed absorptions at 5.2, 7.3, 8.1 and $9.2\ \tau$. What structure is indicated?

A-158 The absorption at 5.2τ is indicative of an ethylenic proton. The hydrocarbon must be an alkene.

Q-159 A compound $C_5H_{10}O$ could be an aldehyde or a ketone. Could the NMR spectrum be used to distinguish between the two possible functional groups? How?

A-159 Yes. The aldehyde would have an absorption in the $0.0-1.0\ \tau$ region.

Q-160 In what region of the spectrum would the labeled protons of the following compound be expected to absorb?

A-160 (*a*) in the aromatic region $(0.5-4\ \tau)$
(*b*) and (*c*) in the region $5-8.5\ \tau$

Q-161 In what region of the spectrum would the labeled protons of the following compound be expected to absorb?

A-161 (*a*) in the $2-5.5\ \tau$ region
(*b*) in the $5-8.5\ \tau$ region
(*c*) in the $8.2-10\ \tau$ region.

Q-162 In what region of the spectrum would the labeled protons of the following compound be expected to absorb?

A-162 (*a*) in the $5-8.5\ \tau$ region
(*b*) in the $8.2-10\ \tau$ region

Q-163 In what region of the spectrum would the labeled protons of the following compound be expected to absorb?

$$CH_3 - CH_2 - CH_2 - \overset{\overset{\displaystyle O}{\|}}{C} - H$$
(*d*)   (*c*)   (*b*)   (*a*)

A-163 (*a*) in the $0.0-1.0\ \tau$ region
(*b*) in the $5-8.5\ \tau$ region
(*c*) and (*d*) in the $8.2-10\ \tau$ region

Q-164 In what region of the spectrum would the labeled protons of the following compound be expected to absorb?

$$CH_3 - \overset{\overset{\displaystyle O}{\|}}{C} - CH_2 - CH_3$$
(*a*)   (*b*)   (*c*)

A-164 (a) and (b) in the $5 - 8.5\ \tau$ region

(c) in the $8.2 - 10\ \tau$ region.

Q-165 In what region of the spectrum would the labeled protons of the following compound be expected to absorb?

$$CH_3 - CH = CH - \overset{\overset{\displaystyle O}{\|}}{C} - H$$
(a)   (b)   (c)   (d)

A-165 (a) in the $5 - 8.5\ \tau$ region

(b) and (c) in the $2.5 - 5.5\ \tau$ region

(d) in the $0.0 - 1.0\ \tau$ region

Q-166 In what region of the spectrum would the labeled protons of the following compound be expected to absorb?

$$Cl_2\ \overset{\overset{\displaystyle O}{\|}}{CHCOCH_2}\ CH_3$$
(a)   (b) (c)

A-166 (a) on the low end of the $5 - 8.5\ \tau$ region (actual 4.1 — note that there are three strong electron pulling groups attached to the carbon bearing the proton)

(b) in the $5 - 8.5\ \tau$ region

(c) in the $8.2 - 10\ \tau$ region

Q-167 In what region of the spectrum would the labeled protons of the following compound be expected to absorb?

$CH_3 CH(NO_2)CH_3$

(a) (b)

A-167 (a) in the $8.2 - 10\ \tau$ region

(b) in the $5 - 8.5\ \tau$ region and probably on the *low* end of the region (actual 5.2)

Q-168 In what region of the spectrum would the labeled protons of the following compound be expected to absorb?

$$H - \overset{\overset{\displaystyle O}{\|}}{C} - \overset{\overset{\displaystyle CH_3}{|}}{\underset{\underset{\displaystyle CH_3}{|}}{N}}$$
(a)   (b)

A-168 (a) in the $0.0 - 1.0\ \tau$ region (Actual $2.0\ \tau$. This is not an aldehydic hydrogen. The compound is a formamide derivative. Formamide protons absorb near $2.0\ \tau$.)

(b) in the $5 - 8.5\ \tau$ region

Q-169 In what region of the spectrum would the labeled protons of the following compound be expected to absorb?

$CH_3 - C \equiv C - H$

(a)   (b)

A-169 (a) in the $5 - 8.5\ \tau$ region

(b) in the $7.0 - 8.2$ (actual 8.2) τ region.

Q-170 In what region of the spectrum would the labeled protons of the following compound be expected to absorb?

$Cl - CH_2 - CH_2 - OH$

(a)   (b)

A-170   (*a*) and (*b*) in the 5 − 8.5 τ region

Q-171   In what region of the spectrum would the labeled protons of the following compound be expected to absorb?

$C_6H_5CH(CH_3)_2$

(*a*) (*b*)   (*c*)

A-171   (*a*) in the 0.5 − 4.0 τ region

(*b*) in the 5 − 8.5 τ region

(*c*) in the 8.2 − 10 τ region

Q-172   In what region of the spectrum would the labeled protons of the following compound be expected to absorb?

$$p - CH_3C_6H_4NH\overset{\overset{\textstyle O}{\|}}{C}CH_3$$

(*a*)   (*b*)   (*c*)

A-172   (*a*) and (*c*) in the 5 − 8.5 τ region

(*b*) in the 0.5 − 4.0 τ region

Q-173   In what region of the spectrum would the labeled protons of the following compound be expected to absorb?

A-173   (*a*) in the 0.5 − 4 τ region

(*b*) and (*c*) in the 5 − 8.5 τ region

R   Chemical shifts expected for various types of protons are given in Table VI in the Appendix.

S-22   Below are listed correlations of proton absorption for hydrogens which are bonded to O, N, and S. Remember that the order of electronegativity is O > N > C.

Proton	Type of molecule	τ value	
OH	Alcohols	4.5 to 9.5	On dilution, gradually shifts to high fields.
	Phenols	2.3 to 6.0	On dilution, gradually shifts to high fields.
	Enols	− 6.0 to − 5.0	Very low fields due to strong intramolecular hydrogen bonds.
	Acids	− 2.0 to − 0.5	Very low fields due to strong intramolecular hydrogen bonds.
N-H	Aliphatic amine	7.8 to 9.7	
	Aromatic amine	5.0 to 7.4	
	Amide	1.5 to 5.0	
S-H	Aliphatic sulfhydryl	8.4 to 8.8	
	Aromatic sulfhydryl	6.4	

Q-174   For the following compound, where would the indicated protons be expected to absorb?

$ClCH_2CH_2OH$

(*a*)   (*b*)

A-174   (*a*) in the $5 - 8.5\ \tau$ region

(*b*) in the $4.5 - 9.5\ \tau$ region

Dilute solutions would show OH absorption at the high field end of this region.

Q-175   For the following compound, where would the indicated protons be expected to absorb?

A-175   (*a*) in the $8.2 \doteq 10\ \tau$ region

(*b*) in the $5 - 8.5\ \tau$ region

(*c*) in the $7.8 - 9.7\ \tau$ region

Q-176   Where would the indicated protons in the following compound be expected to absorb?

A-176   (*a*) in the $0.5 - 4\ \tau$ region

(*b*) in the $5.0 - 7.4\ \tau$ region

(*c*) in the $5 - 8.5\ \tau$ region

Q-177   Where would the protons indicated in the following compound be expected to absorb?

A-177   (*a*) in the $0.5 - 4\ \tau$ region

(*b*) in the $5 - 8.5\ \tau$ region

(*c*) in the $1.5 - 5\ \tau$ region

Q-178   Where would the labeled protons in the compound below be expected to absorb?

A-178   (*a*) in the $5 - 8.5\ \tau$ region

(*b*) in the $0.5 - 4.0\ \tau$ region

(*c*) in the $8.2 - 10\ \tau$ region (low end)

(*d*) in the $2.3 - 6.0$ region. Dilute solutions will absorb in the high field end of this region.

Q-179   In the following compound, the OH proton absorption is at $-1.0\ \tau$, much lower than expected for phenols. Explain.

A-179 There would be a strong intramolecular hydrogen bond in this compound.

This results in a strong down-field shift of the O-H absorption.

S-23 Just as chemical shift values can be used to tell what types of protons are present in a molecule, the magnitude of spin-spin coupling constants can be used for structure and confirmation elucidation. Coupling constants are affected by several factors. Coupling constants of vicinal protons (protons on adjacent carbons, i.e., $-\overset{|}{\underset{H}{C}} - \overset{|}{\underset{H}{C}} -$) will be considered first. The following generalizations are useful.

1) The magnitude of the vicinal coupling constant, J, is a function of the dihedral angle (ϕ). The relationship is given by the Karpus equation

$$J_{(Hertz)} = 4.2 - 0.5 \cos \phi + 4.5 \cos 2\phi$$

2) The dependence of the vicinal coupling constant (J) upon the electronegativity of X ($CH_3 - CH_2 - X$) is given by the equation

$$J_{(Hertz)} = 7.9 - n0.7 (\Delta x)$$

where n is equal to the number of hydrogens replaced by an X group and Δx is equal to ($x_X - x_H$) where x_X and x_H are electronegativities of the substituent and the hydrogen, respectively.

3) The vicinal coupling constant (J) decreases with increasing C-C bond length.

4) The vicinal coupling constants (J) depend upon the carbon-carbon-hydrogen bond angles (θ)

As the angles between the hydrogens are increased, the coupling constant is decreased (bond order remaining the same).

Q-180 The dihedral angle between two protons is zero. What coupling constant would be predicted from the Karpus equation?

A-180 $J = 4.2 - 0.5 \cos \phi + 4.5 \cos 2\phi$

$\cos 0^0 = 1$

$J = 8.2$ Hz

Q-181 What should the coupling constant be when the dihedral angle, ϕ, between protons is $45°, 60°, 90°, 120°, 135°$, and $180°$?

A-181

Angle in degrees	$\cos \phi$	J (Hz)
45	$1/\sqrt{2}$	3.9
60	$1/2$	1.8
90	0	-0.3
120	$-1/2$	2.1
135	$-1/\sqrt{2}$	4.5
180	-1	9.2

Q-182   Sketch on the following graph the dependence of the vicinal coupling constant on the dihedral angle between protons.

A-182

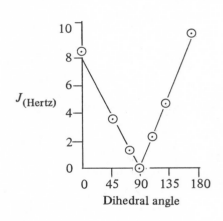

Q-183   Below is a Newman projection (end on view) for the chair form of a cyclohexane ring. Predict the magnitude of the *diaxial* coupling constant.

A-183 $\phi_{aa} = 180°$ $J_{aa} = 9.2$ Hz
(usually 9–13 Hz)

Q-184   Predict the magnitude of the axial-equatorial coupling constant in cyclohexane.

A-184 $\phi_{ae} = 60°$ $J_{ae} = 1.8$ Hz
(usually 2–5 Hz)

Q-185   Predict the magnitude of the di-equatorial coupling constant in cyclohexane.

A-185 $\phi_{ee} = 60°$ $J_{ae} = 1.8$ Hz
(usually 2–5 Hz)

Q-186   Using the Karpus equation predict $J_{a,b}$ for the following compound.

A-186 $\phi_{ab} = 180° \, J_{ab} = 9.2$ Hz

J_{ab} actual = 14 Hz

Q-187 In the last answer, why is the coupling constant larger than predicted by the Karpus equation?

A-187 The Karplus equation is for carbon-carbon single bonds. As the bond order increases, the bond length decreases, causing the coupling constant to increase (rule 3).

Q-188 In which compound would the coupling constant between the indicated protons be larger? Why?

1) R   R'
    C = C   Bond order = 2
   H$_{(a)}$ H$_{(b)}$

2) H$^{(a)}$ H$^{(b)}$

    R   Bond order = 1.67

A-188 Compound 1. The bond order in compound 1 is indicative of a shorter bond length. The coupling constant increases with decreasing bond length.

Actual

Compound 1 J_{ab} = 11.5 Hz

Compound 2 J_{ab} = 8.0 Hz

Q-189 Using the equation given in rule 2, predict the J_{ab} coupling constant in the following compound.

$CH_3 - CH_2 \, Cl$
(a)   (b)

$\chi_H = 2.20$
$\chi_{Cl} = 3.15$

A-189 $J = 7.9 - 0.7 \, (\Delta \chi)$

$J_{ab} = 7.9 - 0.7 \, (0.95) = 7.2$ Hz

observed value = 7.5 Hz

(rule 2)

Q-190 Predict the coupling constant, J_{ab}, in the following compound.

$CH_2 \, Cl - CHCl_2$
(a)   (b)

A-190 $J_{ab} = 7.9 - (3) \, (0.7) \, (0.95) = 5.9$ Hz

Observed value = 6.0 Hz

Q-191 Which of the following compounds has the larger C = C $-$ H bond angle?

H$_a$
H$_b$

R
I

H$_b$ H$_a$

R
II

A-191 Compound II. C = C = 135°

Compound I. C = C = 120°

Q-192 In which of the *compounds* shown in Q-191 will the J_{ab} coupling constant be larger?

A-192   Compound I. (rule 4)

Range for compounds of type I:

$J_{ab} = 5 - 7$ Hz.

Range for compounds of type II:

$J_{ab} = 2.5 - 4.0$ Hz.

Q-193   In which of the compounds given below would the J_{ab} coupling constant be expected to be larger? Why?

I

II

A-193   Compound I. The C = C bond angle in compound I is less than the corresponding bond angle in compound II. (rule 4)

Range for compounds of type **I**:

$J_{ab} = 8.8 - 10.5$ Hz.

Range for compounds of type **II**:

$J_{ab} = 5 - 7$ Hz.

Q-194   1,2 − dihalocyclohexane was found to have a J_{ab} coupling constant of 10 Hz. Is the compound the *cis* or *trans* isomer? What is the conformation of the compound?

I

cis

II

trans

III

trans

A-194   *Trans.* Conformation III. The coupling constant is that usually observed for diaxial interactions.

R   Coupling constants can be used for structure and conformation elucidations. Rules for coupling between vicinal protons are given in S-23. Values for spin-spin coupling constants in some common systems are presented in Table VII of the Appendix.

S-24 Spin-spin coupling is frequently observed between protons (or other nuclei having I > O) separated by more than three bonds. These interactions are called long-range couplings. These coupling constants are on the order of $0 - 3$ Hz and are common in $\pi -$ systems. Examples are:

1) *Substituted benzenes.* The ranges of coupling constants observed in substituted benzenes are summarized below:

$$J_{(ortho)} = 6 - 10 \text{ Hz}$$
$$J_{(meta)} = 1 - 3 \text{ Hz}$$
$$J_{(para)} = 0 - 1 \text{ Hz}$$

2) *Allylic coupling.* Long-range splitting between proton (a) and proton (c) or proton (b) and proton (c) in the unsaturated system shown below is observed.

$$J_{ac \ (trans)} = 1.6 - 3.0 \text{ Hz}$$
$$J_{bc \ (cis)} = 0 - 1.5 \text{ Hz}$$

Q-195 Diagram the splitting pattern for hydrogen (a) in the following compound:

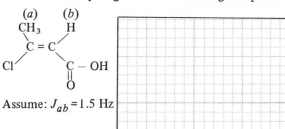

Assume:

$$J_{ab} = 3 \text{ Hz}$$
$$J_{ac} = 1 \text{ Hz}$$

A-195

Q-196 Diagram the splitting pattern for the indicated hydrogens in the following compound.

$$\begin{array}{cc}
(a) & (b) \\
CH_3 & H \\
\end{array}$$

$$C = C$$

Cl ..... C — OH
           ‖
           O

Assume: $J_{ab} = 1.5$ Hz

A-196

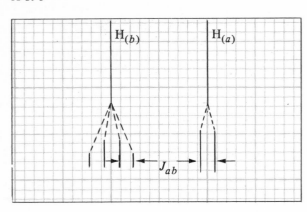

A-197   Doublet.

Long-range splitting with the (b) proton.

$J_{ab} = 1$ Hz

A-198   The (a) proton is split into a doublet by coupling with the (b) proton, J_{ab}, and each of these peaks is split into a doublet by coupling with the (c) proton, J_{ac}.

A-199   The (a) proton is split into a triplet by coupling with the two (b) protons, J_{ab}, and each of these peaks is split into a doublet by coupling with the (c) proton, J_{ac}.

Q-197   Predict the multiplicity for the indicated proton in the following compound.

Q-198   Account for the splitting pattern for the (a) proton in the compound

(a) proton

Q-199   Predict the splitting pattern for the (a) proton in the following compound.

Q-200   In an AMX system containing π-bonds, long-range spin-spin splitting can occur. In the compound below, what coupling constants are involved?

A-200　J_{AM}, J_{AX}, J_{MX}

Q-201　For the compound given in Q-200, which coupling constant, J_{AM}, J_{MX}, or J_{AX} would be expected to be smallest? Why?

A-201　J_{AX} will be smallest. *Meta* coupling constants are smaller than *ortho* coupling constants.

Q-202　In the AMX system illustrated below, would long-range spin-spin splitting be expected?

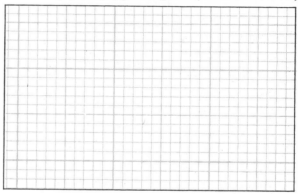

Give all coupling constants for the system.

A-202　Yes.

$J_{AM} \approx 10$ Hz
$J_{MX} \approx 10$ Hz
$J_{AX} \approx 1.6\text{-}3.0$ Hz

Q-203　For the molecule given below,

(M) H⟍⟍⟋⟍ H (X)
(A) H⟍⟍⟋ O ⟍ C – CH₃
　　　　　　　　‖
　　　　　　　　O

assume $J_{AM} = 2.5$ Hz, $J_{AX} = 1.2$ Hz, $J_{MX} = 3.5$ Hz. Diagram the splitting pattern for the (A) and (X) proton peaks (1 Hz = 2 divisions).

A-203

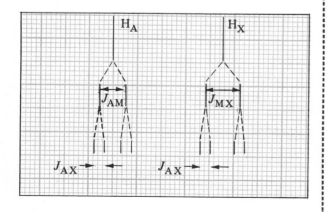

Q-204　Diagram the splitting pattern of the (M) proton in the compound given in Q-203.

A-204

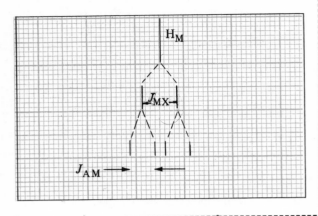

A-205   There should be three groups of lines (one for each type of proton) and each group should have four peaks (two doublets).

A-206   AMX. Each proton will exhibit four peaks (two doublets).

Q-205   What is the multiplicity of the A, the M, and the X proton absorptions in the spectrum of an AMX system in which there is long-range splitting?

Q-206   Establish whether the indicated protons in the following compound make up an AX, AX_2, AMX, A_2, or A_3 case and give the expected spectrum for these protons.

Q-207   Establish whether the protons in the following compound make up an AX, AX_2, AMX, A_2, or A_3 case and give the expected multiplicity for each proton.

A-207   Protons (a), (b), and (c) constitute an AMX case. Each of these protons will exhibit four peaks (two doublets). The (d) protons are an A_3 case and yield a three proton singlet.

Q-208   Long-range spin-spin splitting can give rise to complicating features in the spectra of compounds with protons which make up an A_2X_2 system. In the spectrum of the compound below, the hydrogens give a characteristic quartet with four extra "inside" lines.

What feature of the above compound gives rise to the complications in its spectrum? (Hint: What coupling constants are present?)

A-208   The following spin-spin interactions are present:

The J'_{AX} and J_{AX} coupling constants are not the same. Thus, a complex spectrum results.

Q-209   Establish whether the protons designated in the following compound make up an A_2, A_4, AX, A_2X_2, or AMX system.

A-209 A_2X_2 system where $J_{AX} \neq J'_{AX}$

Q-210   In the A_2X_2 system for the compound below, how many different J_{AX} coupling constants would there be? Why?

(A)H
$\quad$C = C = C$\quad$
(A)H $\qquad$ F(X)
$\qquad\qquad\qquad F$(X)

(Hint: What is the stereochemistry of the compound?)

A-210   One.

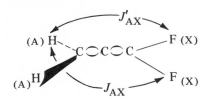

Both spin-spin coupling interactions take place *through the same number and kinds of bonds.*

Therefore, $J_{AX} = J'_{AX}$

A-211   The absorption bands for both A and X will be triplets.

A-212 $J_{AX} \neq J'_{AX}$

The spin-spin interactions operate through a different number of bonds.

A-213 $J_{AX} = J'_{AX}$

There is free rotation about the single bond; therefore, $J_{AX} = J'_{AX}$.

Q-211   What would be the multiplicity of each group in an $A_2 X_2$ spectrum where $J_{AX} = J'_{AX}$?

Q-212   Is the following compound an $A_2 X_2$ system where $J_{AX} = J'_{AX}$ or $J_{AX} \neq J'_{AX}$? Why?

Q-213   Is the following compound an $A_2 X_2$ system where $J_{AX} = J'_{AX}$ or $J_{AX} \neq J'_{AX}$? Why?

(X) H   H (A)
$CH_3 O - C - C - CN$
H   H
(X)   (A)

Q-214   Draw the expected spectrum for the ring hydrogens of the compound:

A-214 A_2X_2 case where $J_{AX} \neq J'_{AX}$.

inside lines
Quartet with 4 inside lines.

R	Long-range splitting (coupling between nuclei separated by more than three bonds) is observed in π-bond systems. These interactions give J values of 0 - 3 Hz.

Characteristic spectra are observed for the AMX and A_2X_2 cases with long-range interactions.

System	Spectrum Characteristics
AMX (long-range coupling)	Each proton exhibits four peaks (two doublets).
A_2X_2 (long-range coupling $J_{AX} \neq J'_{AX}$)	**Four** proton quartet with four additional weak "inside" lines.

S-25   Splitting patterns considered so far have been between interacting nuclei in which δ_{AX} (the difference between the chemical shift of nucleus A and X) is large compared to the size of the coupling constant, J_{AX}. Interacting nuclei for which $\delta_{AX} >> J_{AX}$ are called *first order systems*. First order systems give rise to splitting patterns which are unperturbed by other effects.

Complicating factors arise when the chemical shift value between two interacting nuclei and their coupling constants are of comparable magnitude. Interacting nuclei of this type are designated by the letters A and B. Interacting nuclei for which $\delta_{AB} \cong J_{AB}$ give rise to perturbed peaks in their splitting patterns. In AX cases the ratio δ_{AX}/J_{AX} is larger than about 25. In AB cases the ratio δ_{AB}/J_{AB} is approximately 1.

Q-215   Two protons have chemical shift values of 369 Hz and 120 Hz, respectively. The coupling constant between their protons is 5.0 Hz. Are these protons part of an AX or an AB system?

A-215 $\delta = 360 \text{ Hz} - 120 \text{ Hz} = 240 \text{ Hz}$

$\dfrac{\delta}{J} = \dfrac{240}{5.0} = 48$

This ratio is large; therefore, the protons are a part of an AX system.

Q-216   Two protons have chemical shift values of 6.20 and 6.08 τ. The coupling constant between these protons is 10.0 Hz. Are these protons part of an AX or an AB system? (Assume a 60 MHz oscillator.) (Hint: δ must be in Hz units for comparison.)

A-216 $\Delta \tau = 6.20 - 6.08 = 0.12$ ppm

$\dfrac{(0.12 \text{ ppm}) (60 \text{x} 10^6 \text{ Hz})}{1 \text{ x } 10^6 \text{ ppm}} = 7.2$ Hertz

$\dfrac{\delta}{J} = \dfrac{7.2}{10} = 0.72$

This ratio is small; therefore, the protons are part of an AB system.

Q-217   Two protons have chemical shifts at 6.76 and 6.25 τ. The coupling constant between these protons is 12.0 Hz. Are these protons part of an AX or an AB system? (Assume a 60 MHz oscillator.)

A-217 $\Delta \tau = 6.76 - 6.25 = 0.51$ ppm

$$\frac{(0.51 \text{ ppm}) (60 \times 10^6 \text{Hz})}{(1 \times 10^6 \text{ppm})} = 31 \text{ Hz}$$

$$\frac{\delta}{J} = \frac{31}{12.0} = 2.5$$

This ratio is small enough so that the protons will make up an AB system.

Q-218   Diagram the splitting pattern expected for first order coupling for two protons, A and B, whose chemical shift differs by only 5 Hz while $J_{AB} = 10$ Hz.

A-218

Actually this is not the splitting pattern observed because of perturbation.

R   A first order unperturbed splitting pattern results from the interaction between nuclei where δ_{AX}/J_{AX} is larger than about 25.

An AB system, which gives rise to a perturbed splitting pattern, will result from the interaction between nuclei where δ_{AB}/J_{AB} is approximately 1.

S-26   For a system in which δ_{AB} approaches the magnitude of J_{AB} (See A-218), the intensity and positions of the split lines do not follow the simple first order rules.

For an AB case the inner split lines become more intense at the expense of the outer lines. Furthermore, the splitting pattern is such that the inner peaks do not cross.

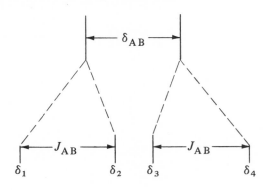

As a result of the perturbation, the difference in chemical shift between protons A and B, δ_{AB}, is given by the equation

$\delta_{AB} = \sqrt{(\delta_1 - \delta_4)(\delta_2 - \delta_3)}$.

The J_{AB} coupling constant is given by the equation

$J_{AB} = \delta_1 - \delta_2 = \delta_3 - \delta_4$.

The relative intensity (I) of the lines is given by the equation

$\dfrac{I_2}{I_1} = \dfrac{I_3}{I_4} = \dfrac{\delta_1 - \delta_4}{\delta_2 - \delta_3}$.

Q-219   A perturbed splitting pattern is given below for an AB system. Will the difference between the midpoints (marked with arrows) of the split lines represent the positions of unsplit lines? Why?

A-219   No. Because the split lines are perturbed and are no longer symmetrical about the original line.

Unperturbed   Perturbed
    case   case

Q-220   On a scale of 1 Hz = 1 division, the splitting pattern for an AB system is diagramed below.

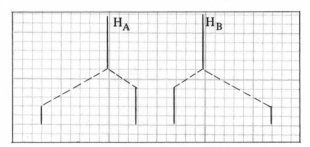

Give the chemical shift difference, δ_{AB}, and the J_{AB} coupling constant for the above splitting pattern.

A-220

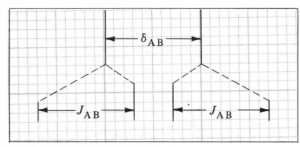

J_{AB} = 10 divisions = 10 Hz

δ_{AB} = 10 divisions = 10 Hz

A-221 $J_{AB} = \delta_1 - \delta_2$ = 10 divisions = 10 Hz

$\delta_{AB} = \sqrt{(\delta_1 - \delta_4)(\delta_2 - \delta_3)}$

$\delta_{AB} = \sqrt{(21)(1) \text{ Hz}^2}$

δ_{AB} = 4.6 Hz

A-222   The uncoupled lines for the A and B protons, separated by 4.6 Hz, are centered between the two outside peaks of the fine structure.

$\delta_1 - \delta_4$ = 21 divisions = 21 Hz

The chemical shift between original peaks is 4.6 Hz. The distance between δ_1 and δ_A

$= \dfrac{21.0 - 4.6}{2} = 8.2$ Hz

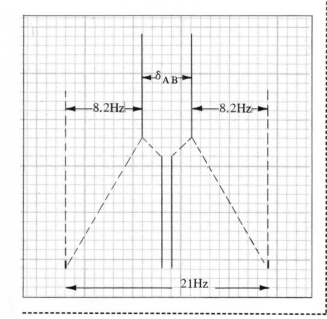

Q-221   For the AB pattern of peaks given below (1 Hz = 1 division), determine the chemical shift difference and the coupling constant between the A and B protons.

Q-222   Indicate on the diagram shown in Q-221 the positions of the uncoupled A and B peaks. What is the distance (in Hz) between the δ_1 and the unsplit δ_A peak?

Q-223   Using the equation given in S-26, calculate the relative intensity of the fine structure peaks for the system described in Q-221.

A-223 $\dfrac{I_2}{I_1} = \dfrac{21 \text{ Hz}}{1 \text{ Hz}} = \dfrac{21}{1}$

Q-224   Analyze the AB splitting pattern given below. Find J_{AB}, δ_{AB}, relative intensity of lines, and positions of unsplit A and B protons.

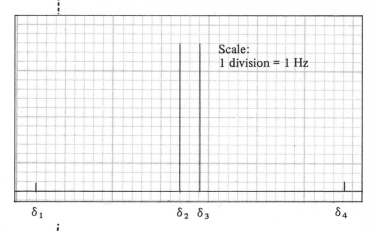

A-224 $J_{AB} = \delta_1 - \delta_2 = 15 \text{ Hz}$

$\delta_{AB} = \sqrt{(\delta_1 - \delta_4)(\delta_2 - \delta_3)} = \sqrt{(32)(2)}$

$= \sqrt{64} = 8 \text{ Hz}$

$\dfrac{I_2}{I_1} = \dfrac{32}{2} = \dfrac{16}{1}$

Distance original peak is from outside peak

$= \dfrac{32\text{-}8}{2} = 12 \text{ Hz}$

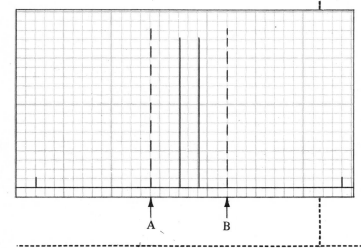

Q-225   Analyze the AB splitting pattern given below. Find J_{AB}, δ_{AB}, relative intensity of lines, and position of unsplit A and B protons.

Scale:
1 division = 1 Hz

δ_1 δ_2 δ_3 δ_4

A-225 $J_{AB} = \delta_1 - \delta_2 = 7$ Hz

$\delta_{AB} = \sqrt{(35)(21)} = \sqrt{735} = 27$ Hz

$\dfrac{I_2}{I_1} = \dfrac{35}{21} = 1.7$

$\delta_1 - \delta_4 = 35$ Hz

Distance original peak is from outside peak

$= \dfrac{35 - 27}{2} = 4$ Hz

H_A H_B

Q-226   A spectrum contains the four lines shown below.

What factor would have to be considered in order to determine if these lines were due to an AB system or the splitting pattern of the X proton in an A_3X system?

A-226   In an A_3X system the four lines are symmetrical with the distance between each line equal to J_{AX}. The peak intensities will be in the ratio of 1 : 3 : 3 : 1. In an AB system the distance between the outside pair of lines will be equal to J_{AB}, but the distance between the inside lines will rarely be equal to J_{AB}. The ratio of intensities will rarely be in the ratio of 1 : 3 : 3 : 1.

Q-227   The following sketch is drawn to scale. Is this an A_3X splitting pattern or an AB splitting pattern?

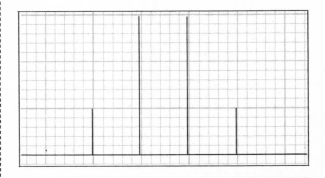

A-227   The distance between each pair of lines is the same and the intensities of the lines are in the ratio of 1 : 3 : 3 : 1. Therefore, this is *most likely* an A_3X system.

Q-228   The following sketch is drawn to scale. Is this an A_3X splitting pattern or an AB splitting pattern?

A-228   Because the distance between the pairs of lines are *not* the same and the ratio of intensities are not 1 : 3 : 3 : 1, this set of lines is, in fact, two doublets of an AB system.

Q-229   For the following compound, $\delta_{2,3} = 35$ Hz and $J_{2,3} = 3.0$ Hz

The spectrum for these protons is drawn below. Explain.

A-229   This spectrum is the result of an AB system where there is very little perturbation, $\delta_{2,3}/J_{2,3} = 11.8$. This system is nearly an AX system.

Q-230   For the following molecule, $\delta_{AB} = 27$ Hz and $J_{AB} = 8$ Hz.

(A)

(B)

Sketch the splitting pattern for the A and B protons.

A-230 $\delta_{AB}/J_{AB} = \frac{27}{8} = 3.3$

The ratio is quite low; therefore, the pattern should show quite a bit of perturbation.

27 Hz

J_{AB}
8 Hz

(not drawn to scale)

A-231

A-232

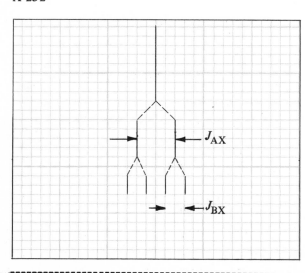

Q-231   In an AB system, the peaks may further be split by coupling with another proton, X. This type of interaction is called an ABX system. Below is drawn the splitting pattern for an AB system. If protons A and B can interact with another proton, X, with coupling constants J_{AX} = 4 Hz and J_{BX} = 2 Hz, diagram the new pattern of lines which would appear for the A and B protons.

Q-232   Diagram the splitting pattern for the X proton of the system described in Q-231.

Q-233   An example of an ABX system is 2,3-lutidine.

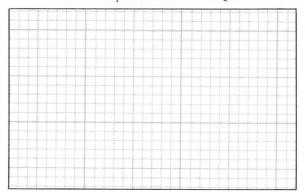

Which protons make up the AB part of the spectrum? Which is the X proton?

A-233

A-234

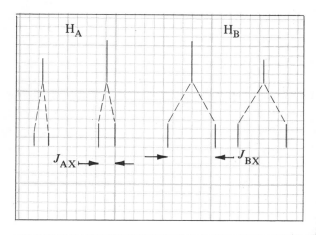

A-235 Four lines (two doublets).

Q-234 The pattern below is for the AB system of 2,3-lutidine (uncoupled to the X proton). If $J_{AX} = 1.3$ Hz and $J_{BX} = 5.0$ Hz, diagram the fine structure for the AB protons resulting from coupling with X.

(Scale: 1 division = 1 Hz)

Q-235 What would be the multiplicity of the X proton in 2,3 - lutidine?

R Analysis of AB type spectrum:

$$\delta_{AB} = \sqrt{(\delta_1 - \delta_4)(\delta_2 - \delta_3)}$$
$$\frac{I_2}{I_1} = \frac{I_3}{I_4} = \frac{\delta_1 - \delta_4}{\delta_2 - \delta_3}$$

In an ABX system the AB splitting pattern is further split by interaction of A and B with X.

S-27   At times, protons that are bonded to a nucleus with a spin quantum number of $I = 1$ or greater will give rise to a broad, unsplit absorption band. This is common for protons bonded to nitrogen. The broad peak in the spectrum below for compound I is due to the two protons on the nitrogen.

When several protons with about the same τ values are present in a molecule, the spectrum may have a large peak with or without fine structure that resembles a haystack. These peaks are very difficult to analyze. The molecule

has the NMR spectrum shown below. The peaks in the 1.6 and 2.2 δ regions are due to the $- CH_2 -$ protons. (The peaks at 5.3 δ are due to an impurity.)

Q-236   The spectrum for propionamide

(a) (b) O

$CH_3 - CH_2 - C$

NH$_2$

(c)

is shown below. Give the τ values for each of the different protons.

A-236   (*a*) 8.9 τ

         (*b*) 7.8 τ

         (*c*) 3.6 τ

Q-237   The spectrum for 1-chloro - 2 - bromoethane

        (*a*)   (*b*)

$ClCH_2 - CH_2 Br$

is shown below. Can the peaks corresponding to the different protons be distinguished in this spectrum?

A-237   No. The (*a*) and (*b*) protons absorb in the 3.6 − 3.8 δ region. This pattern is typical of an A_2B_2 system.

Q-238   The spectrum for 2-pyrrolidone

is shown below. Give the δ value for each of the different protons.

A-238 (a) 3.4 δ

(b) 7.7 δ

(c) (d) 2.1 − 2.3 δ

Q-239   The spectrum for morpholine

(b) H₂C — O — CH₂ (b)

(c) H₂C — | — CH₂ (c)

N

H

(a)

is shown below. Give the τ value for each of the different protons.

A-239   (a) 8.2 τ
         (b) 6.3 τ
         (c) 7.1 τ

Q-240   The spectrum for 1-ethynyl - 1 -
         cyclohexanol

is shown below. Give the δ value for each
of the different protons.

A-240   (a) 2.48 δ

(b) 2.78 δ

(c) (d) (e) 1.4 − 1.8 δ

Q-241   The spectrum for phenacetin

(c)   (d)   (e)
H   H   H

(a)   (b)
$CH_3 - CH_2 - O$ ... N CH_3 (f)

H   H   C
(c)   (d)   ‖
              O

is shown below. Give the δ value for each of the different protons.

δ ppm

A-241   (a) 1.4 δ

(b) 4.0 δ

(c) 6.8 δ

(d) 7.4 δ

(e) 7.9 δ

(f) 2.1 δ

R   Protons bonded to nuclei with $I = 1$ or greater can give rise to broad absorption peaks.

Several protons with approximately the same τ values and complex coupling patterns can give rise to a complicated absorption band referred to as a "haystack".

Chapter 5 | SYNTHESIS OF SPECTRAL DATA

The determination of chemical structure by spectroscopic (or other) methods requires the successful completion of three basic steps, namely:

a) data procurement,
b) interpretation of data, and
c) synthesis of the interpreted data into a chemical structure.

Of the three steps, the synthesis of interpreted data into a chemical structure is by far the most difficult. While every individual will develop his own technique for this synthesizing process, the following chapter demonstrates a systematic method which many chemists employ.

After completing this chapter you should be able to

a) calculate the number of sites of unsaturation in a molecule from the molecular formula of a compound
b) determine the possible molecular formulas of a compound from data provided by molecular weight
c) determine structural and **residual** units present in a molecule
d) combine simple structural units into more complex units
e) arrange simple and complex structural units into molecular structures.

S-1   All compounds containing only C, H, O, or S and having no **units of unsaturation** (multiple bonds or rings) have the general formula $C_nH_{2n+2}O_aS_b$. Each double bond or ring is equivalent to one unit of unsaturation while a triple bond is equal to two units. Each unit of unsaturation reduces the number of hydrogen atoms per molecule by two.

The units of unsaturation in a molecule (Ω) may be calculated from the formula

$$\Omega = 2n+2 - \frac{(\text{number of hydrogen atoms per molecular formula})}{2}$$

where n is the number of carbon atoms per molecule.

structural formula	molecular formula	general formula	Ω
$CH_3CH_2CH=CHCH_2OH$	$C_5H_{10}O$	$C_nH_{2n}O$	1
$S=\langle\rangle - C \equiv C - CH_3$	$C_8H_{10}S$	$C_nH_{2n-6}S$	4

Q-1   Cyclopentanone has the formula C_5H_8O. Calculate Ω for the compound. What is each unit of unsaturation?

A-1 $\Omega = \frac{2n+2-8}{2} = \frac{10+2-8}{2} = 2$

1 double bond + 1 ring

Q-2   Napthalene has the formula $C_{10}H_8$. Calculate Ω for the compound. What is each unit of unsaturation?

A-2 $\Omega = \frac{2n+2-8}{2} = 7$

5 double bonds + 2 rings

Q-3   Furan has the formula C_4H_4O. Calculate Ω for the compound. What is each unit of unsaturation?

A-3 $\Omega = \frac{2n+2-4}{2} = 3$

2 double bonds + 1 ring

Q-4   A compound has the formula $C_6H_{10}O_2S$. Calculate Ω and give all the possible combinations of rings and multiple bonds.

A-4 $\Omega = \frac{2n+2-10}{2} = 2$

2 double bonds **or**

1 triple bond **or**

1 double bond and one ring **or**

2 rings.

Q-5   A compound known to be a carboxylic acid has the formula $C_5H_8O_3$. What are the possible combinations of rings and multiple bonds?

A-5 $\Omega = \frac{2n+2-8}{2} = 2$

In addition to the one unit of unsaturation due to the carbonyl group, there could be one double bond **or** one ring.

R   The units of unsaturation (Ω) in molecules containing only C,H,O,S are given by the expression,

$$\Omega = \frac{2n+2 - (\text{hydrogen atoms per molecule})}{2}$$

S-2   All compounds containing nitrogen and no **units of unsaturation** have the general formula

$C_nH_{2n+2+m}N_m$

Each unit of unsaturation reduces the number of hydrogens by two. The units of unsaturation in a nitrogen-containing compound may be calculated from the formula:

$$\Omega_{N \text{ containing compound}} = \frac{2n+2+m - (\text{number of hydrogen atoms per molecule})}{2}$$

where n and m equal the number of carbon and nitrogen atoms in the molecule, respectively.

structural formula	molecular formula	general formula	Ω
$(CH_3)_3N$	C_3H_9N	$C_nH_{2n+2+1}N$	0
$CH_2 = CH\ CH_2\ NH_2$	C_3H_7N	$C_nH_{2n+1}N$	1
$(CH_3)_2\ C = N - NH\ CH_3$	$C_4H_{10}N_2$	$C_nH_{2n+2}N_2$	1

All compounds containing halogen and no **units of unsaturation** have the general formula $C_nH_{2n+2-x}X_x$

$$\Omega_{\text{halogen containing compounds}} = \frac{2n+2-x-(\text{number of hydrogen atoms per molecule})}{2}$$

Q-6   A compound has the formula C_5H_7N. Calculate Ω for the compound. What are the possible combinations of rings and double bonds?

A-6 $\Omega = \dfrac{2n+2+m-7}{2} = \dfrac{10+2+1-7}{2} = 3$

3 double bonds **or**

1 double and one triple bond **or**

2 double bonds and one ring **or**

1 triple bond and one ring **or**

1 double bond and two rings **or**

3 rings.

Q-7   A compound has the formula $C_6H_{11}N_3$. Calculate Ω.

A-7 $\Omega = \dfrac{2n+2+3-11}{2} = 3$

Q-8   A compound has the formula C_8H_7ClO. Calculate Ω.

A-8 $\Omega = \dfrac{2n+2-1-7}{2} = \dfrac{16+2-1-7}{2} = 5$

Q-9   Could a compound with the formula $C_{10}H_{17}Cl_3$ be aromatic (contain a benzene ring)? Why?

A-9 $\Omega = \dfrac{2n+2 - 3 - 17}{2} = 1$

No. To be aromatic there must be at least four units of unsaturation. This compound has only one.

Q-10   What is the general formula of a compound containing C, H, N, and X?

A-10 $C_nH_{2n+2+m-x}N_mX_x$

Q-11   Calculate Ω for a compound with the formula $C_6H_{11}N_2Cl$.

A-11 $\Omega = \dfrac{2n+2+2-1-11}{2} = 2$

R $\Omega_{\text{N containing compound}} =$

$\dfrac{2n+2+m-(\text{H atoms in molecule})}{2}$

$\Omega_{\text{halogen containing compound}} =$

$\dfrac{2n+2-x-(\text{H atoms in molecules})}{2}$

S-3   From the NMR spectrum, various types of protons present in a molecule may be distinguished. The areas under the NMR peaks are proportional to the number of protons in a particular chemical environment. The total number of protons in the molecule is a multiple of the *sum* of the simplest ratio of these peak areas. Thus, a molecule whose NMR spectrum yields a **three** protron singlet, a **two** proton quartet, and a **three** proton triplet could have 8, 16, 24 . . . protons.

Possible molecular formulas may be determined if the molecular weight, qualitative elemental analysis, and NMR spectrum are available. This information allows the number of carbon atoms per molecule to be calculated by using the formula

$$\#\text{C atoms per molecule} = \frac{\text{molecular weight} - \text{mass of H in molecule} - \text{mass of other atoms}}{12}$$

Q-12   The NMR spectrum of a molecule shows a multiplet (complex splitting pattern), a singlet, a heptet, and a doublet. The peak area ratios are 4 : 3 : 1 : 6. What are the possible number of hydrogens in the molecule?

A-12   The sum of the ratios is $4 + 3 + 1 + 6 = 14$. The number of hydrogens could be 14, 28, 42 . . .

Q-13   The compound described in Q-12 contained only C and H and had a molecular weight of 133 ± 2. How many carbon atoms per molecule are present? What is the formula of the compound?

A-13 $\#\text{C} = \dfrac{133\pm2-14}{12} = 10$

Formula = $C_{10}H_{14}$

Higher multiples of 14 for the number of hydrogens are not possible, i.e.,

$\#\text{C} = \dfrac{133\pm2-28}{12} = 9 \ (C_9H_{28})$

$C_9H_{28} = C_nH_{2n+10}$ (non-existent)

Q-14   The NMR spectrum of a molecule with a molecular weight of 90 ± 2 showed two singlets with a ratio of 1 : 3. The molecule contained only C,H, and O. What are the possible formulas, assuming **one** oxygen atom per molecule?

A-14 C_6H_4O, $C_5H_{12}O$

Using the possible number of hydrogens per molecule to calculate the number of carbon atoms:

$$\#C = \frac{90\pm2-4-16}{12} = 6 \; (C_6H_4O)$$

$$\#C = \frac{90\pm2-8-16}{12} = \frac{66\pm2}{12} \; \text{(not a whole number)}$$

$$\#C = \frac{90\pm2-12-16}{12} = 5 \; (C_5H_{12}O)$$

$$\#C = \frac{90\pm2-16-16}{12} = 5 \; (C_5H_{16}O \text{ non-existent})$$

All higher multiples of hydrogen will give non-existent formulas.

A-15   Possible number of nitrogen atoms per molecule must be even, i.e., N_2, N_4, N_6 . . . . If a compound contains only C, H, and an odd number of N atoms per molecule, the number of hydrogens will be odd. If the molecule contains an even number of N atoms, the number of hydrogen atoms will be even. The compound in this question can have only an even number of hydrogens (6,12,18 . . .).

A-16   Only possible formula is
$C_3H_6N_2$

$$\#C = \frac{70\pm2-6-28}{12} = 3(C_3H_6N_2)$$

Using other possible multiples for hydrogen will yield only non-existent formulas, i.e.,

$$\#C = \frac{70\pm2-18-28}{12} = 2 \quad (C_2H_{16}N_2 \text{ non-existent})$$

A-17 $C_{11}H_{10}$ and $C_{10}H_{20}$

$$\#C = \frac{140\pm3-10}{12} = 11 \quad (C_{11}H_{10})$$

$$\#C = \frac{140\pm3-20}{12} = 10 \quad (C_{10}H_{20})$$

$$\#C = \frac{140\pm3-30}{12} = 9 \quad (C_9H_{30} \text{ non-existent})$$

Q-15   A molecule contained only C, H and N. The NMR spectrum had three peak areas with ratios of 1 : 2 : 3. How many nitrogen atoms per molecule are possible?

(Hint: Will the number of hydrogens in an N containing compound be odd or even? $C_nH_{2n+2+m}N_m$.)

Q-16   The molecule described in Q-15 had a molecular weight of 70±2. What are possible formulas for the molecule, assuming only two nitrogen atoms per molecule?

Q-17   A hydrocarbon has a molecular weight of 140±3 and has two sets of NMR peaks with proton ratios of 3 : 7. What are the possible formulas for the compound?

Q-18   The NMR, IR, and UV spectra for the compound described in Q-17 indicated the presence of an aromatic system. What is the formula of the compound? Give your reasoning.

A-18 $C_{11}H_{10}$

The simplest aromatic system has the general formula C_nH_{2n-6} (three double bonds and a ring). A compound with the formula $C_{10}H_{20}(C_nH_{2n})$ cannot be aromatic. A compound with the formula $C_{11}H_{10}$ (C_nH_{2n-12}) could be aromatic. (It would contain other units of unsaturation in addition to one aromatic ring.)

Q-19   A compound has a molecular weight of 110 ± 3 and does not contain halogen, N or S. The NMR spectrum has two sets of peaks with area ratios of 5 : 3. What are the possible formulas for the compound? (Hint: oxygen *may* be present.)

A-19 C_8H_{16}, C_7H_8O, $C_6H_8O_2$ and $C_3H_8O_4$.

Formulas with no O present:

$$\#C = \frac{110\pm3-8}{12} = \frac{102\pm3}{12} \quad \text{(not a whole number)}$$

$$\#C = \frac{110\pm3-16}{12} = 8 \quad (C_8H_{16})$$

$$\#C = \frac{110\pm3-24}{12} = 7 \; (C_7H_{24} \text{ non-existent})$$

Formula with one O present:

$$\#C = \frac{110\pm3-8-16}{12} = 7 \; (C_7H_8O)$$

Formula with two O present:

$$\#C = \frac{110\pm3-8-32}{12} = 6 \; (C_6H_8O_2)$$

Formula with four O present:

$$\#C = \frac{110\pm3-8-64}{12} = 3 \; (C_3H_8O_4)$$

Q-20   The NMR, IR and UV spectra of the compound described in Q-19 indicate an aromatic system (benzenoid or furanoid). What are the possible formulas for the compound?

A-20 C_7H_8O and $C_6H_8O_2$. If a benzene ring is present, Ω must be 4 or larger. If a furan ring is present, Ω must be 3 or larger.

C_8H_{16} $\Omega = 1$

$C_3H_8O_4$ $\Omega = 0$

R   The total number of protons in a molecule is a whole number multiple of the sum of the simplest ratio of NMR peak areas. The number of carbons in a molecule may be calculated from the formula: $\#C$ = (molecular weight – mass of hydrogen – mass of other atoms)/12.

S-4   The NMR, UV, and IR spectra of a compound yield data which allows identification of *structural units* within the molecule (i.e., a carbonyl group, an ethyl group, a *p*-disubstituted benzene ring, etc.). After the identification of these units, two problems still remain: a) the determination of structural units not identified from spectral data, and b) the possible sequences in which the structural units may be attached.

To help determine **residual** structural units not identified from spectral data, the formulas (or formula weights) of all the *unique* known structural units are subtracted from the formula (or molecular weight) of the compound. The number of sites of unsaturation can also be determined for the **residual** units. The **residual** formula (or formula weight) may also give some indication as to the structure(s) possible for the unknown unit(s). Chemical intuition and other data about the compound, such as odor, mp, or origin may be very helpful in elucidating the possible structures for the **residual** units.

Q-21   The IR spectrum of a compound, $C_9H_{10}O$, indicated the following structural units:

a carbonyl group and

a p-disubstituted benzene ring.

Are all units of unsaturation in the molecule accounted for by the two known structural units? What is the formula of the **residual** unit(s)? What are possible structures for the **residual** unit(s)?

A-21 $\Omega = 5$

The carbonyl and benzene ring account for all 5 units of unsaturation.

	Ω
$C_9H_{10}O$	5
$-C_6H_4$ (aromatic ring)	-4
$-C$ O (carbonyl)	-1
C_2H_6 (residual unit)	0

Residual group(s) can have no units of unsaturation and must be two CH_3 groups.

Q-22   The IR spectrum of a compound, $C_{11}H_{14}O_2$, indicated the following structural units:

a carbonyl group,

a hydroxyl group, and

a monosubstituted benzene ring.

Are all units of unsaturation in the molecule accounted for by the three known structural units? What is the formula of the **residual** structural unit(s)? What are some possible structures for the **residual** unit(s)?

A-22 $\Omega = 5$

The carbonyl and benzene ring account for all 5 units of unsaturation.

	Ω
$C_{11}H_{14}O_2$	5
$-C_6H_5$ (aromatic ring)	-4
$-C$ O (carbonyl)	-1
$-$ H O (hydroxyl)	0
C_4H_8 (residual formula)	0

Possible structures are

$-CH_2(CH_2)_2CH_2-;-CH_2-CH_3,-CH_3$ and

$-\overset{|}{\underset{|}{C}}-;CH_{\overline{3}},-CH_2-CH_{\overline{2}}$, and $-\overset{|}{C}-H$; etc.

Q-23   The IR spectrum of a compound with a molecular weight of 159 ± 3 indicated the following structural units:

a carbon-carbon double bond,

a carboxylic acid group, and

a monosubstituted benzene ring.

What is the formula weight of the **residual** unit(s)? What are some possible structures for the **residual** unit(s)?

A-23 159 ± 3

-45	(COOH)
-77	(C_6H_5)
-24	(C=C)
13 ± 3	(formula weight of residual units)

Possible structures:

$-\overset{|}{\underset{|}{C}}-, -\overset{|}{C}-H, -CH_2-, CH_3-, -O-, \overset{|}{N}-$

(NH and OH would be detected by IR)

Q-24   The NMR spectrum of a compound, $C_8H_6O_3$, had an aldehyde peak, a multiple in the aromatic proton region, and a singlet in the $4.0\ \tau$ region. The ratio of peak areas was $1 : 3 : 2$, respectively. What is the formula of the **residual** unit(s)? (Hint: The aromatic protons could be due to a benzene or furan ring.)

A-24   If the compound contains a benzene ring, the **residual** is O_2 and must contain one unit of unsaturation.

		Ω
$C_8H_6O_3$		6
$- C_6H_3$	(benzene)	-4
$- C\ H\ O$	(aldehyde)	-1
$- C\ H_2$	(4.0 τ singlet)	0
O_2	(residual unit)	1

If the compound contains a furan ring, the residual unit is C_2O with two sites of unsaturation.

		Ω
$C_8H_6O_3$		6
$- C_4H_3O$	(furan ring)	-3
$- C\ H\ O$	(aldehyde)	-1
$- C\ H_2$	(4.0 τ singlet)	0
C_2O	(residual unit)	2

A-25   If the compound contained a benzene ring the **residual** unit would be $- O -$ with no units of unsaturation.

		Ω
$C_8H_8O_3$		5
$- C_6H_3$	(benzene)	-4
$- C\ H\ O$	(aldehyde)	-1
$-\ \ H\ O$	(hydroxyl)	0
$- C\ H_3$	(6 τ singlet)	0
$- O -$	(residual unit)	0

If the compound contained a furan ring, the **residual** unit would be $- C_2 -$ and must have one unit of unsaturation.

		Ω
$C_8H_8O_3$		5
$-C_4H_3O$	(furan)	-3
$-C\ H\ O$	(aldehyde)	-1
$-\ \ H\ O$	(hydroxyl)	0
$-C\ H_3$	(6 τ singlet)	0
$-C_2-$	(esidual unit)	1

Q-25   The NMR spectrum of a compound $C_8H_8O_3$ had an aldehyde peak, a multiple in the aromatic proton region, a broad OH peak and a singlet in the 6 τ region. The ratio of peak areas was $1 : 3 : 1 : 3$, respectively. What is the formula of the **residual** unit(s)?

R   The formula (or formula weight) of the **residual** structural units may be found by subtracting the formula (or formula weight) of all known, *unique* structural units from the formula (or molecular weight) of the compound.

S-5   The preceding sections have demonstrated how functional groups and **residual** units in an unknown compound could be determined from spectral data and a knowledge of the units of unsaturation in the molecule. A more detailed consideration of spectral data yields information about the *neighbors* of the various structural units. Thus, larger structural units may be envisioned and the correct sequence of these units in the molecule may be determined.

Q-26   A portion of the NMR spectrum of a molecule is given below. From the splitting pattern and the position of the peaks, what can be determined about the structure and electronegativity of the neighbors of the protons yielding the absorption?

2 protons

6.5 τ

A-26   The two equivalent protons giving the absorption must have three equivalent neighboring protons and at least one neighbor more electronegative than carbon to cause absorption at such a low τ (i.e., $-CH_2-O$ or $-CH_2-N$).

Q-27   The splitting pattern of a portion of the NMR spectrum for a molecule is given below. The *a* and *b* protons are coupled. Give the structural unit for the *a* protons and the *b* protons separately and then combine them into a single unit. (Hint: The *b* proton is also coupled "long range".)

2 protons
(*b*)

3 protons
(*a*)

8.0 τ 8.5 τ

A-27   (a) protons (two near neighbors)

$$CH_3 \underset{(a)}{-} \overset{\displaystyle H}{\underset{\displaystyle H}{C}} -$$

(b) protons (three near neighbors with long-range splitting by one proton)

$$H-C \overset{\displaystyle R}{\underset{\displaystyle R'}{\diagdown}} C - \underset{(b)}{CH_2} - CH_3$$

or   (R and R' ≠ H)

$$R' - C \overset{\displaystyle R}{\underset{\displaystyle H}{\diagdown}} C - \underset{(b)}{CH_2} - CH_3$$

Combined:

$$H-C \overset{\displaystyle R}{\underset{\displaystyle R'}{\diagdown}} C - \underset{(b)}{CH_2} - \underset{(a)}{CH_3}$$

or

$$R' - C \overset{\displaystyle R}{\underset{\displaystyle H}{\diagdown}} C - \underset{(b)}{CH_2} - \underset{(a)}{CH_3}$$

Q-28   The NMR spectrum of the compound, $C_5H_{10}O_2$, is given below.

What protons are splitting the c proton?

Describe the neighbors of the c proton.

Peak area ratio
1   :   3   :   6

J_{ac} = 4 Hz

5.8 τ   7.9 τ   8.8 τ
(c)   (b)   (a)

A-28   The c proton is being split by the a protons. The c proton must have six equivalent neighbors $(CH_3)_2 \overset{|}{C}-H_{(c)}$. The carbon bearing the c proton must be attached to an atom more electronegative than carbon (i.e., $(CH_3)_2 \underset{\displaystyle H_{(c)}}{\overset{\displaystyle |}{C}} - O -$).

Q-29   Describe the neighbors of the a and b protons for the compound given in Q-28.

A-29   The chemical shift of the b protons indicates a CH_3- group attached to a C = C or C = O group.

The a protons are identical and have one neighbor.

$$\underset{(a)}{CH_3} - \overset{\displaystyle |}{\underset{\displaystyle CH_{3(a)}}{C}} - H$$

Q-30   How many sites of unsaturation are there in the compound described in Q-28? What is the **residual** group(s)?

A-30 $\Omega = 1$

Residual group is oxygen and has one unit of unsaturation.

Q-31 A compound with the formula $C_{10}H_{16}O$ showed a **one** proton multiplet at $4.1\ \tau$, a **three** proton doublet (with very small J) at $8.1\ \tau$, a six proton doublet at $9.2\ \tau$ and a **six** proton "haystack" at $7.2 - 8.0\ \tau$. The UV and IR spectra along with the NMR data given above suggested the following structural units.

$$-\overset{O}{\overset{\|}{C}} - \overset{H}{\overset{|}{C}} = C \diagup \quad \text{or} \quad -\overset{O}{\overset{\|}{C}} - C = C \overset{H}{\diagdown} \quad \text{(acyclic}$$

or six membered ring); $(CH_3)_2 - \overset{|}{C}H$;

$CH_3 - \overset{|}{C} = CH-.$

Which structural units may be combined? Why?

A-31 From the NMR data, only one ethylenic proton can be present in the molecule (peak at $4.1\ \tau$). Therefore, the units,

$$\diagup\overset{O}{\overset{\|}{C}} - \overset{|}{\underset{H}{C}} = C\diagup \quad \text{or} \quad \overset{O}{\overset{\|}{C}} - C = C \overset{H}{\diagdown} \quad \text{and} \quad CH_3\overset{|}{C} = CH-$$

must have some atoms in common and must be combined to give

$$\diagup\overset{O}{\overset{\|}{C}} - \overset{H}{\overset{|}{C}} = C - CH_3 \quad \text{or} \quad \overset{O}{\overset{\|}{C}} - \overset{H}{\overset{|}{C}} = \overset{|}{C} - CH_3$$

Q-32 Determine the **residual** unit for the molecule described in Q-31. What are possible structures for the **residual** unit(s)?

A-32 **Residual** formula: C_3H_5 with one site of unsaturation.

	Ω
$C_{10}H_{16}O$	3
$-C_4\ H_4\ O\ (-\overset{O}{\overset{\|}{C}}-\overset{|}{CH}=CCH_3)$	-2
$\underline{-C_3\ H_7\quad ((CH_3)_2\,\overset{|}{C}H)\ (9.2\ \tau\ \text{doublet})}$	$\underline{0}$
$C_3\ H_5$	1

Because there is only one ethylenic proton,

the **residual** must be $-CH_2-\overset{H}{\overset{|}{C}}-CH_2-$ or

$-CH_2-CH_2-\overset{|}{CH}$ or $-\overset{|}{CH} - CH_2 -$ and $-\overset{|}{CH}$,

etc., and be part of a saturated ring structure

$(-\overset{H}{\overset{|}{\underset{|}{\underset{H}{C}}}}-\overset{|}{C}-CH_3$ is not probable because of the

lack of a three proton triplet in the NMR).

Q-33 A compound, with the formula $C_{10}H_{14}O$, gave the following NMR spectra.

Peak area ratios:

Other spectral evidence indicated the following features:

$$\overset{H}{\underset{R}{\diagdown}}C=\overset{R}{\overset{|}{C}}-\overset{O}{\overset{\|}{C}}-\quad \text{(acyclic or six membered ring)}$$

and a terminal double bond, $\diagup C=CH_2$. Give structural units and some possible **residual** units.

A-33

or

or

or

Reasoning: Only three ethylenic protons are present in the molecule. At least one of the CH_3 groups (and perhaps both CH_3 groups giving the 6 proton peak at 8.2 τ) must have long-range splitting.

Residual unit: C_3H_5 with one unit of unsaturation. Because none of the hydrogens of the residual unit can be ethylenic, the unsaturation unit must be a ring. Residue could be $-CH_2-CH-CH_2-$, $-CH_2-CH-$ and $-CH_2-$, etc.

R   Detailed analysis of spectra may yield information about neighbors of structural units, allowing larger, more complex structural units to be constructed.

S-6   When constructing structural formulas from structural units, **polyvalent** units are combined first in all possible ways, then **monovalent** groups are attached in all possible ways. Finally, the various possible structures are checked to see if they are consistent with all known information about the compound. An example of the reasoning used in combining structural units follows.

Structural Units: $-C\equiv N$; $-\overset{\overset{\displaystyle O}{\|}}{C}-$; CH_3-ns; $-O-$; $ns'-CH_2-CH_2-ns''$ (ns = non-splitting group)

Step One: Combine polyvalent units in all possible ways.

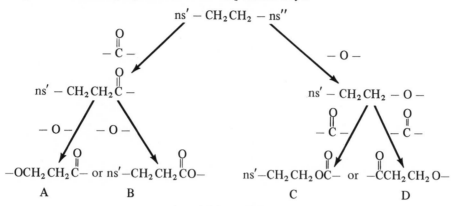

A and D are identical.

Step Two: Combine the units resulting from step one in all possible ways with monovalent units.

A $\xrightarrow[-CN]{CH_3-}$ $CH_3OCH_2CH_2\overset{\overset{\displaystyle O}{\|}}{C}CN$ or $N\equiv COCH_2CH_2\overset{\overset{\displaystyle O}{\|}}{C}OCH_3$
$\qquad\qquad\qquad\qquad\quad A_1 \qquad\qquad\qquad\qquad A_2$

B $\xrightarrow[-CN]{CH_3-}$ $N\equiv C\ CH_2CH_2\overset{\overset{\displaystyle O}{\|}}{C}-OCH_3$ (note that only $-CN$ is a non-splitting group)
$\qquad\qquad\qquad\qquad\qquad B_1$

C $\xrightarrow[-CN]{CH_3-}$ $N\equiv C\ CH_2CH_2O\overset{\overset{\displaystyle O}{\|}}{C}CH_3$
$\qquad\qquad\qquad\qquad\qquad C_1$

Step Three: Check possible structures with other data. In the preceding case, the compound yielded acetic acid on hydrolysis. The structure C_1 is the only structure consistent with this piece of evidence.

Q-34   A compound with the formula $C_{12}H_{14}O_2$ had the following structural units:

CH_3O-; CH_3-CH_2-ns; C_6H_5-;

$\overset{\displaystyle}{C}=O$; $\overset{\displaystyle}{C}=C\overset{\diagup H}{\diagdown}$.

Give the possible structures for the compound.

A-34

$$C_6H_5, \quad \overset{O}{\overset{\parallel}{C}} - CH_2CH_3$$
$$C = C$$
$$H \qquad CH_3$$

$$CH_3O \qquad \overset{O}{\overset{\parallel}{C}} - CH_2CH_3$$
$$C = C$$
$$H \qquad C_6H_5$$

$$C_6H_5 \qquad \overset{O}{\overset{\parallel}{C}} - CH_2CH_3$$
$$C = C$$
$$CH_3O \qquad H$$

$$CH_3O \qquad \overset{O}{\overset{\parallel}{C}} - CH_2\ CH_3$$
$$C = C$$
$$C_6H_5 \qquad H \qquad\qquad , etc.$$

Reasoning process:

$$\overset{}{C} = C \overset{H}{\diagdown} \quad + \quad \overset{O}{\overset{\parallel}{C}}$$

$$\overset{}{C} = C \overset{H}{\underset{C=O}{\diagdown}} \quad or \quad \overset{}{C} = C \overset{H}{\underset{-C \overset{O}{\diagdown}}{\diagup}}$$

$$\overset{}{C} = C \overset{H}{\underset{\underset{C_2H_5}{C=O}}{\diagdown}} \quad \cdot \quad \overset{}{C} = C \overset{H}{\underset{\underset{C_2H_5}{C=O}}{\diagup}}$$

(no long-range splitting of ethyl group)

Further possible combinations of phenyl and methoxyl give structures above.

Q-35   A compound, with the formula $C_6H_{12}O_2$, had the following structural units:

CH_3—ns (three identical); CH_3—ns;

$\overset{}{\underset{}{C}} = O$; residual CO with no units of unsaturation. Give all the possible structures.

A-35

$$(CH_3)_3 \ C-\overset{\overset{\displaystyle O}{\|}}{C}-O-CH_3$$

$$(CH_3)_3 \ C-O-\overset{\overset{\displaystyle O}{\|}}{C}-CH_3$$

Reasoning process:

Residual unit(s) could be

$-\overset{|}{\underset{|}{C}}-$ and $-O-$ or $-\overset{|}{\underset{|}{C}}-O-$

Combine the multivalent groups:

$$-\overset{\overset{\displaystyle O}{\|}}{\underset{|}{C}}-\overset{|}{\underset{|}{C}}-O- \quad -\overset{|}{\underset{|}{C}}-O-\overset{\overset{\displaystyle O}{\|}}{C}- \quad -O-\overset{\overset{\displaystyle O}{\|}}{C}-\overset{|}{\underset{|}{C}}- \quad -\overset{\overset{\displaystyle O}{\|}}{C}-\overset{|}{\underset{|}{C}}-O-$$

A   or   B   or   C   or   D

A and D are identical

Combine with monovalent groups:

A $\xrightarrow[\text{CH}_3-]{3 \ \text{CH}_3-}$ Cannot have three equivalent methyl groups.

B $\xrightarrow[\text{CH}_3-]{3 \ \text{CH}_3-}$ $(CH_3)_3 \ CO\overset{\overset{\displaystyle O}{\|}}{C}CH_3$

C $\xrightarrow[\text{CH}_3-]{3 \ \text{CH}_3-}$ $CH_3 \ O\overset{\overset{\displaystyle O}{\|}}{C}C \ (CH_3)_3$

Q-36   A compound, with the formula $C_{10}H_{13}NO$, had the following structural units:

$$CH_3CH_2- \ ; \ -NH; \ -\overset{\overset{\displaystyle O}{\|}}{C}-N\overset{\diagup}{\diagdown} ; \ CH_3-ns;$$

$p-C_6H_4\overset{\diagup}{\diagdown}$; no **residual** unit.

Hydrolysis of the substance yielded a base soluble, acid insoluble material with a mp of 179-180°. Give all possible structures indicated by the spectral data. Give the structure indicated by spectral and chemical data.

A-36   From spectral data alone, the following structures are indicated:

$CH_3C_6H_4CONHC_2H_5$ A

$C_2H_5C_6H_4CONHCH_3$ B

$CH_3CONHC_6H_4C_2H_5$ C

$C_2H_5CONHC_6H_4CH_3$ D

From spectral and chemical data, the only structure possible is A.

Reasoning process:

multivalent groups combined first

(only one N atom per molecule)

Further combinations of methyl and ethyl give compounds A–D. On hydrolysis, the substance yielded an acid with a mp of 179-180°. Only A & B would yield solid acids. p-Toluic acid melts at 179°. p-Ethyl benzoic acid melts at 112°.

Q-37   A compound, with the formula C_8H_8O, had the following structural units: C_6H_5-;

residual unit O with one site of unsaturation. Give all the possible structures. (No aldehydic proton was observed.)

A-37

Reasoning process:

$$ns-\overset{H'}{\underset{ns}{C}}-\overset{H}{\underset{ns}{C}}-\overset{H''}{\underset{ns}{C}}-ns \text{ is not a possible unit (too}$$

many carbons).

$$ns-\overset{H'}{\underset{ns}{C}}-\overset{H}{\underset{ns}{C}}-H''$$

$\downarrow -O-$

$$ns-\overset{H}{\underset{ns}{C}}-\overset{H'}{\underset{O}{C}}-H'' \text{ or } ns-\overset{H}{\underset{O}{C}}-\overset{H'}{\underset{ns}{C}}-H''$$

$\downarrow C_6H_5$

(H′ and H″ are not identical because C_6H_5- is *cis* to H″ and *trans* to H′.)

Q-38

A compound, with the formula $C_4H_6Cl_2O_2$, had the following structural units:

$$Cl-; \quad Cl-; \quad -\overset{O}{\overset{\|}{C}}-; \quad CH_3CH_2-O-; \quad H-\overset{ns}{\underset{ns}{C}}-ns$$

Give possible structures.

A-38

$$CH_3CH_2O\overset{O}{\overset{\|}{C}}-\overset{H}{\underset{Cl}{C}}-Cl \text{ or } CH_3CH_2O\overset{H}{\underset{Cl}{C}}-\overset{O}{\overset{\|}{C}}-Cl$$

Reasoning process:

$$H-\overset{|}{C}-$$

$\downarrow$

$$-\overset{O}{\overset{\|}{C}}-$$

$$H-\overset{|}{\underset{|}{C}}-\overset{O}{\overset{\|}{C}}-$$

$\downarrow 2Cl-, CH_3CH_2O-$

$$H-\overset{Cl}{\underset{Cl}{C}}-\overset{O}{\overset{\|}{C}}-O-C_2H_5 \text{ or}$$

$$H-\overset{Cl}{\underset{OC_2H_5}{C}}-\overset{O}{\overset{\|}{C}}-Cl$$

Q-39

A compound, with the formula $C_9H_{10}N_4O_4$, had the following structural units: $-NO_2$; CH_3-ns (attached to double bond carbon); CH_3-ns (attached to double bond carbon); $\overset{\diagdown}{C}=N; \overset{\diagup}{N}-H$; 1, 2, 4- trisubstituted C_6H_3; residual unit NO_2 with one site of unsaturation. Give some possible structures.

A-39

NO₂ NO₂ ... $N-N=C$ with CH₃, CH₃

NO₂ CH₃ ... $N-N=C$ with NO₂, CH₃

NO₂ ... $N=C$ NO₂, CH₃ ... N–CH₃   **and other combinations.**

Reasoning process:

The residue is most likely $-NO_2$, but could also be $-N=O$, and $-O-$, etc. Combining the multivalent units in all possible ways gives many structural units. Some are

or   or $C=N$ etc.

$N-N=C$ $N=C$ with H–N–

or   or

$N=C$ / $N-H$ $N-H$ / $N=C$

etc.   etc.

Q-40   A compound, with the formula $C_{10}H_{14}O$, had the following structural units:

$$R-\overset{O}{\underset{}{C}}-C(CH_3)=C\overset{H}{\underset{R}{}}$$ (acyclic or six membered ring);

$CH_2=CCH_3\,R$; C_3H_5 with one site of unsaturation. Give some possible structures for the compound. Only three ethylenic protons were indicated in the NMR spectrum.

A-40

Using the residual unit $-CH_2\overset{|}{C}HCH_2-$ as part of a ring structure the following analysis results:

$-CH_2CHCH_2- \rightarrow -CH_2CHCH_2-\overset{O}{C}-\overset{CH_3}{C}=C\overset{H}{}$

Using the residual unit $>CHCH_2CH_2-$, and a similar analysis to that shown above yields the other two structures.

WAVELENGTH IN MICRONS

Beckman IR-4
liquid sample
thin layer

% Transmittance

WAVENUMBER IN CM⁻¹

% Transmittance

millimicrons

Beckman DB

Varian A-60A

SOLVENT			
TEMPERATURE		°C	
FILTER BANDWIDTH		Hz	
R.F. FIELD		mG	
SWEEP TIME		sec	
SWEEP WIDTH		Hz	
SWEEP OFFSET		Hz	
SPECTRUM AMP.			
INTEGRAL AMP.			
REMARKS:			

Q-41   On this page are the spectra of a compound which contains C, H, and Cl and has a molecular weight of 125±3.
What structural units are indicated?
What is the formula of the residual unit(s)?
What structures are possible?

(Hint: The ratio of the area under the NMR peaks is 4.4:1.7 or 2.6:1 or 5:2.)

←1.7 cm→

←——4.4 cm——→

PPM (δ)

A-41   **Structural Units:**
Cl$-$; C_6H_5-; ns$-CH_2-$ns
Residual units: none.
Possible formula
$C_6H_5CH_2Cl$.

Chapter 6 | PRACTICE PROBLEMS

This chapter contains the IR, UV, NMR spectra and the elemental analysis, molecular weight, or molecular formula of 31 organic compounds. Other chemical data may also be included.

Determine a structure consistent with the data given for each compound.

After the first few problems the answer and a detailed analysis of the data are given. For the latter questions, the answers are given on page 236. The time required to solve successfully each of these problems will vary. Some will require as little as five minutes while others may require thirty or more minutes of diligent work. Do not give up on a problem too soon. It is not necessary to attempt the problems in the order presented.

While each individual is likely to develop his own unique method of determining molecular structure by the interpretation of spectral data, the following step-wise approach is used by many chemists.

Step 1: A cursory examination of all the data to note the presence or absence of various structural features such as, OH, C=O, aromatic protons, sites of unsaturation, etc.

Step 2: A detailed examination of the spectra to determine the kinds of structural features present. (The NMR spectrum is perhaps the best to start with since it allows not only the determination of structural fragments but also the calculation of possible molecular formulas if one is not available.)

Step 3: Prepare a list of all the structural fragments and molecular formulas determined. Elimination or combination of structural fragments by the restrictions of the molecular formula or, conversely, elimination of possible molecular formulas through the requirements of the structural fragments may be possible.

Step 4: Determine the residual formula and then combine fragments in all possible ways.

Step 5: Examine the possible structures derived in Step 4 to see if any can be eliminated on the basis of other data that might be available.

% Transmittance

millimicrons

Beckman DB

WAVENUMBER CM⁻¹

Beckman
Microspec

liquid sample
thin layer

WAVELENGTH IN MICRONS

% Transmittance

Problem 1:

The compound does not contain halogen,
nitrogen, nor sulfur. Its molecular weight
was found to be 108 ± 2.

Varian A-60A

SOLVENT				°C
TEMPERATURE				cps
FILTER BANDWIDTH				mG
R.F. FIELD				sec
SWEEP TIME				cps
SWEEP WIDTH				cps
SWEEP OFFSET				
SPECTRUM AMP.				
INTEGRAL AMP.				
REMARKS:				

PPM (δ)

Answer Problem 1: Spectra are of $C_6H_5CH_2OH$.

Step 1: *Cursory Examination of the Data:*

The UV spectrum indicates that a conjugated system is present. The IR spectrum indicates the presence of OH, absence of C=O, and the presence of an aromatic system. The NMR spectrum indicates the presence of aromatic protons (7.1 δ) and protons attached to carbons carrying a strong electron withdrawing group(s) (4.3 δ).

Step 2: *Detailed Analysis of Data:*

NMR Spectrum

POSITION	MULTIPLICITY	INTEGRATION CURVE HEIGHT	RATIO	SMALLEST WHOLE NUMBER RATIO
7.1 δ	Singlet	9.2 cm	5.1	5
5.1 δ	Singlet	1.8 cm	1	1
4.3 δ	Singlet	3.7 cm	2.1	2

The compound contains eight or some multiple of eight hydrogens and may contain oxygen. The IR indicates OH(3400 cm^{-1} band). Calculations of molecular formulas assuming one or more oxygens and multiples of eight hydrogens yield the following:

$$\#C = \frac{108 \pm 2 - 16 - 8}{12} = 7.2 - 6.8 \quad C_7H_8O$$

$$\#C = \frac{108 \pm 2 - 16 - 16}{12} = 6.5 - 6.2 \quad \text{Does not yield a whole number.}$$

$$\#C = \frac{108 \pm 2 - 16 - 24}{12} = 5.8 - 5.5 \quad \text{Does not yield a whole number.}$$

Other multiples of eight hydrogens and one oxygen produce nonexistent formulas.

$$\#C = \frac{108 \pm 2 - 32 - 8}{12} = 5.8 - 5.5 \quad \text{Does not yield a whole number.}$$

$$\#C = \frac{108 \pm 2 - 32 - 16}{12} = 5.2 - 4.8 \quad C_5H_{16}O_2 \text{ nonexistent } (C_nH_{2n+6})$$

$$\#C = \frac{108 \pm 2 - 48 - 8}{12} = 3.7 - 3.3 \quad \text{Does not yield a whole number.}$$

$$\#C = \frac{108 \pm 2 - 48 - 16}{12} = 3.0 - 2.7 \quad C_3H_{16}O_3 \text{ nonexistent } (C_nH_{2n+10})$$

$$\#C = \frac{108 \pm 2 - 64 - 8}{12} = 3.2 - 2.8 \quad C_3H_8O_4$$

$$\#C = \frac{108 \pm 2 - 80 - 8}{12} = 1.8 - 1.5 \quad \text{Does not yield a whole number.}$$

Other multiples of eight hydrogens and more than five oxygens produce nonexistent formulas. The formula of the compound must be C_7H_8O or $C_3H_8O_4$.

Analysis of the 7.1 δ singlet:

The position of the singlet is strongly suggestive of aromatic protons. A five proton singlet is suggestive of a monosubstituted ring with an aliphatic carbon attached to the ring; i.e.

Analysis of the 5.1 δ singlet:

The OH proton would account for this peak.

Analysis of the 4.3 δ singlet:

A two proton singlet is indicative of $ns-\overset{}{C}-ns$. The position of the peak indicates that one of the ns groups attached must be a strong electron withdrawing group; i.e., $ns-C-O-$.

UV Spectrum

The absorption substantiates the presence of an aromatic ring and eliminates $C_3H_8O_4$ (no sites of unsaturation) as a possible formula.

IR Spectrum

Absorption at 3400 cm^{-1} indicates OH and strong absorptions in the 1600 cm^{-1} region further confirms an aromatic ring.

Step 3: *List of Structural Fragments:*

The fragments found were:

$$ns-\overset{H}{\underset{H}{C}}-O- , \quad -OH, \quad$$

Since the formula is C_7H_8O, the oxygen atoms of the fragments must be common, $ns-CH_2-OH$.

Step 4: *Residual Formula and Combination of Fragments*

The fragments $ns-CH_2OH$ and account for all atoms in the formula C_7H_8O. The compound must be $-CH_2OH$.

WAVELENGTH IN MICRONS

WAVENUMBER IN CM⁻¹

% Transmittance

% Transmittance

millimicrons

Beckman DB

Beckman IR-4

liquid sample
thin layer

Varian A-60A

SOLVENT	CCl₄	
TEMPERATURE	40	°C
FILTER BANDWIDTH	4	cps
R.F. FIELD	.02	mG
SWEEP TIME	250	sec
SWEEP WIDTH	500	cps
SWEEP OFFSET	0	cps
SPECTRUM AMP.	1.0	cps
INTEGRAL AMP.	25	
REMARKS:		

Problem 2:
The compound did not contain halogen,
nitrogen, nor sulfur, and had a molecular
weight of 105 ± 2.

Answer Problem 2: Spectra are of *p*-xylene.

Step 1: *Cursory Examination of the Data:*

The UV spectrum indicates a conjugated system. The IR spectrum indicates the lack of OH and C=O and the presence of an aromatic system. The NMR spectrum indicates the presence of aromatic protons and aliphatic protons with non-splitting groups attached.

Step 2: *Detailed Analysis of the Data:*

NMR Spectrum

POSITION	MULTIPLICITY	INTEGRATION CURVE HEIGHT	RATIO	SMALLEST WHOLE NUMBER RATIO
7.0 δ	Singlet	6.8 cm	1	2
2.2 δ	Singlet	10.4 cm	1.5	3

Because the compound does not contain halogen or nitrogen, the number of hydrogens must be even. Thus, the hydrogens in the molecule must be a multiple of 10. Calculations of molecular formulas assuming the absence or presence of oxygen (although the IR gives no evidence that oxygen is present) and multiples of ten hydrogens yield the following:

$$\#C = \frac{105 \pm 2 - 10}{12} = 8.1 - 7.8 \quad C_8H_{10}$$

$$\#C = \frac{105 \pm 2 - 20}{12} = 7.3 - 6.9 \quad C_7H_{20} \text{ nonexistent } (C_nH_{2n+6})$$

$$\#C = \frac{105 \pm 2 - 16 - 10}{12} = 6.8 - 6.4 \quad \text{Does not yield a whole number.}$$

$$\#C = \frac{105 \pm 2 - 16 - 20}{12} = 5.9 - 5.6 \quad C_6H_{20}O \text{ nonexistent } (C_nH_{2n+8})$$

$$\#C = \frac{105 \pm 2 - 32 - 10}{12} = 5.4 - 5.1 \quad C_5H_{10}O_2$$

$$\#C = \frac{105 \pm 2 - 32 - 20}{12} = 4.6 - 4.3 \quad \text{Does not yield a whole number.}$$

$$\#C = \frac{105 \pm 2 - 48 - 10}{12} = 4.1 - 3.8 \quad C_4H_{10}O_4$$

All other combinations of oxygen and multiples of ten hydrogens give nonexistent formulas.

The formula of the compound must be one of the following:

C_8H_{10}
$C_5H_{10}O_2$
$C_4H_{10}O_4$

Analysis of the 7.0 δ Singlet:

The position of the peak is indicative of aromatic protons. The number of protons (4) is indicative of a disubstituted ring. The singlet nature of the peak is indicative of a symmetrical *para* substitution (substituents identical).

Analysis of the 2.2 δ Singlet:

The six proton singlet is indicative of $(ns - CH_3)_2$ or $(ns - CH_2 - ns)_3$

UV Spectrum

Absorption indicates a conjugated system thus eliminating the formula $C_4H_{10}O_4 (\Omega = 0)$. The UV spectrum supports the NMR evidence that an aromatic ring is present.

IR Spectrum

The absorption bands at 1520 and 800 cm^{-1} are further indications that an aromatic ring is present. The substantial evidence that an aromatic ring is present in the molecule (UV, IR, NMR) excludes $C_5H_{10}O_2$ as a possible formula.

Step 3: *List of Structural Fragments:*

The fragments identified are:

and $(ns - CH_3)_2$ or $(ns-CH_2-ns)_3$

Step 4: *Residual Formula and Combination of Fragments*

Because the formula of the compound is C_8H_{10}, the fragments must be and $(ns-CH_3)_2$.

The compound must be $CH_3$$CH_3$.

WAVELENGTH IN MICRONS

% Transmittance

Beckman IR-4

liquid sample
thin layer

WAVENUMBER IN CM⁻¹

millimicrons

Beckman DB

% Transmittance

Varian A-60A

SOLVENT
TEMPERATURE   °C
FILTER BANDWIDTH   cps
R.F. FIELD   mG
SWEEP TIME   sec
SWEEP WIDTH   cps
SWEEP OFFSET   cps
SPECTRUM AMP.
INTEGRAL AMP.
REMARKS:

Problem 3:
C₆H₁₀O₃

Answer Problem 3: Spectra are of $CH_3COCH_2COOC_2H_5$.

Step 1: *Cursory Examination of the Data:*

The formula indicates two sites of unsaturation. The UV spectrum indicates conjugation. The IR spectrum indicates the absence of OH but the presence of two different carbonyl groups. The NMR indicates the possible presence of an ethoxyl group (quartet at 4.1 δ and triplet at 1.2 δ with identical coupling constants).

Step 2: *Detailed Analysis of the Data:*

NMR Spectrum:

POSITION	MULTIPLICITY	INTEGRATION CURVE HEIGHT	NUMBER OF PROTONS
4.1 δ	Quartet	4.0 cm	2
3.5 δ	Singlet	3.5 cm	2
2.2 δ	Singlet	5.4 cm	3
1.2 δ	Triplet	5.9 cm	3

18.8 cm/10 protons = 1.9 cm/proton

Analysis of the 4.1 δ Quartet:

The multiplicity and area under the peaks indicate $-CH_2-CH_3$. The position of the quartet indicates $-O-CH_2CH_3$.

Analysis of the 3.5 δ Singlet:

The multiplicity and area indicate ns $- CH_2 -$ ns.

The position indicates that electron withdrawing groups are attached to the carbon, but the electron withdrawing groups must not be oxygen (oxygen would shift absorption further downfield).

Analysis of the 2.2 δ Singlet:

The multiplicity and area indicate $CH_3 -$ ns. The position indicates a weak electron withdrawing group attached to the methyl. The position is appropriate for

$$CH_3\overset{\overset{\text{O}}{\|}}{C}-$$

Analysis of the 1.2 δ Triplet:

The multiplicity, area and position are indicative of $\underline{CH_3}CH_2 - $.

The *J* value is identical to that of the 4.1 δ quartet, thus, these two groups must be coupled. The fragment present must be CH_3CH_2O-.

UV Spectrum:

A conjugated system is indicated.

IR Spectrum:

The bands at 1720 and 1750 cm^{-1} indicate $-\overset{\overset{\text{O}}{\|}}{C}-$ and $-\overset{\overset{\text{O}}{\|}}{C}-$.

Step 3: *List of Structural Fragments:*

The fragments indicated are:

$-\overset{\overset{\text{O}}{\|}}{C}-$, $-\overset{\overset{\text{O}}{\|}}{C}-$, CH_3CH_2O-, $-CH_2-$, and CH_3-

Step 4: *Residual Formula and Combination of Fragments:*

The formula $C_6H_{10}O_3$ indicates two sites of unsaturation, and both are accounted for by the fragments shown above. The above fragments also account for all atoms. Combining the fragments:

Structure (3) requires that four protons absorb in the 3.8 — 4.5 region (a two proton quartet at 4.2 δ and a two proton singlet still further downfield). Because only two protons absorb in this region, structure (3) may be rejected. Structure (4) requires a two proton quartet in the 4.2 region ($CH_3\underline{CH_2}O-$) and a two proton quartet in the 2.0 δ region ($\overset{\overset{\text{O}}{\|}}{C}\underline{CH_2}CH_3$). Because only a two proton singlet is observed in the 2.0 δ region, structure (4) may be rejected. Only structure (5) is consistent with all the data. (Enolization accounts for conjugation.)

WAVELENGTH IN MICRONS

Beckman IR-4

liquid sample
thin layer

% Transmittance

WAVENUMBER IN CM⁻¹

Ultraviolet:
No appreciable
absorption.

SOLVENT	$DCCl_3$		°C
TEMPERATURE	40		
FILTER BANDWIDTH	4		cps
R.F. FIELD	.02		mG
SWEEP TIME	250		sec
SWEEP WIDTH	500		cps
SWEEP OFFSET	0		cps
SPECTRUM AMP.			
INTEGRAL AMP.	2.0		
REMARKS:	16.0		

Varian A-60A

PPM (δ)

Problem 4:

The compound contains chlorine and has
a molecular weight of 146 ± 2.

Answer Problem 4: Spectra are of ClCH₂CHClCH₂Cl.

Step 1: *Cursory Examination of the Data:*

The UV indicates that no conjugated system is present. The IR indicates no OH, C=O, aliphatic, or aromatic double bond stretch. The NMR indicates that no aromatic protons are present and that all protons are either ethylenic (inconsistent with IR) or attached to carbons carrying a strong electron withdrawing group.

Step 2: *Detailed Analysis of the Data:*

NMR Spectrum:

POSITION	MULTIPLICITY	INTEGRATION CURVE HEIGHT	RATIO	SMALLEST WHOLE NUMBER RATIO
4.3 δ	Multiplet	2.8 cm	1	2
3.9 δ	Singlet	6.8 cm	2.4	5
3.85 δ	Singlet	4.1 cm	1.5	3
		OR		
4.3 δ	Multiplet	2.8 cm	1	1
3.9 δ	Doublet	10.9 cm	3.9	4

If there are three sets of NMR peaks of ratio 2:5:3, then there must be an even number of halogens, i.e., Cl₂, Cl₄, etc. Because of the molecular weight restriction only Cl₂ is possible. The calculation of molecular formulas assuming two chlorines and a multiple of ten hydrogens yields only nonstoichiometric formulas, i.e.,

$$\#C = \frac{146 \pm 2 - 71 - 10}{12} = 5.6 - 5.3 \text{ Does not yield a whole number.}$$

$$\#C = \frac{146 \pm 2 - 71 - 20}{12} = 4.8 - 4.4 \text{ Does not yield a whole number.}$$

If there are two sets of NMR peaks of ratio 1:4 and the molecule has odd multiples of five hydrogens, then there must be an odd number of halogens, i.e., Cl, Cl₃, Cl₅, etc. Because of the molecular weight restriction only Cl and Cl₃ are possible. The calculation of molecular formulas assuming one or three chlorines and odd multiples of five hydrogens yields the following:

$$\#C = \frac{146 \pm 2 - 35.5 - 5}{12} = 9.0 - 8.6 \ C_9H_5Cl$$

$$\#C = \frac{146 \pm 2 - 35.5 - 15}{12} = 8.1 - 7.8 \ C_8H_{15}Cl$$

$$\#C = \frac{146 \pm 2 - 35.5 - 25}{12} = 7.3 - 7.0 \ C_7H_{25}Cl \text{ nonexistent } (C_nH_{2n+11})$$

$$\#C = \frac{146 \pm 2 - 106.5 - 5}{12} = 3.0 - 2.7 \ C_3H_5Cl_3$$

$$\#C = \frac{146 \pm 2 - 106.5 - 15}{12} = 2.2 - 1.9 \ C_2H_{15}Cl_3 \text{ nonexistent } (C_nH_{2n+11})$$

One of the following must be the formula of the compound:

C₉H₅Cl	Ω = 7
C₈H₁₅Cl	Ω = 1
C₃H₅Cl₃	Ω = 0

Analysis of the 3.9 δ Doublet:

The four (or 12) proton doublet (3.9 δ) is indicative of (ns $-$ CH₂ $-$ $\overset{\displaystyle |}{\underset{\displaystyle |}{CH}}$ $-$)₂ or ₆.

The position of the doublet (3.9 δ) suggests an electron withdrawing group attached to the carbon (Cl $-$ CH₂ $-$ CH $-$)₂ or ₆.

Because six chlorines in the molecule are not possible (mole wt), only two fragments, (ClCH₂CH $-$)₂, are possible.

Analysis of the 4.3 δ Multiplet:

The one (or 3) proton multiplet is indicative of (sp $-$ $\overset{\displaystyle H}{\underset{\displaystyle |}{C}}$ $-$ sp)₁ or ₃ (sp = splitting group).

The position of the multiplet suggests an electron withdrawing group attached to the carbon

(sp $-$ $\overset{\displaystyle H}{\underset{\displaystyle |}{\underset{\displaystyle Cl}{C}}}$ $-$ sp)₁ or ₃.

UV Spectrum:

The lack of any significant absorption eliminates the possibility of conjugated systems. This strongly suggests that C₉H₅Cl(Ω=7) is not the molecular formula.

IR Spectrum:

The lack of aliphatic and aromatic unsaturation is significant.

Step 3: *List of Structural Fragments:*

The fragments found were:

$$\underset{A\ \ H}{ClCH_2\overset{\displaystyle |}{\underset{\displaystyle |}{C}}} \ + \ \underset{A\ \ H}{ClCH_2\overset{\displaystyle |}{\underset{\displaystyle |}{C}}} \ + \text{ one or three } sp - \underset{B}{\overset{\displaystyle Cl}{\underset{\displaystyle H}{\overset{\displaystyle |}{\underset{\displaystyle |}{C}}}}} - sp$$

These fragments dictate that at least three chlorines must be present in the molecule. Therefore, the only formula possible is C₃H₅Cl₃. Thus, the $-\overset{\displaystyle |}{\underset{\displaystyle |}{C}}-$ group of each "A" fragment must be common to fragment B.

Step 4: *Residual Formula and Combination of Fragments:*

$$\underset{A}{ClCH_2} - \underset{B}{\overset{\displaystyle H}{\underset{\displaystyle Cl}{\overset{\displaystyle |}{\underset{\displaystyle |}{C}}}}} - \underset{A}{CH_2Cl}$$

WAVELENGTH IN MICRONS

WAVENUMBER IN CM⁻¹

% Transmittance

Problem 5:
$C_{12}H_{16}O_3$

Beckman IR-4

liquid sample
thin layer

Beckman DB

millimicrons

Varian A-60A

SOLVENT
TEMPERATURE
FILTER BANDWIDTH
R.F. FIELD
SWEEP TIME
SWEEP WIDTH
SWEEP OFFSET
SPECTRUM AMP.
INTEGRAL AMP.
REMARKS:

PPM (τ)

PPM (δ)

Answer Problem 5: Spectra are of

[structure: ortho-substituted benzene with OH and $-C(=O)-OCH_2CH_2CH(CH_3)_2$]

Step 1: *Cursory Examination of the Data:*

The formula $C_{12}H_{16}O_3$ indicates five sites of unsaturation (an aromatic ring may be present). The absorption in the UV indicates a conjugated system. The IR indicates the presence of OH, and the low frequency (3200 cm⁻¹) is suggestive of a phenol. The IR is also indicative of an aromatic ring and a conjugated carbonyl. The NMR indicates the presence of aromatic protons (7 δ region), aliphatic protons attached to carbon carrying a strong electron withdrawing group (4.1 δ region), and other aliphatic protons.

Step 2: *Detailed Analysis of the Data:*

NMR Spectrum:

POSITION	MULTIPLICITY	INTEGRATION CURVE HEIGHT	NUMBER OF PROTONS
7.1 δ	Multiplet	4.7 cm	4
4.2 δ	Triplet	2.1 cm	2
1.5 δ	Multiplet	3.9 cm	4
0.9 δ	Doublet	6.7 cm	6
		17.4 cm/16 protons = 1.1 cm/proton	

Analysis of the 7.1 δ Multiplet:
The position of the peak is indicative of an aromatic ring. The four proton area is indicative of a disubstituted ring.

Analysis of the 4.2 δ Triplet:
The position of the two proton peak is indicative of $-O-\underline{CH_2}-$.
The multiplicity of the peak is indicative of $-O-\underline{CH_2}-CH_2-$.

Analysis of the 1.5 δ Multiplet:
The position and multiplicity of the peak are indicative of aliphatic protons. The OH proton (presence confirmed from IR) may also absorb in this region.

Analysis of the 0.9 δ Doublet:
The position and multiplicity of the peak is indicative of

[structure: $\underset{CH_3}{\overset{CH_3}{C}}\!\!-\!H$]   or $ns-CH_3$ and $ns'-CH_3$

UV Spectrum:
The absorption indicates a conjugated system and is consistent for the spectrum of an aromatic system.

IR Spectrum:
The peak at 3200 cm⁻¹ is indicative of OH and its low frequency suggests a phenol. The presence of a conjugated carbonyl (1680 cm⁻¹), an aromatic system (1620 and 1580 cm⁻¹), and an *ortho* disubstituted benzene ring (760 cm⁻¹) are all indicated.

Step 3: *List of Structural Fragments:*
The fragments indicated are:

[structure: C_6H_4], [structure: $-C(=O)-$ (conj)], OH (possible phenol)

$O-CH_2CH_2-$ and $(CH_3)_2CH-$ or CH_3-ns plus CH_3-ns'.

Step 4: *Residual Formula and Combination of Fragments:*
The formula $C_{12}H_{16}O_3$ indicates five sites of unsaturation. The fragments account for all five sites.
The residual units are found by subtracting the sum of the known fragments from the formula.

SUM OF FRAGMENTS:

C_6H_4
C   O
H   O*
C_2H_4 O*
C_3H_7 or C_2H_6

$C_{12}H_{16}O_3$(A) or $C_{11}H_{15}O_3$(C)
    or
$C_{12}H_{16}O_2$(B) $C_{11}H_{15}O_2$(D)

* These oxygens may be common, i.e., OH and $-OCH_2CH_2-$ may be combined to give the fragment $HOCH_2CH_2-$

Formula A requires no residual unit.
Formula B requires O as the residual unit, and assumes $HOCH_2CH_2-$ is a fragment.
Formula C requires CH as the residual unit.
Formula D requires CHO as the residual unit and assumes $HOCH_2CH_2-$ is a fragment.

The low frequency of the OH band in the IR (3200 cm⁻¹) is a strong indication of phenolic OH. If the assumption is made that the OH is, indeed, phenolic, then formula B and D can be rejected and a new fragment [structure: phenol –OH] can be postulated.

Combining units using formula A:

$-\overset{O}{\overset{\|}{C}}-O-CH_2CH_2-$ →   or $-\overset{O}{\overset{\|}{C}}-CH_2CH_2O-$ →

(1) [structure: ortho-OH benzene with $-C(=O)-OCH_2CH_2CH(CH_3)_2$]
or
[structure: benzene with $-C(=O)-OCH_2CH_2CH(CH_3)_2$ and OH]

(2) $(CH_3)_2CHCOCH_2CH_2-$ [with phenol OH]

(3) [structure: $-C(=O)-CH_2CH_2O-$ benzene OH]   or   [structure: $(CH_3)_2CHCHCH_2CH_2O-$ with benzene OH]

(4) [structure: benzene OH with $-C(=O)-CH_2CH_2O-$]

Structures (2) and (4) do not account for the conjugated carbonyl (IR spectrum) and can be rejected. Structure (3) requires that three protons absorb in the 3.8 – 4.5 region of the NMR. Because only two protons absorb in this region, structure (3) may be rejected. Only structure (1) accounts for all the data.

Combining units using formula C:

(5) [structure: $-C(=O)-\overset{H}{\underset{\|}{C}}-\overset{O}{\overset{\|}{C}}-$]

(6) [structure: $-\overset{O}{\overset{\|}{C}}-COCH_2CH_2-$ or $-\overset{H}{\underset{\|}{C}}-\overset{O}{\overset{\|}{C}}-C-CH_2CH_2O-$ or $-CH_2CH_2O-$ or $-O-CH_2CH_2-C-$]

(7) [structure: $-\overset{H}{\underset{\|}{C}}-\overset{O}{\overset{\|}{C}}-C-$ or $-O-CH_2CH_2-\overset{O}{\overset{\|}{C}}-$]

(8) [structure: $CH_3OCH_2CH_2-\overset{H}{\underset{\|}{C}}-\overset{O}{\overset{\|}{C}}-C\cdot CH_3$ with phenol OH]

Structures (5) and (6) may be rejected because neither will account for a conjugated carbonyl. Structure (7) may be rejected because the remaining fragments ($ns-CH_3$, $ns'-CH_3$, and OH) cannot be accommodated.

(9) [structure: benzene OH with $-C(=O)-OCH_2CH_2CH\overset{CH_3}{\underset{CH_3}{}}$]

Structure (9) requires that five protons absorb in the 3.8 – 4.5 region of the NMR (CH_3-O-CH_2-). Because the NMR spectrum shows only two protons in this region, structure (9) may be rejected. The only structure accounting for all the data is

[structure: ortho-OH benzene with $-C(=O)-OCH_2CH_2CH(CH_3)_2$]

% Transmittance

millimicrons
Beckman DB
2 mg/100 ml ethanol

Beckman IR-4
liquid sample
thin layer

WAVELENGTH IN MICRONS
WAVENUMBER IN CM⁻¹
% Transmittance

SOLVENT	neat
TEMPERATURE	38
FILTER BANDWIDTH	4
R.F. FIELD	0.06
SWEEP TIME	500
SWEEP WIDTH	500
SWEEP OFFSET	—
SPECTRUM AMP.	1.6
INTEGRAL AMP.	—
REMARKS:	—

Varian A-60A

Problem 6:

$C_{10}H_{14}O$, a cyclic terpene found in mandarin peel, spearmint, and gingergrass oils.

Answer Problem 6: Spectra are of *l*-carvone.

Step 1: *Cursory Examination of the Data:*

The IR spectrum indicates a conjugated carbonyl and a geminal disubstituted alkene. The NMR indicates ethylenic hydrogens. The UV indicates a conjugated system. Either a diene system or an $\alpha\beta$-unsaturated ketone must be present. Six membered rings are common cyclic terpene structures.

Step 2: *Detailed Analysis of the Data:*

NMR Spectrum:

POSITION	MULTIPLICITY	INTEGRATION CURVE HEIGHT	PROTONS
6.8 δ	Multiplet	2.6 cm	1
4.8 δ	Multiplet	5.2 cm	2
2.5 δ	Multiplet	14.1 cm	5
1.8 δ	Multiplet	16.0 cm	6

37.9 cm/14 protons = 2.7 cm/proton

The formula $C_{10}H_{14}O$ indicates four sites of unsaturation.

Analysis of 6.8 δ Multiplet:
The position, area and multiplicity of the peak indicate $\ce{>C=C<}$ with long-range splitting. The low field position of the proton must be explained by an anisotropic or an inductive effect.

Analysis of 4.8 δ Multiplet:
The position, area and multiplicity of this peak indicate

$\left(\ce{>C=C<} \right)_2$ or, more likely, $\ce{>C=CH_2}$.

Analysis of 2.5 δ and 1.8 δ Multiplets:
The fact that no peaks appear below 1.5 δ is indicative that all methyl groups, if any are present, must be attached to an electron withdrawing group such as C=C or C=O. The six proton multiplet at 1.8 δ is strongly suggestive of

CH_3 — $C=CH$ (*cis* or *trans*) , CH_3 — $C=CH$ (*cis* or *trans*)
with long-range splitting.

UV Spectrum:
The absorption maxima of 238 $m\mu$ is indicative of

H, R, O — C=C–C–

Parent system	215 $m\mu$
α substituent	10 $m\mu$
β substituent	12 $m\mu$
	237 $m\mu$

Step 3: *List of Structural Fragments:*

The fragments which are strongly indicated from the spectral data are:

CH$_3$(1.8 δ)

(6.8 δ) (1) , CH_3 * H — $C = C$ (2) , and $\ce{>C = CH_2}$ * (3)

*Carbons in these groups may be common.

Step 4: *Residual Formula and Combination of Fragments:*

Combination of fragments yields:

or   or

Actual spectra are of *l*-carvone.

WAVELENGTH IN MICRONS

Beckman IR-4

liquid sample
thin layer

% Transmittance

WAVENUMBER IN CM⁻¹

Varian A-60A

SOLVENT		°C
TEMPERATURE	40°	
FILTER BANDWIDTH	4	cps
R.F. FIELD	.02	mG
SWEEP TIME	250	sec
SWEEP WIDTH	500	cps
SWEEP OFFSET	0	cps
SPECTRUM AMP.	1.0	
INTEGRAL AMP.	2.0	
REMARKS:		

Problem 7:
The compound does not not contain nitrogen, halogen, nor sulfur, and has a molecular weight of 100 ± 2.

Ultraviolet:
No appreciable absorption.

Answer Problem 7: Spectra are of *i*-propyl acetate.

Step 1:   *Cursory Examination of the Data:*

$CH_3 \underset{\underset{O-}{|}}{CH} CH_3$ (5.0 δ septet, 1.2 δ doublet), $\underset{/}{\overset{\backslash}{C}} = O$ (1750 cm^{-1})

Step 2:   *Detailed Analysis of the Data:*

POSITION	PROTON RATIO
5.0 δ	1
1.9 δ	3
1.2 δ	6

Possible formula: $C_5H_{10}O_2$.

Step 3:   *List of Structural Fragments:*

$-\overset{\overset{O}{\|}}{C}-$ (1750 cm^{-1}, IR), $CH_3 \underset{\underset{O-}{|}}{C}HCH_3$ (NMR), CH_3 -ns (NMR)

Step 4:   *Residual Formula and Combination of Fragments:*

$CH_3 \overset{\overset{O}{\|}}{C}-O-CH\,(CH_3)_2$

Problem 8:
The compound did not contain nitrogen, halogen, nor sulfur, and had a molecular weight of 196 ± 4. The compound is a minor constituent of chenopodium oil.

Beckman IR-4
liquid sample
thin layer

Beckman DB

Varian A-60A

Answer Problem 8: Spectra are of dibenzyl ether.

Step 1: *Cursory Examination of the Data:*

No OH nor C=O, but the presence of an aromatic system and C–O– (1100 cm^{-1} band) is indicated by the IR. A conjugated system is indicated (UV). Aromatic protons and aliphatic protons attached to strong electron withdrawing groups (4.3 δ) are indicated by the NMR.

Step 2: *Detailed Analysis of the Data:*

POSITION	PROTON RATIO
7.2 δ	5
4.3 δ	2

There must be 14 or a multiple of 14 hydrogens in the compound.

Possible formula:

(A) $C_{14}H_{14}O$ $\Omega = 8$
(B) $C_{13}H_{28}O$ $\Omega = 0$
(C) $C_{13}H_{14}O_2$ $\Omega = 7$
(D) $C_{10}H_{14}O_4$ $\Omega = 4$
(E) $C_9H_{14}O_5$ $\Omega = 3$
(F) $C_6H_{14}O_7$ $\Omega = 0$

The presence of an aromatic system (NMR, IR, UV) eliminates formula (B), (E), and (F).

Step 3: *List of Structural Fragments:*

Fragments indicated are: , ns –CH$_2$–ns, –O–

Step 4: *Residual Formula and Combination of Fragments:*

Because the fragments indicate only seven carbons and seven hydrogens and all hydrogens are accounted for in the NMR, the actual C:H ratio must be some multiple of C_7H_7, i.e., $C_{14}H_{14}$, $C_{21}H_{21}$, etc. The only formula which fits a multiple of C_7H_7 is $C_{14}H_{14}O$.

Fragments: , (ns – CH$_2$ – ns)$_2$, – O –

Combining the fragments gives ns – CH$_2$–O– or ns–CH$_2$–CH$_2$–ns →

$$\text{ns–CH}_2\text{–O–CH}_2\text{–ns} \quad \text{or} \quad \text{ns–CH}_2\text{–CH}_2\text{–O–}$$
$$\qquad\qquad (1) \qquad\qquad\qquad\qquad (2)$$

Structure (2) will not account for the singlet at 4.3 δ and may be rejected.

Structure of compound must be

CH$_2$OCH$_2$

WAVELENGTH IN MICRONS

%Transmittance

WAVENUMBER IN CM⁻¹

Beckman IR-4
liquid sample
thin layer

Ultraviolet:
No appreciable
absorption.

Varian A-60A

SOLVENT	DCCl₃	
TEMPERATURE	40	°C
FILTER BANDWIDTH	4	cps
R.F. FIELD	.02	mG
SWEEP TIME	250	sec
SWEEP WIDTH	500	cps
SWEEP OFFSET	0	cps
SPECTRUM AMP.	6.3	
INTEGRAL AMP.	6.3	
REMARKS: Impurity 1.58		

PPM (δ)

Problem 9:
C₁₀H₁₆ monocyclic terpene.

Answer Problem 9: Spectra are of

Step 1: *Cursory Examination of the Data:*

Aliphatic double bond stretch (1650 cm^{-1}), a geminal disubstituted alkene ($>$C=CH$_2$, 890 cm^{-1}) are indicated in the IR spectra. The NMR indicates two different types of ethylenic hydrogens. If methyl groups are present, they must be attached to C=C (no absorption in the NMR below 1.5 δ). Six membered rings are very common to cyclic terpenes.

Step 2: *Detailed Analysis of Data:*

POSITION	NUMBER OF PROTONS
5.4 δ	1
4.7 δ	2
2.0 δ	7
1.7-1.5 δ	6

Fragments from the spectrum: $/$CH=C$\big\langle$, $\big\rangle$C=CH$_2$, $/$C=C$\big\langle^{CH_3}$ (methyl indicates long-range splitting), $^{CH_3}/$C=C$\big\langle^{*}$ (methyl indicates long-range splitting).

*Suggested by the six proton peaks at 1.7 − 1.5 δ. The double bonds may be common to those in the first two fragments.

Step 4: *Residual Formula and Combination of Fragments:*

The formula C$_{10}$H$_{16}$ indicates three sites of unsaturation. At least two sites are indicated by the fragments above. The third site of unsaturation must be a ring. The compound is a monocyclic terpene.

Assuming a six membered ring, the fragments indicated are:

(A) [six membered ring], $-\overset{H*}{\underset{}{C}} = C\overset{CH_3}{\underset{}{\diagdown}}$ or $\overset{H}{\underset{}{C}} = C\overset{/}{\underset{CH_3}{\diagdown}}$, and $\overset{CH_3}{\underset{H}{C}} = CH_2$

or

(B) [six membered ring], $-\overset{H}{\underset{}{C}} = C(CH_3)_2$, and $\overset{*}{C} = CH_2$

*Carbon atoms of these groups may be common with ring carbons. Note that any possible combination of set B fragments yields a C$_{11}$ compound. Combinations of set A fragments yield:

[structure with CH$_3$, =CH$_2$, CH$_3$] or [structure with CH$_3$, CH$_3$, CH$_2$] or [structure with CH$_3$, CH$_3$, C, CH$_2$] or [structure with CH$_2$, C, CH$_3$, CH$_3$]

Spectra are of *d*-limonine,

[structure of limonene with CH$_3$, C, CH$_3$, CH$_2$]

% Transmittance

millimicrons

Beckman DB

WAVENUMBER CM⁻¹

Beckman Microspec

solid sample

nujol mull

% Transmittance

WAVELENGTH IN MICRONS

Varian A-60A

SOLVENT	DCCl₃	°C
TEMPERATURE	38°	Hz
FILTER BANDWIDTH	1	mG
R.F. FIELD	0.02	
SWEEP TIME	500	sec
SWEEP WIDTH	500	Hz
SWEEP OFFSET	0	Hz
SPECTRUM AMP.	16	
INTEGRAL AMP.	—	
REMARKS:		

Problem 10:

C₇H₅NO (Hint: Nujol gives IR peaks at
2900-3000 cm⁻¹, 1450 cm⁻¹, and 1375 cm⁻¹.)

Answer Problem 10: Spectra are of *p*-cyanophenol.

The OH band is shifted to 2950 cm^{-1}. The C$\equiv$N band is at 2210 cm^{-1}. Indication of a *p*-disubstituted ring is given by aromatic proton absorption in the NMR.

WAVELENGTH IN MICRONS

% Transmittance

WAVENUMBER IN CM⁻¹

Beckman IR-4

liquid sample
thin layer

Varian A-60A

SOLVENT		°C
TEMPERATURE		cps
FILTER BANDWIDTH		mG
R.F. FIELD		
SWEEP TIME		sec
SWEEP WIDTH	500	cps
SWEEP OFFSET	0	cps
SPECTRUM AMP.		
INTEGRAL AMP.		
REMARKS:		

Ultraviolet:
No appreciable
absorption.

Problem 11:

C₃H₄O is a skin irritant and sometimes
causes depression of the central nervous system.

Answer Problem 11: Spectra are of propargyl alcohol.

The IR spectrum should have given an indication of $-OH$ and $C\equiv C$. The NMR indicates three peaks with ratios of $1:2:1$. The peak whose position is solvent and concentration dependent must be due to the OH proton. The two proton peak must be coupled to the 2.7 δ proton, long range. The system $\underbrace{H-C\equiv C-}_{1.8\ \delta}\underbrace{CH_2-OH}_{4.3\ \delta}$ is strongly indicated.

% Transmittance

millimicrons

Beckman DB

WAVELENGTH IN MICRONS

% Transmittance

WAVENUMBER IN CM⁻¹

Beckman IR-4

liquid sample
thin layer

SOLVENT
TEMPERATURE
FILTER BANDWIDTH
R.F. FIELD
SWEEP TIME
SWEEP WIDTH
SWEEP OFFSET
SPECTRUM AMP.
INTEGRAL AMP.
REMARKS:

Varian A-60A

PPM (δ)

Problem 12:

Contains only   carbon, hydrogen, and oxygen,
and has a molecular weight of 110 ± 2.

Answer Problem 12: Spectra are of anisole.

The analysis of the IR spectrum should have suggested an aromatic system. The NMR gives evidence of a mono-substituted benzene ring and a methoxyl group.

WAVELENGTH IN MICRONS

% Transmittance

WAVENUMBER IN CM⁻¹

Beckman IR-4

liquid sample
thin layer

Varian A-60A

PPM (τ)

PPM (δ)

SOLVENT	neat	
TEMPERATURE	38°	°C
FILTER BANDWIDTH	4	Hz
R.F. FIELD	0.02	mG
SWEEP TIME	500	sec
SWEEP WIDTH	500	Hz
SWEEP OFFSET	0	Hz
SPECTRUM AMP.	0.5	
INTEGRAL AMP.	—	
REMARKS:		

Problem 13:

The compound did not contain halogen, nitrogen, nor sulfur, and dissolved in cold concentrated sulfuric acid. Its molecular weight was found to be 103 ± 2.

Ultraviolet:
No appreciable
absorption.

Answer Problem 13: Spectra are of di-*i*-propyl ether.

Strong bands at 1100 cm^{-1} are indicative of C—O bonds. Identification of $(CH_3)_2CH$—O— from the NMR and the calculation of the possible formula should have made this an easy one.

Ultraviolet:
No appreciable
absorption.

Varian A-60A

SOLVENT		
TEMPERATURE	40	°C
FILTER BANDWIDTH	4	cps
R.F. FIELD	.02	mG
SWEEP TIME	250	sec
SWEEP WIDTH	500	cps
SWEEP OFFSET	0	cps
SPECTRUM AMP.	0.8	
INTEGRAL AMP.	20.0	
REMARKS:		

Beckman
Microspec

liquid sample

thin layer

WAVENUMBER CM⁻¹

WAVELENGTH IN MICRONS

% Transmittance

Problem 14:
C₄H₇NO

Answer Problem 14: Spectra are of 3-methoxypropionitrile.

A nitrile is indicated by peak at 2250 cm^{-1}. The C–O bond is indicated by a strong band at 1100 cm^{-1}. The fragments $\underline{CH_3}O-$ (3.3 δ singlet), $-O-\underline{CH_2}CH_2-$ (3.5 δ triplet), and ns$-CH_2-CH_2-$(where ns could be nitrogen or a multiple carbon bond) should be recognizable from the NMR spectrum.

WAVELENGTH IN MICRONS

% Transmittance

WAVENUMBER IN CM⁻¹

Beckman IR-4

liquid sample
thin layer

Ultraviolet:
No appreciable
absorption.

SOLVENT	neat					
TEMPERATURE	38°	°C			
FILTER BANDWIDTH	4	Hz			
R.F. FIELD	0.02	mG			
SWEEP TIME	500	sec			
SWEEP WIDTH	500	Hz			
SWEEP OFFSET	—	Hz			
SPECTRUM AMP.	2.0				
INTEGRAL AMP.	—				
REMARKS:					

Varian A-60A

Problem 15:

The compound did not contain halogen,
nitrogen, nor sulfur, and had a molecular
weight of 99 ± 2.

PPM (δ)

WAVELENGTH IN MICRONS

WAVENUMBER IN CM⁻¹

% Transmittance

Beckman IR-4
liquid sample
thin layer

millimicrons

Beckman DB

% Transmittance

Varian A-60A

SOLVENT	neat		
TEMPERATURE	38°	°C	
FILTER BANDWIDTH	4	Hz	
R.F. FIELD	0.02	mG	
SWEEP TIME	500	sec	
SWEEP WIDTH	500	Hz	
SWEEP OFFSET		Hz	
SPECTRUM AMP.	1.25		
INTEGRAL AMP.			
REMARKS:			

PPM (δ)

Problem 16:

The compound contained nitrogen, but not halogen nor sulfur. The compound was readily soluble in dilute hydrochloric acid, and had a molecular weight of 149 ± 3.

Beckman IR-4

liquid sample
thin layer

Beckman DB

% Transmittance

millimicrons

Varian A-60A

SOLVENT	$DCCl_3$	
TEMPERATURE	40	°C
FILTER BANDWIDTH	4	cps
R.F. FIELD	.02	mG
SWEEP TIME	250	sec
SWEEP WIDTH	500	cps
SWEEP OFFSET	0	cps
SPECTRUM AMP.	1.25	
INTEGRAL AMP.	32.0	
REMARKS:		

Problem 17:

The compound did not contain nitrogen, halogen, nor sulfur, and had a molecular weight of 107 ± 2.

WAVELENGTH IN MICRONS

WAVENUMBER IN CM⁻¹

% Transmittance

Beckman IR-4

liquid sample

thin layer

Varian A-60A

SOLVENT	neat	
TEMPERATURE	38°	°C
FILTER BANDWIDTH	4	Hz
R.F. FIELD	0.02	mG
SWEEP TIME	500	sec
SWEEP WIDTH	500	Hz
SPECTRUM AMP.	0	Hz
INTEGRAL AMP.	1.6	
REMARKS:		

Ultraviolet:
No appreciable
absorption.

Problem 18:
$C_{10}H_{23}NO$

% Transmittance

millimicrons

Beckman DB

WAVELENGTH IN MICRONS

% Transmittance

Beckman IR-4

liquid sample

thin layer

WAVENUMBER IN CM⁻¹

PPM (τ)

SOLVENT	neat		°C
TEMPERATURE	38°	38°	°C
FILTER BANDWIDTH	4	4	Hz
R.F. FIELD	0.02	0.02	mG
SWEEP TIME	1000	1000	sec
SWEEP WIDTH	500	500	Hz
SWEEP OFFSET		120	Hz
SPECTRUM AMP.	1.0	1.0	
INTEGRAL AMP.			
REMARKS:			

Varian A-60A

PPM (δ)

Problem 19:

The compound contained only carbon, hydrogen, and oxygen, and had a molecular weight of 71 ± 2.

Problem 20:

The compound was readily soluble in dilute hydrochloric acid, and had a molecular weight of 106 ± 2.

% Transmittance

millimicrons

Beckman DB

WAVELENGTH IN MICRONS

% Transmittance

Beckman IR-4
liquid sample
thin layer

WAVENUMBER IN CM⁻¹
PPM (τ)

Varian A-60A

SOLVENT	neat
TEMPERATURE	38 °C
FILTER BANDWIDTH	4 Hz
R.F. FIELD	0.02 mG
SWEEP TIME	500 sec
SWEEP WIDTH	500 Hz
SPECTRUM AMP.	—
INTEGRAL AMP.	10
REMARKS:	

PPM (δ)

WAVELENGTH IN MICRONS

% Transmittance

WAVENUMBER IN CM⁻¹

Beckman IR-4

liquid sample
thin layer

% Transmittance

millimicrons

Beckman DB

Varian A-60A

SOLVENT _neat_
TEMPERATURE _38°_ °C
FILTER BANDWIDTH _4_ Hz
R.F. FIELD _0.02_ mG
SWEEP TIME _500_ sec
SWEEP WIDTH _500_ Hz
SWEEP OFFSET _—_ Hz
SPECTRUM AMP. _2.0_
INTEGRAL AMP. _—_
REMARKS:

PPM (τ)

PPM (δ)

Problem 21:

The compound gave negative tests for
nitrogen, halogen, and sulfur, and had a
molecular weight of 121 ± 2.

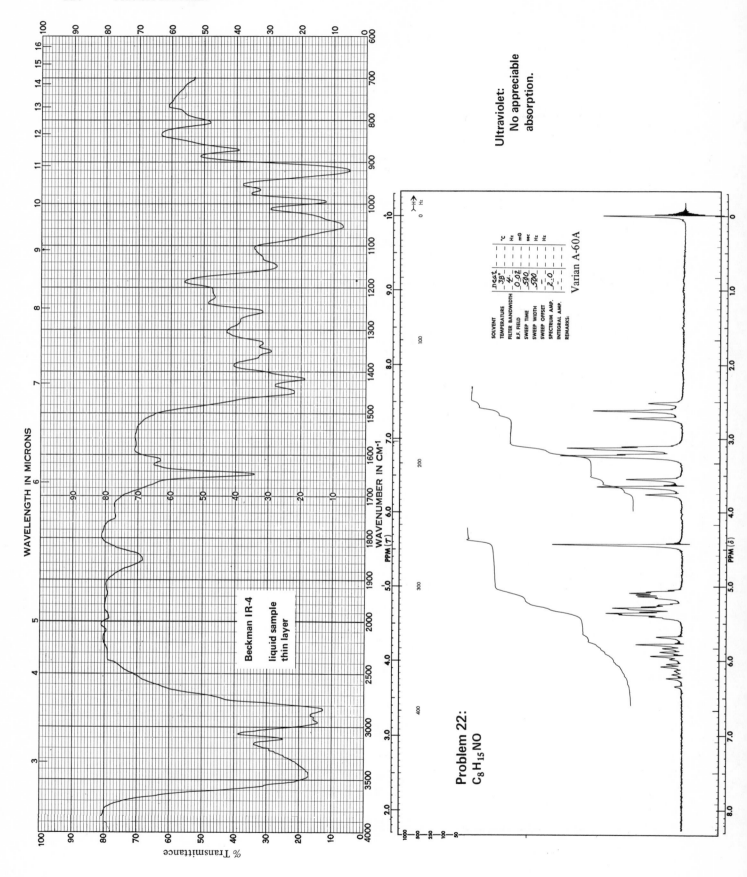

WAVELENGTH IN MICRONS

% Transmittance

WAVENUMBER IN CM⁻¹

Beckman IR-4
liquid sample
thin layer

Ultraviolet:
No appreciable
absorption.

SOLVENT	neat	
TEMPERATURE	38°	°C
FILTER BANDWIDTH	4	Hz
R.F. FIELD	0.02	mG
SWEEP TIME	500	sec
SWEEP WIDTH	500	Hz
SPECTRUM AMP.	—	Hz
INTEGRAL AMP.	2.0	
REMARKS:		

Varian A-60A

PPM (δ)

Problem 22:
$C_8H_{15}NO$

WAVELENGTH IN MICRONS

% Transmittance

Beckman IR-4
liquid sample
thin layer

WAVENUMBER IN CM⁻¹

Ultraviolet:
No appreciable
absorption.

SOLVENT		°C
TEMPERATURE	40	
FILTER BANDWIDTH	4	cps
R.F. FIELD	.02	mG
SWEEP TIME	250	sec
SWEEP WIDTH	500	cps
SWEEP OFFSET	0	cps
SPECTRUM AMP.	063	cps
INTEGRAL AMP.		
REMARKS:		

Varian A-60A

PPM (δ)

Problem 23:
Contained bromine, but not nitrogen, nor
sulfur, and had a molecular weight of 185 ± 4.

WAVELENGTH IN MICRONS

% Transmittance

Beckman IR-4

liquid sample
thin layer

Problem 24:

The compound contained nitrogen, but not halogen, nor sulfur, and had a molecular weight of 53 ± 1.

WAVENUMBER IN CM⁻¹

PPM (τ)

Varian A-60A

PPM (δ)

SOLVENT		
TEMPERATURE		°C
FILTER BANDWIDTH		cps
R.F. FIELD		mG
SWEEP TIME		sec
SWEEP WIDTH		cps
SWEEP OFFSET		cps
SPECTRUM AMP.		
INTEGRAL AMP.		

REMARKS: Ethanol impurity

WAVELENGTH IN MICRONS

% Transmittance

WAVENUMBER IN CM⁻¹

Beckman IR-4

liquid sample

thin layer

Ultraviolet:
No appreciable
absorption.

SOLVENT	neat			°C
TEMPERATURE	38°			Hz
FILTER BANDWIDTH	4			mG
R.F. FIELD	0.02			sec
SWEEP TIME	500			Hz
SWEEP WIDTH	500			Hz
SWEEP OFFSET				
SPECTRUM AMP.	/.0			
INTEGRAL AMP.				
REMARKS:				

Varian A-60A

PPM (δ)

Problem 25:

Contained only carbon, hydrogen, and oxygen,
and had a molecular weight of 161 ± 3.

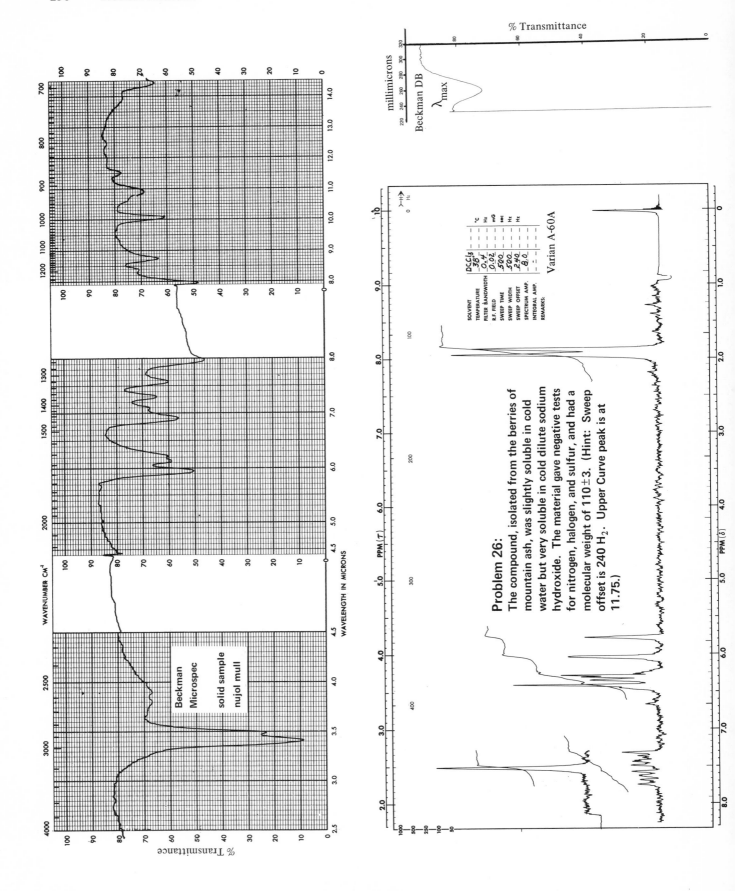

% Transmittance

millimicrons

Beckman DB

λ_{max}

WAVENUMBER CM⁻¹

WAVELENGTH IN MICRONS

% Transmittance

Beckman

Microspec

solid sample

nujol mull

Varian A-60A

SOLVENT	DCCl₃
TEMPERATURE	38°
FILTER BANDWIDTH	0.4
R.F. FIELD	0.02
SWEEP TIME	500
SWEEP WIDTH	500
SWEEP OFFSET	240
SPECTRUM AMP.	8.0
INTEGRAL AMP.	—
REMARKS:	

Problem 26:

The compound, isolated from the berries of mountain ash, was slightly soluble in cold water but very soluble in cold dilute sodium hydroxide. The material gave negative tests for nitrogen, halogen, and sulfur, and had a molecular weight of 110 ± 3. (Hint: Sweep offset is 240 H_2. Upper Curve peak is at 11.75.)

WAVELENGTH IN MICRONS

WAVENUMBER IN CM⁻¹

Beckman IR-4
solid sample
nujol mull

% Transmittance

millimicrons

Beckman DB

33 mg in 100 ml ethanol

SOLVENT	DCCl₃	°C
TEMPERATURE	38°	Hz
FILTER BANDWIDTH	4	mG
R.F. FIELD	0.02	
SWEEP TIME	500	sec
SWEEP WIDTH	500	Hz
SWEEP OFFSET	0	Hz
SPECTRUM AMP.	1.0	
INTEGRAL AMP.	-	
REMARKS:		

Varian A-60A

Problem 27:
$C_8H_{12}O_2$

WAVELENGTH IN MICRONS

% Transmittance

Beckman IR-4

liquid sample

thin layer

WAVENUMBER IN CM⁻¹

PPM (τ)

Ultraviolet:
No appreciable
absorption.

Varian A-60A

SOLVENT	DCCl₃	
TEMPERATURE	40	°C
FILTER BANDWIDTH	2	cps
R.F. FIELD	.02	mG
SWEEP TIME	250	sec
SWEEP WIDTH	500	cps
SWEEP OFFSET	0	cps
SPECTRUM AMP.	12.5	
INTEGRAL AMP.	5.0	
REMARKS:		

PPM (δ)

Problem 28:

Contains only carbon, hydrogen, and oxygen,
and has a molecular weight of 101 ± 2.

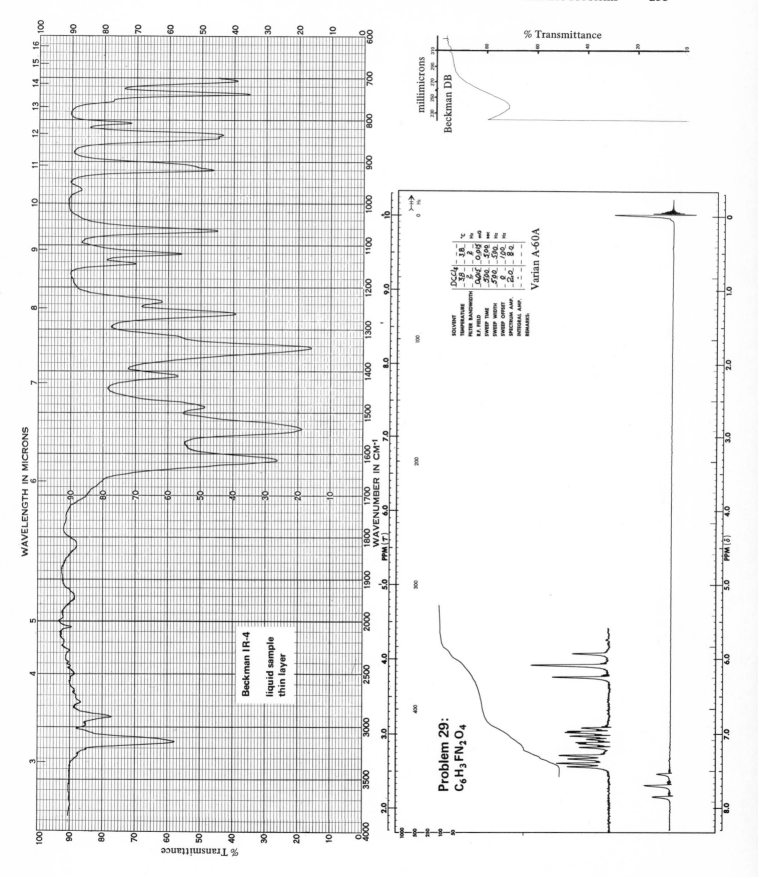

WAVELENGTH IN MICRONS

% Transmittance

Beckman IR-4

liquid sample
thin layer

WAVENUMBER IN CM⁻¹

millimicrons

Beckman DB

% Transmittance

Varian A-60A

SOLVENT	DCCl₄	38 °C
TEMPERATURE	38	2 Hz
FILTER BANDWIDTH	2	0.005 mG
R.F. FIELD	0.005	500 sec
SWEEP TIME	500	500 Hz
SWEEP WIDTH	500	100 Hz
SWEEP OFFSET	0	8.0
SPECTRUM AMP.	2.0	
INTEGRAL AMP.	1	
REMARKS:		

Problem 29:
C₆H₃FN₂O₄

Beckman Microspec

liquid sample

thin layer

Varian A-60A

SOLVENT	CCl_3	°C
TEMPERATURE	40	cps
FILTER BANDWIDTH	4	mG
R.F. FIELD	.01	sec
SWEEP TIME	250	cps
SWEEP WIDTH	500	cps
SWEEP OFFSET	0	
SPECTRUM AMP.	1.6	
INTEGRAL AMP.	25.0	
REMARKS:		

Problem 30:

The compound contained fluorine but neither nitrogen, nor sulfur, and had a molecular weight of 125 ± 2.

Ultraviolet:
No appreciable
absorption.

Beckman Microspec

solid sample
nujol mull

WAVENUMBER CM⁻¹

WAVELENGTH IN MICRONS

PERCENT TRANSMISSION

BECKMAN INSTRUMENTS INC., FULLERTON, CALIFORNIA, U.S.A.

WHEN REORDERING SPECIFY CHART NO. 130452

PRINTED IN U.S.A.

SOLVENT	DCCl₃	
TEMPERATURE	38°	°C
FILTER BANDWIDTH	0.4	Hz
R.F. FIELD	0.02	mG
SWEEP TIME	500	sec
SWEEP WIDTH	500	Hz
SPECTRUM AMP.		Hz
INTEGRAL AMP.	2.5	
REMARKS:	CHCl₃ peak at	
	7.3δ	

Varian A-60A

Problem 31:
C₃H₅NO

The compounds whose spectra appear in problems 15 through 31 are given below:

Problem 15   cyclohexanone

Problem 16   *N,N*- diethylaniline

Problem 17   *o*-xylene

Problem 18   *N,N*-di-*n*-butylethanolamine

Problem 19   crotonaldehyde

Problem 20   benzylamine

Problem 21   *p*-methylanisole   (methyl-*p*-tolyl ether)

Problem 22   N,N-diallylethanolamine

Problem 23   1,2-dibromoethane

Problem 24   acrylonitrile

Problem 25   diethyl malonate

Problem 26   sorbic acid

Problem 27   2,2,4,4-tetramethyl-1,3-cyclobutanedione

Problem 28   tetrahydrofurfuryl alcohol

Problem 29   1-fluoro-2,4-dinitrobenzene

Problem 30   *p*-fluoroanisole.

Problem 31   acrylamide

APPENDIX

Table I

Rules for Diene Absorption

Value assigned to parent heteroannular or open chain diene	214 mμ
Homoannular diene	36 mμ
Increment for	
(a) each alkyl substituent or ring residue	5 mμ
(b) the exocyclic nature of any double bond	5 mμ
(c) a double bond extension	30 mμ
(d) auxochrome $-$OAcyl	0 mμ
$-$OAlkyl	6 mμ
$-$SAlkyl	30 mμ
$-$Cl, $-$Br	5 mμ
$-$NAlkyl$_2$	60 mμ
Total	λ calc

(Reprinted with permission from A.I. Scott, *Interpretation of the Ultraviolet Spectra of Natural Products,* Pergamon Press, Oxford, 1964.)

Table II

Rules for αβ-unsaturated Ketone and Aldehyde Absorption

$$\overset{\delta}{C} = \overset{\gamma}{C} - \overset{\beta}{C} = \overset{\alpha}{C} - C = O$$

ϵ values are usually above 10,000 and increase with the length of the conjugated system.

Value assigned to parent αβ-unsaturated six-ring or acyclic ketone			215 mμ
Value assigned to parent αβ-unsaturated five-ring ketone			202 mμ
Value assigned to parent αβ-unsaturated aldehyde			207 mμ
Increments for			
(a) a double bond extending the conjugation			30 mμ
(b) each alkyl group or ring residue	α		10 mμ
	β		12 mμ
	γ and higher		18 mμ
(c) auxochromes			
(i) —OH	α		35 mμ
	β		30 mμ
	δ		50 mμ
(ii) —OAc	α, β, δ		6 mμ
(iii) —OMe	α		35 mμ
	β		30 mμ
	γ		17 mμ
	δ		31 mμ
(iv) —SAlk	β		85 mμ
(v) —Cl	α		15 mμ
	β		12 mμ
(vi) —Br	α		25 mμ
	β		30 mμ
(vii) —NR$_2$	β		95 mμ
(d) each exocyclic double bond			5 mμ
(e) homoannular diene			39 mμ
			——— EtOH
		Total	λcalc

(Reprinted with permission from A.I. Scott, *Interpretation of the Ultraviolet Spectra of Natural Products,* Pergamon Press, Oxford, 1964.)

Table III

Rules for αβ-unsaturated Acid and Ester Absorption
ϵ values are usually above 10,000

β-monosubstituted	208 mμ
αβ- or ββ-disubstituted	217 mμ
αββ-trisubstituted	225 mμ
Increment for	
(a) a double bond extending the conjugation	30 mμ
(b) exocyclic double bond	5 mμ
(c) when the double bond is endocyclic in a five- or seven-membered ring	5 mμ
Total	λcalc

(Reprinted with permission from A.I. Scott, *Interpretation of the Ultraviolet Spectra of Natural Products,* Pergamon Press, Oxford, 1964.)

Table IV

Rules for the Principal Band of Substituted Benzene Derivatives
$R-C_6H_4-COX$

	Orientation	λ_{calc}^{EtOH} mμ
Parent Chromophore:		
X = alkyl or ring residue		246
X = H		250
X = OH or OAlkyl		230
Increment for each substituent:		
R = alkyl or ring residue	*o-, m-*	3
	p-	10
R = OH, OMe, OAlkyl	*o- m-*	7
	p-	25
R = O$^-$	*o-*	11
	m-	20
	p-	78
R = Cl	*o-, m-*	0
	p-	10
R = Br	*o-, m-*	2
	p-	15
R = NH$_2$	*o-, m-*	13
	p-	58
R = NHAc	*o-, m-*	20
	p-	45
R = NHMe	*p-*	73
R = NMe$_2$	*o-, m-*	20
	p-	85

(Reprinted with permission from A.I. Scott, *Interpretation of the Ultraviolet Spectra of Natural Products,* Pergamon Press, Oxford, 1964.)

Table V

Characteristic infrared group frequencies. (Courtesy of N.B. Colthup, Stamford Research Laboratories, American Cyanamid Company, and the editor of the Journal of the Optical Society.) Overtone bands are marked 2 *ν*.

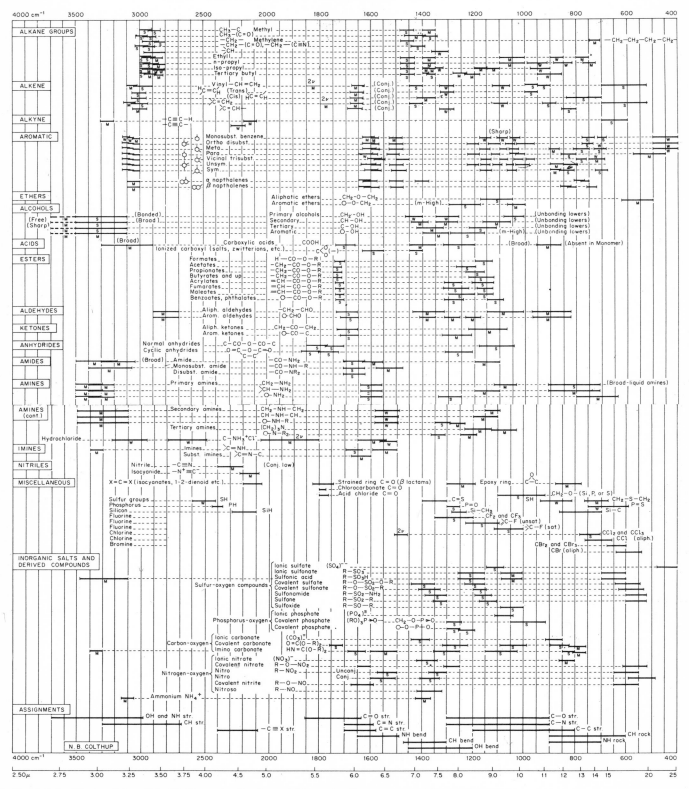

Reprinted with permission, John R. Dyer, *Applications of Absorption Spectroscopy of Organic Compounds,* 1965, Prentice-Hall, Inc., Englewood Cliffs, N.J.

Table VI

Absorption positions of protons in various structural environments.

STRUCTURAL TYPE   τ VALUE AND RANGE†

		Structural Type
1.	TMS, 10.0000
2.	–CH₂–, cyclopropane, 9.78
3.	CH₄, 9.767
4.	ROH, monomer, very dilute solution, *ca* 9.5
5.	CH₃–C– (saturated), (8.7)9.05-9.15(9.3)
6.	R₂NH‡, 0.1-0.9 mole fraction in an inert solvent, (7.8)8.4-9.6
7.	CH₃–C–C–X (X = Cl, Br, I, OH, OR, C=O, N), (8.8)8.90-9.10
8.	–CH₂– (saturated), 8.65-8.80
9.	RSH‡, 8.5-8.9
10.	RNH₂‡, 0.1-0.9 mole fraction in an inert solvent, (8.2)8.5-8.9
11.	–C–H (saturated), 8.35-8.60
12.	CH₃–C–X (X = F, Cl, Br, I, OH, OR, OAr, N), (8.0)8.1-8.8(9.0)
13.	CH₃–C=C, 8.1-8.4
14.	CH₃–C=O, 7.4-7.9(8.1)
15.	CH₃Ar, 7.5-7.75(7.9)
16.	CH₃–S–, 7.2-7.9
17.	CH₃–N, 7.0-7.9
18.	H–C≡C–, nonconjugated, 7.35-7.55
19.	H–C≡C–, conjugated, 6.9-7.2
20.	ArSH‡, 6.0-7.0
21.	CH₃–O–, (6.0)6.2-6.5(6.7)
22.	ArNH₂‡, ArNHR‡, and Ar₂NH‡, (5.7)6.0-6.6(6.7)
23.	ROH‡, 0.1-0.9 mole fraction in an inert solvent, 4.8-7.0
24.	CH₂=C, nonconjugated, 5.0-5.4
25.	H,C=C, acyclic, nonconjugated, (4.1)4.3-4.8(4.9)
26.	H,C=C, cyclic, nonconjugated, 4.3-4.8
27.	CH₂=C, conjugated, (3.75)4.3-4.7
28.	ArOH‡, polymeric association, 2.3-5.5
29.	H,C=C, conjugated, (2.25)3.3-4.3(4.7)
30.	H,C=C, acyclic, conjugated, (2.9)3.5-4.0(4.5)
31.	H–N–C=O, 1.5-4.5
32.	ArH, benzenoid, (0.5)2.0-3.4(4.0)
33.	ArH, nonbenzenoid, (1.0)1.4-3.8(6.0)
34.	RNH₃⁺, R₂NH₂⁺, and R₃NH⁺ (trifluoroacetic acid solution), 2.3-2.9
35.	H–C=O, 1.9-2.1
36.	H–C=O, 1.8-2.0
37.	ArNH₃⁺, ArRNH₂⁺, and ArR₂NH⁺ (trifluoroacetic acid solution), 0.5-1.5
38.	C=N–OH‡, ¬0.2-1.2
39.	RCHO, aliphatic, α,β–unsaturated, 0.35-0.50
40.	RCHO, aliphatic, 0.2-0.3(0.5)
41.	ArCHO, (-0.1)0.0-0.3(0.5)
42.	ArOH, intramolecularly bonded, (-5.5)-2.5 - -0.5
43.	–SO₃H, -2 - -1
44.	RCO₂H, dimer, in nonpolar solvents, (-3.2)-2.2 - -1.0(0.3)
45.	Enols, -6 - -5

†Normally, absorptions for the functional groups indicated will be found within the range shown. Occasionally, a functional group will absorb outside this range. Approximate limits for this are indicated by absorption values in parentheses and by shading in the figure.

‡The absorption positions of these groups are concentration-dependent and are shifted/to higher τ values in more dilute solutions.

Reprinted with permission, John R. Dyer, *Applications of Absorption Spectroscopy of Organic Compounds,* 1965, Prentice-Hall, Inc., Englewood Cliffs, N.J.

Table VII

Spin-spin coupling constants

Type	J, cps	Type	J, cps
H_2†	280	$\diagup$C=CH—CH=C$\diagdown$	9–13
CH_4†	12.4	H—C≡C—H †	9.1
$\diagup$C$\diagdown^H_H$	12–15	$\diagdown$CH—C≡C—H	2–3
$\diagdown$CH—CH$\diagup$	2–9	$\diagdown$CH—C$\diagdown^H_O$	1–3
—C—(—C—)$_n$—C— H H	~0	$\diagup$C=C$\diagdown^H$ C ‖ O	6–8
CH_3—CH_2—X	6.5–7.5		
$CH_3 \atop CH_3$ CH—X	5.5–7.0	(benzene ring)	o– 6–9 m– 1–3 p– 0–1
H—C—C—H X Y	a,a 5–10 a,e 2–4 e,e 2–4	(furan ring, O)	$\alpha\beta$ 1.6–2.0 $\alpha\beta'$ 0.6–1.0 $\alpha\alpha'$ 1.3–1.8 $\beta\beta'$ 3.2–3.8
$\diagup$C=C$\diagdown^H_H$	0.5–3		
$^H_{\diagdown}$C=C$^H_{\diagup}$	7–12	(pyrrole ring, N–H)	$\alpha\beta$ 2.0–2.6 $\alpha\beta'$ 1.5–2.2 $\alpha\alpha'$ 1.8–2.3 $\beta\beta'$ 2.8–4.0
$^H_{\diagdown}$C=C$_{\diagup}^H$	13–18		
$\diagdown$C=C$^H_{\diagup}$ —C—H	4–10	(thiophene ring, S)	$\alpha\beta$ 4.6–5.8 $\alpha\beta'$ 1.0–1.8 $\alpha\alpha'$ 2.1–3.3 $\beta\beta'$ 3.0–4.2
$\diagdown$C=C$\diagdown^{C—H}$ H	0.5–2.5	(pyridine ring, N)	$\alpha\beta$ 4.9–5.7 $\alpha\gamma$ 1.6–2.6 $\alpha\beta'$ 0.7–1.1 $\alpha\alpha'$ 0.2–0.5 $\beta\gamma$ 7.2–8.5 $\beta\beta'$ 1.4–1.9
$^H_{\diagdown}$C=C$\diagdown^{C—H}$	~0		

† The coupling constant for these molecules, which contain only equivalent protons, has been determined from the spectra of the partially deuterated substances.

DATE DUE

GAYLORD   PRINTED IN U.S.A.